SoulQuest

———

A TRAIL GUIDE TO LIFE

———

Pamela Anne Bro
Ph.D.

WWW.SOULQUESTNOW.COM

SOULQUEST

ISBN ISBN-13: 978-1478239468

ISBN-10: 1478239468

Cover image courtesy of Phil Neff
Cover design by Kaitlyn Bro Benetz

Printed in the United States of America

SOULQUEST
Pamelabro22@hotmail.com

Dedication

To my sweet *John*,
companion on the Quest,

to my precious daughters,
Chelsea and Kaitlyn,
without whom this book
would never have been conceived,

and to my vibrant friend,
Chantal Dejou, without whose
financial and spiritual generosity,
this book would never have come to birth.

My Prayer

With the words you give me,
Wakan Tanka,*
May the young be liberated,
The world transformed.

*Great Spirit
In the Lakota Indian tradition

CONTENTS

Preparing for the Quest

6

A Quester for Others

I will not die an unlived life.
      I will not go in fear
      of falling or catching fire.
I choose to inhabit my days,
      to allow my living to open to me,
      to make me less afraid,
      more accessible,
to loosen my heart
      until it becomes a wing,
      a torch, a promise.
I choose to risk my significance:
      to live
      so that which comes to me as seed
            goes to the next as blossom,
            and that which comes to me as blossom
            goes on as fruit.

                      –Davna Markova

SoulQuest

———

A trail guide to life

———

ONE

___

Prep Notes from Your Trail Guide

It was December 26, 1982. Tall, slim, clad in a peacock blue woolen dress, auburn hair curled, blue eyes shining, I stood on the small stage in the front of the sanctuary, shivering with excitement. The pastor was preparing to place the sacred stole upon my shoulders to signify that I was now ordained to the priesthood—making me the sixth generation pastor on my father's side. My dad had just preached a powerful sermon. My mom, having raised five children and now one of the first wave of ordained female ministers in the country, prepared to deliver the charge, the same one my grandmother had given her on her ordination day: lift up the women in our faith, tell their forgotten stories, celebrate their gifts, and widen the spaces for them to shine and serve in their church and in the world.

How did I end up here?

As a skinny little girl with glasses growing up in the 1950's in an all-white model suburb south of Chicago, I sat at the feet of my grandmother, Margueritte Harmon Bro, spellbound by her stories. She and her husband, Albin, had been educational missionaries in Nanjing, China from 1919 to1924. My petite and energetic Granny spoke of going out on the hillsides to rescue infant girls who had been left there to die *just because they were female*. She remembered the times that Chinese women accepted Jesus Christ. Some came to her to have their tiny wrapped feet *unbound*.

Years later, I learned that foot binding had been a Chinese custom for almost one thousand years. A young girl's feet were broken across the arches, then bound tightly so that when she grew up, her small feet, though misshapen and terribly painful, would be sexually appealing to men. I assumed that having their feet unbound would relieve their pain, but Granny exclaimed, "Oh, no, Pam. The pain of being unwrapped was excruciating!"

Granny continued. Sometimes Chinese men would have to restrain a furious husband from preventing his wife from having her feet unbound or from having his daughter's feet broken. These brave, newly baptized women wanted to stand tall on their own two feet to help bring in the kingdom of God. As I listened to these stories, I thought to myself, "If this is what the Christian faith is all about, I want to be a part of it."

A feminist methodology demands that an author reveal her social context. I consider myself a feminist mystic/activist, universal Christian pastor, preacher and teacher. Now that's a mouthful, but let me explain. I am a white, middle-class woman of Scandinavian heritage born in 1947 in the Midwest, the eldest of five children, four girls and a boy. My father, Harmon H. Bro, born in Nanjing in 1919, was a theologian, author, Jungian psychologist, professor and preacher. Thirteen years after his death, people still tell me how reading one of his seven books saved their lives. My mother, June, trained as a concert pianist, still plays with great power and grace at the ripe old age of ninety. In her fifties, after raising five children, she went on to obtain her Master's and Doctorate of Divinity degrees. She currently attends peace rallies, has an insatiable curiosity, and is the "belle of the ball" at any social gathering.

My parents gave me several strong pillars to support my young life. First, they instilled Democratic values in me: helping the unfortunate, sharing the wealth, saving the planet. While discussing the news and spoofing television commercials, they taught me the skills of political and economic analysis. Second, they gave me the tools of Jungian psychology to analyze my dreams, understand my psychological challenges and demons, and help me to build a healthier self.

As Christians, they taught me to respect the goodness and equality of all races and faiths, based on the Biblical pronouncement that God created each human being in God's image with *love*. Jesus' injunction, "As you do it to the least of these, you do it unto me" (Matthew 25) resonated strongly within me. As long as I can remember, I have been concerned for the "least of these," especially women and children.

When I was thirteen, my parents told me of a man named Edgar Cayce who had strongly influenced their lives. Little did I know that my grandmother, Margueritte, had not only met Mr. Cayce and received several diagnostic readings from him, but she had written an article about him, entitled *"Miracle Man of Virginia Beach",* for the national publication, *Coronet Magazine."* My parents later had the opportunity to work with the Cayce's for almost a year in 1943. Cayce's mystical and prophetic Christian worldview strongly colors my understanding of my life's purpose and meaning.

I came of age in the explosive decade of the 1960s. An activist from my teens, I was highly influenced by the idealism of John F. Kennedy and the Peace Corps. In my college years, I joined the civil rights movement. In 1967, a year before Dr. Martin Luther King, Jr.'s tragic death, I marched with him in downtown Chicago for better housing for African-Americans—still a highlight of my life some forty years later. During the Vietnam War, I worked hard in the peace (anti-Vietnam war) movement and was jubilant when the war was declared over.

In 1970, I graduated with honors in English and Drama from Drake University and headed west, I mean *really* west, to what was then West Berlin, Germany, to get my Master's degree in Children's Theater. Back home in the States in 1972, I helped to form a women's liberation consciousness-raising group with a radical, fun-loving group of seven women, and proudly became a self-taught feminist.

I visited my sister who lived in New York City and regularly participated in the worship and community life of Judson Church in Greenwich Village. One Sunday, she took me to a service. I was floored. As I walked into the sanctuary, I was delighted to see theater lights suspended from the ceiling! I found the liturgy relevant, deep and moving, and I marveled at one of their outreach ministries—accompanying prostitutes as they walked the streets throughout the night. The churchwomen were not trying to convert or shame the prostitutes. They were there solely to show these women that, no matter what, *they* cared and *God* cared.

"Wow!" I exclaimed to my sister. "If there were a church community like that in Virginia Beach, I'd join it!"

In one of those rare prophetic moments, she looked me dead in the eyes, and with a twinkle dared me, "Why don't you start one?"

Initially I snorted with disdain. But never one to shrink from her dares (being her elder by scarcely a year), I took the bait. I informed her I would *only* apply to the divinity school that the Associate Pastor at Judson, who had written and directed all the church musicals, had attended, no matter where it was in the United States.

Much to my surprise, that school turned out to be the world-famous Union Theological Seminary in New York City. What seemed a miracle I know now was God's desire. I was accepted. I became actively involved in social justice programs at Riverside Church, under the inspiring leadership of Rev. William Sloane Coffin, who became my treasured mentor and friend.

Following graduation from Union, I moved back to Virginia Beach. After spending a year "in care" with the church, I now stood at the threshold of my ordination, my mother's arm outstretched over me. Would I be able to fulfill the large responsibility of that charge?

Almost thirty years later, this book is my attempt to be faithful to my charge and promise: I would strive to empower women and join them in making a difference in our world.

In 1982, I met and married my husband, John. Because Virginia Beach was largely a military, fundamentalist and still racially-segregated area, John and I wanted to create an alternative faith community, like the one at Union Seminary or Riverside Church—one that applied a feminist critique and was dedicated to peace and justice for all. Together with six other couples, John and I founded Christpoint Community Church, a house church modeled upon early Christian house churches.

When I asked the Disciples and the United Church of Christ denominations for support, both monetarily and morally, they told me I had to wait a year while they did a feasibility study. I couldn't, or truthfully *wouldn't*, wait a year because I was on fire with the Spirit's enthusiasm and vision. So Christpoint Community Church joined the International Council of Community Churches and we set to work: working with Habitat for Humanity, serving the homeless and people dying from AIDS. At Christmastime, we caroled in hospitals and homes for the elderly. We lobbied and wrote letters after worship services to change national policies that hurt poor mothers and children. We supported *Witness for Peace* in Nicaragua. Every Sunday after worship, we gathered in a circle to lay hands on whoever asked for healing. Sometimes, in place of regular sermons, we performed theater pieces.

I proudly pastored Christpoint for seven years—some of the most challenging and creative years of my life. Each of us grew in spiritual depth, while together we exercised our various gifts, locally and globally. My experience as pastor of Christpoint Community Church continues to inform my vision of the love, joy and spiritual gifts such a community can offer.

While pastoring Christpoint, I continued to teach college as well as to participate in two blessed events—giving birth to two daughters, Chelsea and Kaitlyn. As my daughters grew within our church community, I became increasingly frustrated with the lack of female imagery in Christian hymns and prayers. Nowhere did I see my lovely daughters' faces reflected in the Divine face. After much prayer and inner struggle, I resigned from Christpoint and headed off to Chicago to get my doctorate in Theology and Women's Studies.

During the next seven years, I changed my major from Women's Studies to Anthropology. I studied "mission-as-reconciliation" with the Lakota Indians on the reservations of Pine Ridge and Rose Bud in South Dakota, finally earning my doctorate in 1999.

Surpassing my wildest dreams, I ended up as one of two pastors for the Church of Christ in Yale University, the pulpit of such Christian luminaries as William Sloane Coffin, Dr. Martin Luther King, Jr., and Archbishop Desmond Tutu of South Africa. A few years into my service there, I came to believe that the church was resting on its considerable laurels. I begged the head pastor for a vision to serve, to grow the congregation. None was forthcoming. After agonizing deliberation, I resigned. A year later, the pastor, together with Yale's president, disbanded the 257-year-old congregation, ostensibly to make the campus more multi-religious. Though I supported a multi-religious campus ministry, I would never have abandoned my people at the Church of Christ in Yale. I was glad I resigned when I did.

In 2003, I participated in a week's training in "mindfulness" with the great Vietnamese Buddhist activist and peace-maker, Thich Nhat Hanh or Thây as we disciples call him ("teacher" in Vietnamese). In the fall of 2005, our family moved back home to Virginia Beach and within a year, I founded and continue to pastor the spiritual community *Living Waters Sanctuary*. I continue to engage in interfaith dialogue between Jews, Christians, Muslims, Native Americans and Wiccans. Twice a year, I train Disciple and United Church of Christ missionaries in cross-cultural sensitivity in Indianapolis, the very city in which my grandparents were trained as missionaries to China almost a century ago. God sure has a sense of humor!

Why this book?

I began this book as a love story to my sweet, strong daughters, Chelsea and Kaitlyn, as my spiritual legacy to them; as a testimony of my trials and triumphs, and as a guide to some of the pitfalls and joys I've encountered in making of my life a conscious spiritual quest. Now I'm expanding the audience to include you, the reader. I hope that the people and stories that inspired me on my journey will shed light on your own spiritual path, especially during the tough times.

Even though we modern-day Americans would never consider breaking and binding our little girls' feet, like the Chinese did in my grandmother's day, many of our daughters are still not free to stand tall or to walk safely. I will do whatever I can, literally or symbolically, to prevent my daughters' feet, or *any* of our daughters' feet, from being broken and bound. The courage of Granny's Chinese women friends has inspired me my whole life to be an advocate for all people: to help them stand tall, walk, run, jump or even dance for joy. My heart's desire is that this trail guide will help you walk confidently upon the earth as you travel your unique and precious path to discover your soul.

Years ago, I saw a statue of Kwan Yin, the Buddhist goddess of mercy, depicted with a sword.

"Oh, no!" I agonized. "Someone always has to put a violent spin on everything. Now they've ruined the goddess Kwan Yin for me."

However, as I continued to contemplate the painting, I realized that the sword in Kwan Yin's usually merciful hand did not have to be used to destroy others, but could be used to liberate people from inner bondage.

I believe that the goal of feminism is to *advocate for all women*: to speak up and stand up for their rights, gifts and glorious personhood; and to work on liberating both men and women from society's bonds as well as from our own internal dungeons. Our ultimate pursuit of our souls must include partnering, men and women together, to create a safe and kinder world for all.

Goals of *SoulQuest*

One major goal of this *SoulQuest* is to find and claim your God-given talents so that you can help change the world in some significant way. At times, your talents will spring out at you like tigers leaping forth from jungle-like bushes. At other times, they may flit before you like fireflies in twilight, and you'll want to capture them in a jar to study them before trusting in your own inner light and setting the fireflies free. Oh, my daughters, there are so many delightful surprises awaiting you on your wilderness trail.

The spiritual path is often strewn with paradoxes. While you are on a personal quest to identify your particular passions, fears, dreams and desires and to find and claim your gifts—know that you benefit not only yourself but *every person on this planet*. We are that inter-connected. You have a specific mission, a purpose, to benefit the whole world—a purpose only *you* can fulfill. You may have the healing oil for someone's pain, the song to cheer, the dance to delight, the sense to build a business, the courage to seek justice.

Another paradox—your quest will require performing both hard work and boring tasks. It may take you on tortuous treks to reach sublime heights, or you may find yourself stalled, lying dead in the water. At other times, you may feel hopelessly lost, that you have veered "off the path." I used to think about my own spiritual journey in those terms. Recently, I heard someone announce the extraordinary good news that "the whole world is the path," so we can never stray from it. We are never a failure—only students, learning from our mistakes to make wiser and more loving choices.

A final paradox—the goal lies not merely at the end of the journey but *includes the journey* itself. So no matter what you have suffered or experienced so far in your life, you can use it for good. Each of us has a responsibility to leave the world a better place than when we entered it.

Why a Trail Guide?

As you know, a trail guide receives education and training from the best teachers she can find, and then using her own hard-won wisdom, volunteers to take others on similar journeys. She can:
- help you prepare for what you might encounter;
- point out pitfalls or traps to avoid, and breathtaking views you shouldn't miss;
- be a companion, comforting you when you fall; inspiring you when you feel you can't go another step; cheering you up, and rooting for you when you're tempted to give up or give in.

Please remember, dear readers, this book is only a map. Though a map can be extremely helpful, even necessary at times, *it is never wise to confuse the map with the territory*. Please know, sweet friends, that I held your faces before me as I wrote. As your trail guide, I desire that you become the most wondrous selves you can be.

The Lure of the Wilderness

My daughter, Chelsea, and I decided we needed a "bonding" experience before she headed off to college. It was time to test what we were made of, and have some fun to boot. We decided to go tubing down a local rural river. We picked the site, Devil's Rapids—not its real name, but the word "Devil" was in the name, which should have forewarned us. It didn't.

It was a nice August day, though overcast. In our bathing suits, we joined the other adventurous tubers at the river's edge. Lowered down the rough ravine-like bank by cute male teenagers, we climbed into our tubes, bottoms first. The water was freezing. It must have been about 60 degrees. The "guides" (I use that term loosely) admitted the water was pretty cold for our two hour trip down the river.

Chelsea and I questioned each other: "Should we get out and go another day?"

Heck, we weren't going to let a cold river scare us. Or the fact that we'd never even tubed before.

The guides assured us they'd have someone positioned on the riverbank a few yards downstream if we decided to change our minds and get out. Past that point, however, we'd be on our own for the rest of the trip. That should have raised a red flag, too. It didn't. We'd only traveled a few yards when the rapids flipped Chelsea over on her back. Ever the good sport, she yelled she was OK. We waved gaily to the one remaining guide as we rushed by him.

Then came the *big* rapids. (After our trip, one guide admitted that the river had been too low to safely allow tubing that day, but that didn't stop them from renting to us.) Because of the low water level and the roiling water, my tube caught on a large submerged rock and flipped me over. My head was underwater several seconds. My right leg hit a large rock and pain seared through my shinbone. I came up for air, grasping my tube and the rock for dear life. I wanted *out*. Now.

A few yards further down river from me, four men and women had pulled off to the side on a low bank to get warm in the fickle sun. Chelsea kicked her tube hard in their direction, and they pulled her out of the rolling rapids as she sped by.

"Come on, Mom!" she yelled. "You can make it over here!"

My leg felt like it might be broken, but the water was so cold, I decided to let go of the rock, hoping to catch one of the men's hands as I zoomed by. They all cheered as he caught me and pulled me out.

One man was an EMT, as luck (or God) would have it. He examined the little white piece sticking out of my shin.

"Looks like bone—can't be sure," he offered. "Someone had better go for help."

But where? We were the last of the tubers that day on a deserted river with only an overgrown unpaved path barely visible on the river's other bank.

The kind man volunteered to get help. Miraculously, he made it across the rapids and was gone for half an hour. I kept my leg submerged in the river. No blood, thank goodness, but no feeling either. However, I felt strangely calm. You see, usually when I'm hurt, I freak out. But not this time. Chelsea was upbeat; our new friends were kind and supportive.

The man returned.

"No luck," he reported.

What should we do? I couldn't make it the two hours down the river to the pickup place.

An hour later, my leg was so numb from the cold water, I couldn't feel it. Some teenagers biked by us on the opposite side of the river. We shouted to them in an effort to flag them down, but apparently they thought we were just saying hi and off they rode. The kind man decided to go chase them down, so they could go for help.

An hour or two later, I was hypothermic but still amazingly calm, even enjoying the day. Then we heard a siren. Unbelievably, an ambulance was making its way through the rough, narrow, brush-covered path. The EMT team leader told me that he had brought all of his team because their department so rarely got an emergency call and they needed the practice. All ten slid down the opposite ravine and bravely forged the rapids, almost dropping the stretcher once or twice. After reaching me and strapping me in, they carried me back across the rapids and up the steep incline. I tried not to laugh when they almost tipped me over several times, shouting to each other, "Watch out! Be careful!"

As the team brought me up alongside the back of the ambulance, a medic inside the truck called out, "Wait a minute! I'm almost finished taking care of the other guy!"

The other guy?

Though my teeth were chattering because I was indeed hypothermic with a 94 degree temperature (at 92 degrees, your brain freezes and you die), I listened intently as they wrapped me in silver space suit material to warm my body. Here's the bizarre story.

Just before Chelsea and I had gotten into our river tubes, a young man had jumped in to go tubing with his friends. At one point down the river, the man got so cold that he swam over to the bank to warm up, planning to catch up with his friends when he did. However, his body was so cold that he decided to head up the steep bank to get help. Passing out several times on the way up, he finally collapsed, unconscious, at the side of the path just as the ambulance passed by on its way to rescue me. Without the ambulance coming to my aid, he would surely have *died* there.

Aha. That explained why, during the whole ordeal, I had felt overshadowed by a calming, even angelic, presence. This rescue was about *him*, not me. I was just the vehicle.

Chelsea and I warmed up together in one emergency room bed, shivering under warm woolen blankets. The attending physician gave us the good news—what looked like a bone fragment sticking out of my shin was just a piece of flesh which would easily heal. He was stern, however, with the young man in the bed beside us, telling him how close he'd come to dying. The young man was rather blasé, remarking how he couldn't wait to join his buddies later for a beer.

On hearing this, Chelsea and I just shrugged and hugged each other closer. We both agreed—the next time we wanted to "bond," we'd go out and get our nails done!

So you see, daughters, you can choose to view your life as coincidence or chance with little meaning. Or you can choose to view your life as a purposeful, meaningful, Spirit-filled journey, as an act of bravery or even faith. Approaching your day-to-day life as a quest implies that you are seeking to discover yourself, others, the world and the mysterious Creator. Such a journey will lead you into uncharted and unfamiliar territory—into the very wilderness itself. The choice is yours.

Trapped!

During my training as an anthropologist, I learned that people in indigenous cultures, consciously or not, usually juxtapose the area of "wilderness" against the area of their "culture." The "culture" always resides in the *center* of the town or village where the homes are located, while the "wilderness" lies in the area outside: on the margins, the fringes surrounding the safe center. In the overgrown wilderness of forest, jungle or desert, ghosts, dead ancestors, and witches roam, haunting or sometimes attacking, a lost or careless native. There are plenty of taboos and rituals to protect a native until he arrives safely back home to his family and village.

Most of us live in a "safe" and familiar round of life; the Internet, iPods, the constant thrum of music, noise and images assault our senses at every turn. Is it possible to become our fullest selves if we always play it safe in the arms of our culture or our close-knit circle of family and friends?

Are you familiar with the process a trainer uses to teach an elephant to be docile and obedient? The trainer takes the baby elephant, ties one end of a rope onto the shackle around the baby's ankle, and the other end to a pole in the ground, limiting the baby elephant's movement to a small circle. As the elephant grows older and larger, the trainer puts on a bigger shackle, extending the lead, and allowing the elephant to roam in a slightly larger circle. After this "training," the trainer can remove the shackle, but that full-grown elephant, weighing one to two tons and possessing incredible strength, will venture no farther—ever—than that small circle.

Or did you know that when a scientist takes a pot of boiling water and tosses a frog into it (I know this sounds cruel), the frog will jump about frantically to get out and save its life. But if the scientist places the frog into a pot of nice, cool water, the frog will start to swim around, and as the scientist slowly turns up the heat, the frog, never suspecting its life is in danger, will boil to death.

One final image. The ancient Greek philosopher Plato suggested that human beings lived their lives as though inside a cave. Seeing shadows thrown up on the cave walls caused by people passing in front of the fire outside the cave, they mistook the *shadows* of those persons for the actual flesh-and-blood ones. Seldom did a person have the courage to leave the false comfort of the cave to venture outside into the blinding light of reality.

We Westerners have something in common with the elephant, the frog and Plato's cave dwellers, don't you think? Might we too often settle for running around in circles or staying in place until we boil to death of boredom? Do we too often cling to our small, safe, restricted, one-room life rather than risking the vast unknown to discover our unique path and purpose? Do we tend to believe that our conception of reality is the only reality?

12

Years ago, my then ten-year-old nephew Michael, after reading the Old Testament, had been assigned by his teacher to read the New Testament. As a Christian pastor, I chuckled out loud when I heard him groan:

"Mom, I don't think I'm going to like the New Testament. The Old Testament was about the journey of a whole people, while the New Testament is only about one guy and his pals!"

Oh, my dear Michael. On the surface, you are quite correct. Certainly, Jesus was a part of family, friends, and Jewish culture and faith life. But he didn't stay long in that cozy, familiar circle. He went further out—wa-a-a-y out! Jesus epitomized the boldness of venturing into the wilderness, outside the margins of society and propriety. My dear friend and colleague, anthropologist and theologian Tony Gittins, observes that Christians should be willing to be led

> ...to encounters on the margins and not at the centers, in unhabituated places rather than by familiar landmarks. It is where our personal space or territory or turf is opened up to others, and where others invite us into their own world.

> For Jesus, it happens at the water's edge, in graveyards, in deserted places, by a well, at a bedside or a tomb, up a mountain, in a dark garden, on a cross; it is manifest in the breaking of bread, at a supper, a breakfast, with a hungry crowd, at a marriage feast, and in myriad spontaneous and surprising encounters.

Almost every faith tradition understands the wilderness to be an auspicious place to encounter one's demons and angels. The important notion I hope you will grasp, dear ones, while reading this trail guide, is that your journey is part of a much *larger* human journey—wilderness and all.

As *SoulQuesters*, we are called to find our gifts and use them for the common good. We are not called to play it safe, at least not often. It is imperative that we challenge the aspects of our culture and the *status quo* that devalue and damage women *just because* they are women. It means we will rethink and transform harmful stereotypes of what it means to be male in our culture. It means we will purposely head out into the wilderness at some time in our lives: a wilderness outside of us or, more likely, the wilderness within us.

The call of the wilderness brings us to a land where dangers lie in wait and temptations lurk in the shadows. But it is also where the action is—the healing, restoring, renewing and transforming action of Love. At this fragile time in human history, when we hold the nuclear potential to blow up the world at least thirteen times, as sisters and brothers of spirit on an intentional quest, we must not show forth the *love of power*. No. We are destined to show forth the *power of love*.

Using Power on the Quest

Power in general has to do with the use of strength, force. It has to do with agency, a sense of control over one's life choices. It has to do with passion, purpose, and confidence. There are basically three types of power, as Wiccan theologian Starhawk observes: "power over," "power within" and "power with." "Power over" others has been the dominant strategy in the West for thousands of years. As you know, while those with power over others flourish, those under them usually suffer.

The "power within" has several names. Quakers call it the "inner light"; others might call it God's spirit or the Holy Spirit. You can think of the "power within" as your conscience, your own inner knowing, a still small voice within you. At times, it may guide you gently yet clearly. At other times, you may feel a rush of power, or tingling, or a surge of energy pushing you towards the right next thing to do. Though it takes time and effort to work with this "power within," I believe this power, which seeks only good for our souls and others, is constantly available to each one of us.

"Power with" focuses on *sharing* power between persons. For example, it means that a leader empowers people under her or his care. "Power with" includes respecting others: employees, bosses, friends, and listening carefully to them. The act of paying attention is one of the greatest gifts we can give another human being. The mode of "power with" works best in building relationships, whether in work or in love. In using our "power with," we build up and support others, while accepting their support and encouragement.

I believe that many women hesitate, if not downright resist taking on their spiritual power. For the first half of my life, I refused to take on my own spiritual power. Why? Because the "power over" model was the only model available, and I'd seen enough abuse done by male priests, fathers, and other males in positions of authority. I wanted no part of that kind of power.

For example, as a newly ordained pastor thirty years ago, I was interviewed by a group of male counselors to join their team of pastoral counselors. After polite introductions, some of the men began to make fun of my smile. They claimed I couldn't be helpful to anyone in counseling because, as a woman, I only knew how to smile and be nice. They assumed I had no inner strength to deal with people in crisis. I was so shocked by their harsh judgments that I sat there in stunned silence at the unexpected turn of the interview.

Finally, one of the pastors spoke up, chiding his colleagues.

"What are we doing here, guys? She is new to our group. She's only smiling to be polite and friendly. Yet we're tearing her apart for it! We should apologize and get back to focusing on her qualifications for the job."

The group didn't apologize but did re-focus on my resume.

When the interview was over, I left the office, fuming, and jumped into the car my husband had pulled up. I spilled out the story to him. He was totally supportive. The following day, when the men called me to offer me the position, I was still so outraged that I told them there was no way I would want to work with those "power-hungry" males.

It wasn't long, though, before the naive and self-righteous young me discovered that males aren't the only gender susceptible to the abuse of power. In the words of British Lord Acton, "Absolute power corrupts absolutely." So all of us must ask the following questions about any situation, especially when we are directly involved:

- Who has the power? Who doesn't?
- Who are the chosen leaders? Who are the role models?
- What role does gender play?
- Who is suffering? Why?
- How can the situation be changed, so that safety, respect and human dignity belong to not just those in power, but to all persons involved?

Whether we are mommies or CEOs, daddies or department heads, we must be ruthlessly honest with ourselves about how we are using our power: over, within or with.

Sacred Landscape vs. Secular Landscape

As a child, my society and family taught me that the two worlds of sacred and secular were opposites, and never the twain shall meet. So I divided the areas of my life into either sacred or secular. Throughout the last 2000 years, the West has identified the sacred or "spirit" world with gods, deities, angels, *devas*, fairy spirits, and the like. The realm of "the spiritual" is concerned with "Spirit" or God, whatever the image of he/she/it might be. It also refers to the highest human values: love, peace, hope, courage, justice, kindness. The spiritual includes a sense of the "numinous"—drawing out our feelings of mystery, awe, wonder, the indescribable, and the un-nameable. The realm of the sacred encompasses practices such as prayer, meditation, fasting, tithing, and service to foster a spiritual life growing toward more awareness of, and ultimately union with, God.

On the other hand, the secular world, which some spiritual traditions call the "profane," includes the non-spirit world: people, creatures, and matter like rocks and machines. It also includes everyday mundane human activities, such as washing cars, working, raising children, playing the stock market, getting married or getting sick. (I'm not equating these last two, you understand.)

Over the past several decades, my parameters of "spiritual" have radically changed. I now include everything that I used to consider secular *within* the realm of the "spiritual." Perhaps you think of God as "immanent," that is, *within* all created persons and objects, even nature; or as "transcendent," above and *outside* of all created matter. Some people, including myself, hold the view of *panentheism* which considers God to be both immanent and transcendent. The Lakota people have taught me that all "things," even the Stone People and the Cloud People, are alive in some sense. Each has a spark of *"wakan,"* the holy, within them, placed there by the Creator, *Wakan Tanka*. Other mystical traditions affirm a similar truth.

What do you think, sacred sisters, holy brothers?

The Stakes of Your Quest

Currently, there are so many ideological hot spots of conflict on our planet, many religion-based, planned, led and fought mainly by men. Many men, it seems, are motivated by fear of women and feel a sense of scarcity around sharing power with them. Recently, for example, the Vatican has begun to undermine the women who are risking being "ordained" to the priesthood by brave but "invisible" priests. The Vatican is placing these faith-filled women—who feel called by God to exercise their leadership gifts in Catholic communities with the shortage of male priests—into the category of sinning that includes priests who are pedophiles. This is an unconscionable last ditch effort by male church leaders to keep women out of their millennia-old, patriarchal power structures.

In our country, some males will get threatened when you take on your spiritual power and begin to apply your gifts and talents in the corporate world. I truly believe that men stand to benefit greatly from women exercising their creativity, brains, strength, heart, and moral and spiritual vision, in places of work and worship. Also, when women are freed from damaging stereotypes about their gender, men will be free from such debilitating stereotypes, as well. Thank goodness, many strong and visionary men, on their own or collaborating with strong, visionary women, are engaged in new models of partnership, both in the United States and around the globe.

Strangely, at least it seemed strange to me for many years, some women and men resist taking on their own power and simultaneously make trouble for women who are. Perhaps you've noticed this characteristic in some of your female friends or co-workers already. The term "internalized oppression" describes this attitude and can apply to any marginalized or oppressed group. A woman growing up in a sexist society that has put her down her whole life may identify herself with the culture's demeaning stereotype of women rather than seize the opportunity to exhibit her powerful, talented self in a realm of equality. Sounds like the frog or the elephant type to me.

But remember—as a woman, you have received a rich heritage, one that has cost others dearly to obtain and then hand down to you. For example, think of your foremothers, who fought to keep their families going during the Great Depression or struggled to keep their various faith traditions alive and vital during two world wars. Think of the early feminists who fought to win women the right to vote in 1920—less than one hundred years ago.

Women of my Baby Boomer generation suffered ridicule or ostracism as they led or participated in the Women's Movement, ultimately gaining you women readers access to traditionally all-male professions, where you have a pretty good chance of earning equal pay and prestige. They have helped guarantee you your constitutionally protected reproductive rights as well as freedom from sexual harassment in your place of work or study.

After reading this chapter's first draft, my daughter Chelsea suggested that I invite you right now, before you read any further, to get out your cell phone and give your Grandma, your mom or your aunt a call. Thank them for all the work they have done to pave the road for you so you can risk, succeed and become your best self in the world. Invite them to share their stories of the sacrifices they have made in the trenches so that you can soar.

Blest on the Quest

So, my daughters and sons, with your bold intentions and bright eyes, do you accept my invitation to undertake a perilous, daunting, exciting and surprising journey through the wilderness of life? Know that every *trail* can easily transform into a *trial*. The quest will demand all of your energy, will power and determination to find and claim your gifts so you can use them to transform your corner of the world.

No one can guarantee what will happen on our journey, but we do not travel alone. We can rely on the courage and vision of those who have gone before us, as well as those on the path next door or a million miles away. As you quest, my earnest prayer is that my signposts and stories will be helpful and inspiring, blessing you on your way.

On the outskirts of a vast and scary wilderness, a young woman and her elder guide prepare to undertake a perilous journey.

The young woman cries out in panic, *"But I don't see a path!"*

The wise older woman responds, *"Do not worry, my daughter. As we walk together, the path will appear."*

Are you excited, brave *SoulQuesters*? Let's prepare for the adventure!

18

TWO

You Matter!

"You've Come a Long Way, Baby"[1] but...

When my mother was pregnant with her first child—me—her friend Hazel whispered in one of those mysterious, knowing moments: "June, there's going to be something *wonderful* about this child." As a young girl, I never tired of asking my mom to tell this story. I thought if I heard it enough times, it would come true, and I would finally believe that I *was* wonderful.

I'm not unique in this desire. Each of us wants to believe that our existence matters in the whole crazy scheme of things. We long to know that not only were we wanted and cherished as infants, but that even as teenagers and adults, we matter. We long to believe that without our existence on the planet, the light would not shine so brightly, nor the laughter sound as lovely or the tears glisten so keenly. We long to express our unique gifts and talents. No matter our fussing, fumbling or failures, *we want our existence to matter.*

When I first moved to New Haven in November of 2000 to begin my job as Associate Pastor at the Church of Christ in Yale University, I was informed I needed to attend a state-wide clergy meeting. I went eagerly. As the day's activities went on, I noticed how lively the gathering was, with scores of pastors happily greeting each other with warm recognition. I began to feel more and more invisible.

That evening, all two hundred of us gathered to celebrate communion. Forlornly, I walked down the aisle and stood before the man serving the communion cup. As I looked into his eyes, he offered, "Pamela, the cup of blessing." I was stunned, amazed. How did this man know my name? Then it dawned on me—he had read my nametag! I had to laugh at myself and my longing to be known. *But every human being wants to be seen, to matter.*

Women are still at risk

---

[1] The old *Virginia Slims* cigarette slogan celebrating women's equal right to smoke, even to have her own brand of cigarette

Still, today in our advanced, first-world culture, women are at risk *just because they are female*. Even after winning the right to vote in 1920, and even after the First and Second Waves of feminism that advocated for women's equal rights with men, *even* after the Sexual Revolution with the advent of birth control pills, so that a woman's destiny is no longer tied solely to her anatomy, too many women are invisible, nameless and voiceless *just because they are women*.

Think about it. You enter your college orchestra's practice room. The walls are plastered with pictures of famous composers—all males. You enter your child's English or art classroom and masculine names and faces confront you. You turn on the TV to watch the latest report on a world summit meeting on some vital issue like economics or nuclear proliferation—and you see mostly men making the decisions. If you're a member of four of the five major world religions—Islam, Christianity, Judaism or Buddhism—chances are you will hear prayers uttered to God the Father, seldom to God the Mother.

What about women in leadership positions?

Take our great country, America. How visible are women in leadership? Though we pride ourselves on being the most highly evolved nation in the world, several other countries have beaten us in electing their first female president: India, Great Britain, Germany, Brazil and even an African nation, Liberia. Men occupy 84% of governorships. In the U.S. House and Senate, only 73 of the 535 members of both houses are female, a mere 17%. It's ironic that the new Iraqi constitution, backed by U.S. advisors, calls for 25% of its representation to be female. Why don't we here at home aim for that number?

In the corporate world, 88% of top corporate leadership positions are held by males. Routinely, glass ceilings—stained glass or otherwise—smack us women in the forehead on our way up the corporate ladder. Why don't we raise the bar here in the States for women's corporate leadership?

Economic security for women?

The Global Fund for Women reports (echoing a United Nations report in 1980) that around the globe, although women perform two-thirds of all labor and produce more than half of the world's food, they own only about one percent of the world's assets and 1/100th of the land. Women represent 70 percent of those living in absolute poverty. Two thirds of the world's uneducated children are girls, and two-thirds of the world's illiterate adults are women.

Economically in the U.S., women fare better, but not as well as you'd think. For example, according to the *U.S. Women's Bureau and the National Committee on Pay Equity* report of 2008, women in 1951 made about 64 cents for every dollar earned by men. The gender wage gap has narrowed and now women earn about 77 % of the salaries earned by their male counterparts. Are you satisfied with that?

Let me break it down for you in a hypothetical case.

- If you're a young woman who graduated from high school in the summer of 2009, you will earn *$700,000 less* over your working life than the young man standing in line with you to get his diploma.
- If you graduated from college, throughout your career, you stand to earn *$1.2* million <u>less</u> than the man getting his degree alongside you.
- If you graduated from law school, medical school, or got an MBA last summer, you could lose income of up to$2 million over your lifetime, just because you are <u>female</u>.

That two million dollars represents food you can't buy, credit cards you can't pay off, lessons your children won't be able to have, and retirement savings you can't put away.

Outrageous, right?

Let's face it. If we don't act now, if we don't teach our daughters to stand up proud and tall as they present themselves and their gifts to the world, how much leadership power and economic security will they hold in the future?

When my daughters, four and eight years old, headed off to the school bus, I sometimes asked them in a teasing voice, "What is your name?"

The eldest would respond rather timidly, "Chelsea Katrina Bro Benetz."

Pretending to be stern this time, I would again ask, "What is your name?"

She would answer a bit louder, "Chelsea Katrina Bro Benetz."

Finally the third time I asked her, she would throw her head back and shout with glee, "Chelsea Katrina Bro Benetz and proud of it!"

"Hurray!" I'd yell back.

Try this with you own kids or grandkids and see how they grow in stature, right before your eyes.

How's Your Self-Esteem?

Do you feel that people in your daily life take the time to listen to you? Do they value what you have to say? Do they invite you to make a contribution to the discussion, then verbally acknowledge your input? Do you have a few family members or friends who "get" you, who understand and love the real you? Are you even allowing the real you to shine forth for people to see? If your answer to many of these questions is "no," you may be suffering from low self-esteem.

One vivid instance from my life springs to mind. While slaving on my doctoral thesis about ten years ago, I had argued for hours with my adviser, trying to make him see the validity of the point I was making, but he just couldn't get it. Claiming it was my fault for being unclear, he sent me home to rewrite the chapter for the umpteenth time. I felt I had written extremely clearly and that *he* was the problem.

I stomped out of his office. As my car sped along the Dan Ryan Expressway, I fumed: "Why doesn't he get it? Does anybody see the point I'm making? Is it a good one? Or is he right and I'm the one who's crazy? I feel totally invisible. Do I even matter? Is anybody there? Does anybody care?"

As I zoomed along, I happened to glance to the far right lane. Covering the whole side of a large white semi-tractor-trailer were these letters in bold black print—"**P A M.**" Nothing else. No other words to explain the acronym.

I burst out laughing at God's timing. I could almost hear God chuckle: "*I* see you, Pam. You are certainly not invisible to me. You have some great ideas, too advanced for most people. Hang in there! I know you, PAM. And spell that out BIG!"

A sense of humor goes a long way in bolstering one's self-worth.

Causes of Low Self-Esteem

There are many causes of low self-esteem, as you know. Obviously, some major causes are childhood experiences of abuse or neglect (by parent or significant others), belligerent or indifferent teachers, critical peers, verbally abusive partners, and a culture which too often treats women as sex objects or potential victims of violence.

I want to briefly focus here on our fears, fears that keep us from acknowledging our own value.

1. Pleasing others while losing your true self

It's ironic, but I believe that as much as we want to matter—to ourselves, to others, and to God—we also fear becoming who we are called to be. We are afraid to "individuate"—the term the depth psychologist, Carl Jung, created for becoming the unique and special individual each of us can be—unique in all of history. To please our parents, spouse or boss, we may even try desperately to become someone else. We dread discovering that, no matter what we do, our authentic self will not be good enough.

Or perhaps we fear that when we look deep within ourselves, we will find no one home.

I experienced this for years. I played any role my parent, teacher or boyfriend asked of me because I wanted to be liked by others more than I wanted to be authentically me. Years later, when I finally decided to find out who I truly was, I didn't even know what color I liked, or what style of clothes I wanted to wear. Worse than that, I realized I didn't have a clue about what made me laugh or cry, what activities bored or thrilled me. Without feedback from boyfriend or sister, I had no idea who I was. Listen to this story from the Jewish mystical tradition.

> Zusya was a man intent on serving his God. So all of his life he tried to model himself after the leaders of his faith—Moses or Joshua. One day, his rabbi corrected him, saying,
>
> "Zusya, when you die, the Lord will not ask you, 'Why were you not Moses, or why were you not Joshua?'
>
> "He will demand of you, 'Why were you not Zusya?'"

Who are *you*, my one-of-a-kind friend?

2. Fear of deepening

Another fear that may hold us back from valuing ourselves is that while we live in adult bodies, at heart, we're really still children. If we're rich, maybe we love playing the role of the spoiled brat. If we grew up in the '60s (as I did), we might still be rebels in that hippie style. The term "Flower *Child*" denoted innocence, playfulness and trust. None of us wanted to be called a "Flower *College Student*" or "Flower *Adult*," especially an adult who waged war for profit. Our motto was "Make love, not war."

As the Vietnam War years dragged on, taking too many young lives, both American and Vietnamese, we took our young, fragile bodies to the streets in protest, and finally halted that terrible war. Afterwards, reluctantly, many of us finally decided to mature.

A wonderful fantasy story that addresses the fear of deepening is the children's book, *A Wind in the Door,* by my favorite children's author, Madeleine L'Engle. Twelve-year-old Meg Murry is worried about her brother Charles Wallace, a six-year-old genius and telepath who is shunned and bullied at school. On top of that, Meg discovers that Charles Wallace has a fatal disease which is leaving him short of breath. Their mother, a microbiologist, suspects it may have something to do with his cells' mitochondria (fact) and the "Farandolae" (fictional) that live within them.

Through the adventure to save Charles Wallace's life, Meg learns that the survival of our galaxy is being threatened by beings called *Echthroi*, who seek to erase the entire universe by un-Naming people, extinguishing their uniqueness and their ability to love. The Echthroi have targeted Charles Wallace and are destroying his farandolae. Meg and her friends travel inside one of his mitochondria, named Yadah, and finally convince a young farandola, against the urgings of an *Echthros*, to take root, deepen, and accept its role as a mature fara. Though Meg is nearly "Xed" herself, her friends name each other and the deepening farandolae, even the Darkness, and succeed in saving Charles Wallace's life.

If you're plagued by refusing to deepen in your life, you might glean keen insights from reading this book. I know it inspired me, and you'll love the many-winged, many-eyed cherubim hero, *Proginoskes*.

Later in L'Engle's life, a reporter asked her if she felt she had finally matured, like her character, Charles Wallace. L'Engle responded that her goal as an adult was to keep her inner child alive and joyful as well as to mature. This reminds me of the English mystic/poet, William Blake, who described the development of human life as a progression from innocence to experience to "wise innocence." I love that.

24

My former psychology professor in seminary, Jungian analyst Ann Ulanov, opened my eyes one day. I had been telling her how difficult it was for me to deepen. I had played the role of "Miss Superficiality" in our seminary community with great success; practically everyone liked me. But I found myself growing bored and restless. I longed to go deeper in understanding myself, especially in my relationships.

Even my faith life was being affected. I was afraid that if I deepened in my convictions as a Christian, I would become arrogant toward those of other faiths. So I refused to deepen. After listening intently to me, perched precariously on the sharp horns of my dilemma, Ann offered this alternative.

> Pam, imagine that each of the five fingers on my hand are the five major world religions. They are unique and different, though they are all fingers. As you choose to deepen in one tradition, it looks like you will be missing out on getting to know the other traditions, but as you can see, if you keep traveling deeper down your finger, you will end up in your palm. So will they.

> Your palm is the "Ground of Being," theologian Paul Tillich's name for God. That is the place where you can meet others from their distinctive traditions, not on the surface but at the deepest level.

I chose to deepen that very day.

Years later, I found the works of the eloquent Persian mystic poet, Rumi. When he died in December of 1273, representatives of every major religion attended his funeral to honor him. Why? In the midst of the Crusades with violent conflict on every side, he had come to this conclusion, "I go into the Moslem mosque and the Jewish synagogue and the Christian church and I see *one* altar." Rumi had found his way to the palm of God, and in the process, created a holy space where others of various faiths could join him.

3. A final (and surprising) fear

Some years ago, I read this passage by spiritual writer Marianne Williamson in her book *Return to Love*. Her truth resonated strongly with me.

Our deepest fear is not that we are inadequate. Our deepest fear is that we are powerful beyond measure. It is our light, not our darkness, that most frightens us.

We ask ourselves, "Who am I to be brilliant, gorgeous, talented, fabulous?" Actually, who are you *not* to be? You are a child of God. Your playing small does not serve the world. There is nothing enlightened about shrinking so that other people won't feel insecure around you.

We are all meant to shine, as children do. We were born to make manifest the glory of God that is within us. It is not just in some of us; it is in everyone. And as we let our own light shine, we unconsciously give other people permission to do the same.   As we are liberated
from our own fear, our presence automatically liberates others.

Yes! Each time one of us claims we are a child of God and lets that light shine, it's infectious. Somebody else realizes, "Oh, my! I'm a child of God, too!"   They start letting *their* light shine, so the collective light grows brighter and brighter. To use another metaphor, a flower does not beg for fragrance. It just releases its essence. That's our calling, too—to release our God-selves with our luscious fragrance. We matter. We must reclaim our self-worth.

An Exercise with Your Imagination

I have been doing this imaginative exercise with groups for thirty years because it reveals so much about one's self-image so quickly. Please keep in mind that there are no wrong answers. Rather, this exercise is designed to help you get to know the language and symbols of your psyche, your subconscious, that deep place within you that often knows what's going on with you more than your conscious self does.

To do this exercise, you may want to prepare a tape of yourself reading these directions, or have a friend read them to you. Don't force anything to appear in your mind's eye. Trust that as your mind becomes still, images will automatically float to the surface. It's best to finish the whole guided imagery exercise before you write anything down. I think you will be surprised. (And if you do this exercise again in a year, your symbols will most likely change.)

Take three deep breaths, breathing in calmness and breathing out stress.

Now, imagine that you are walking down a path. What kind of path is it? Is it curved or straight? Wide or narrow? What is it made of—concrete, dirt, pebbles, pine needles? Have you seen it before or is it a new path? What surrounds it?

Let a path present itself in your imagination. Later, jot down your answer on these pages or in your journal.

Walking leisurely along, you look down on the path ahead of you, and you see a cup. You stoop to pick it up. What kind of cup is it? What is it made of? What does it look like? How does it feel as you cup it in your hands or hold it delicately by the handle?

After you examine it closely, you put it in your back pack and go on.

Then as you're walking slowly down the path, looking around at everything around you, you find a key. What kind of key is it? What door might it open? What might you do with it?

Then you put the key in your pocket and continue walking down the path. You come to a body of water. What kind of water is it? A tiny stream, a roaring river, a lake, a waterfall, the ocean? What, if anything, do you do with this water?

You know that you can come back to this water any time, so you continue walking along. You come to a large obstruction in the road. What is it? Natural or human-made? What, if anything, do you do about the obstacle? Does the path continue on the other side? If so, can you get around the obstacle? Do you want to?

Now slowly come back to yourself in your room, your chair, and take some deep breaths. Go back in your mind's eye, and write down any details you remember.

Next, apply the following symbolic analysis. But remember what my dad used to say, quoting depth psychologist, Carl Jung: "Always interpret the *dreamer*, not the dream." In this case, take everything I suggest in the following paragraphs and check it against your own experience, guts and intuition. Why? Your psyche has chosen each symbol specifically for you and you alone, based on your "lived experience" (an anthropologist's term for honoring the embodied nature of experience), in order to reveal the workings of your inner life.

The path

The path symbolizes your current situation in life. What clues does your path provide about how you see your life right now? For example, is your path straight? Then you probably know right where you're going in the coming weeks or months. If your path is winding or going up hill and you can't see far ahead, perhaps you feel that your life in the next months or so is somewhat uncertain, maybe even challenging.

Pay attention to the composition of the path. Is it concrete, hard and paved—a well-traveled road, perhaps showing you that you prefer traditional paths? Or is it a grassy dirt path, one less traveled, indicating you may be more comfortable with charting your own unusual course rather than following the crowd?

Is the path familiar, for example, the one you walked with your grandmother on her farm? If so, what qualities do you associate with your grandmother or her farm? Perhaps the path that appeared is brand new to you. For some people, that is a good thing, signifying adventure and the unknown. For others, anxiety may arise.

Each of the aspects of your path can reveal your subconscious understanding of your life situation right now. Don't be afraid to dialogue with your images. They arose in your mind's eye to reveal something specific *just* for you.

The cup

The cup symbolizes your self-worth. Since a cup allows us to offer someone a drink, it can symbolize how we offer ourselves to the world. What kind of cup did you find?   Perhaps it was a family cup from your childhood.   Then how you picture yourself will have something to do with family ties, values, or cherished or troubling memories. Maybe you found a delicate teacup. That might mean you see yourself as fragile, or at least sensitive, in how you present yourself to others. Tea is a calming, civilized and soothing beverage, so your subconscious may be affirming that you have the gift of calming others.

Perhaps you have imagined a white paper cup, or seemingly worse, a Styrofoam cup. Don't panic! Keep reflecting upon your associations and feelings. This doesn't mean your self-worth is necessarily low. Of course, since a paper cup is easily crushed and disposed of, your psyche's choice of this symbol might mean that you don't value yourself, that you see yourself as easily expendable or somehow cheap. On the other hand, the positive aspects of a paper cup could indicate that you are easily available to help others; without fanfare or much ado, you offer your "cup of cold water," as the Bible urges readers to do. What a gift!

If you have envisioned a silver or golden goblet, then most likely you have a precious sense of your self-worth. *Caution*: always ask yourself what the symbol or color or material means *to you*, in light of your life's experience. It is *your* subconscious, after all.

Twenty-five years ago, I had breakthrough about my self-worth. One Saturday, I went to hear a spiritual leader give a talk in downtown Manhattan. He asked the audience: *"Imagine that you are a cup. What does the cup look like?"* (Sound familiar?)

A particular cup presented itself to my mind's eye. It was unremarkable. Actually, it was worse than that. It was broken, chipped, and dirty. I wondered what other people were imagining. I suspected most of them visualized a beautiful china teacup, or perhaps a crystal goblet. My cup, by comparison, was in terrible shape.

The leader continued,

> Now imagine you're out on the desert and somebody comes up to you, desperately thirsting for a drink of cold water. You have a cup and it's the only cup around. It's you. You have water—God's spirit, right?—God's love which only you can pour out.

But you refuse to give it to the person, claiming, "I can't give you any water or relief. My cup's all cracked and dirty."

That exercise really set me to thinking about how I viewed my self. I realized that God can use even a chipped and broken cup to provide a needy person with the relief of cold water. Any kind of cup can be of service; you do not have to wait until your self-esteem is high before you offer your gifts to a hurting world. I love Martin Luther's pithy saying, penned almost five hundred years ago: "God can ride the lame horse and carve the rotten wood. What more, then, can he do with us?"

Years after this experience, after working hard with self-talk, visualization, and inviting God and some beloved friends to fill my heart's cracked cup with love, I performed this exercise once again. This time, as I walked down the path of my imagination, there at my feet lay a beautiful golden goblet, inlaid with priceless jewels. What a confirmation of all my hard work. You can transform your self-image, too, in your own way and time.

The key

The key is a commonly recognized symbol for knowledge. What are you seeking answers for in your life right now? What is important to you to learn more about? Often students of mine tell me they have found an old-fashioned skeleton key. Since a skeleton key's function is to open many doors, it makes sense that they are seeking knowledge of not just one but many subjects. There's also the common association of the skeleton key with "skeletons in the closet." Perhaps there is something in your life or your heart long hidden away that now begs to be discovered and healed. In another case, if you pictured a key to your dwelling, most likely this symbolizes that your home, or the relationships in our home, are important to you at this point on your journey. Get the idea? Have fun. Be creative.

The body of water

The body of water is such a rich symbol that it can stand for several things. Did you imagine a well, fountain or waterfall? An ocean, a lake? Dialogue with this symbol. First, the body of water can stand for your *sexuality*--your juiciness, wetness, fluidity. Second, the body of water may stand for your *emotional* life, since our emotions are constantly changing. Last but not least, the body of water can symbolize your *spiritual* life, for water is the most vital element for our planet's and our human existence. It is the source of all life. Ask yourself: is the body of water smooth and calm, or stormy and rough? Is the water threatening or reassuring or alluring?

Look at how you responded to the water. Did you leap right in, even stripping down to your skin? (Many of my college students report this in their exercise.) Or did you place a timid toe in? Was it more comfortable, even safer, to sit and just watch the water? Did you take a clear, cool drink with the cup you found on your path? What are these clues telling you about yourself and your relationship to your sexuality, emotions or your relationship to Spirit: Perhaps a combination?

Remember, my companions, there is no right or wrong to this exercise. The goal is to better understand the dynamics of your inner landscape right here, right now.

The obstruction on the path

The obstruction can symbolize at least two levels. At one level, the type of obstruction can reveal some information about what type of obstruction or challenge you are currently facing on your life's path. For example, was the obstruction man-made (bulldozer or brick wall), or natural (dead tree or living tree fallen over, dead animal, boulder, etc.) Does the obstruction symbolize something you have helped to create? Recall more details of your encounter with the obstruction. Do you sit and wait for the problem to resolve itself? Do you get up and climb around it? Do you avoid it altogether, or are you somehow creative and courageous in navigating around the obstruction so you can continue on your path?

On a deeper level, the obstruction can stand for your unconscious image of death. Is the concept of death man-made, an artificial construction like a brick wall or a bulldozer? Or is it natural, like a huge boulder or a dead tree trunk, fallen over? Ask yourself, does the path continue beyond the obstruction, perhaps indicating some kind of belief in an after-life? Again, look at your response to the obstruction.

If you share this exercise with a trusted friend, you will probably obtain richer insights than by doing it alone. The goal is to get some insight into your life right now, so that you can assess what step you want to take next—whether it's healing a specific part of your self-worth, or celebrating how far you've come. This is a great party game, but be sure your guests feel truly safe with each other.

Some Ways to Heal Low Self-Worth

There are many ways to heal low self-worth. One is to read a book on raising self-esteem. Or you can join a support group—this is usually free and can be a wonderful boost if the group and group leader are right for you. If you have the money and choose to adopt the sentiment of the L'Oreal commercial—"Because you're worth it!"—you can treat yourself to a one-day workshop or months of therapy. These can help you identify the sources of damage to your self-esteem as well as explore strategies for building a more confident and happy you. I've used the following four techniques over the years to bolster my self-esteem.

1. Invite other women to fill the holes in your heart.

Many years ago when my children were little, I began to miss my mother terribly. She and my dad lived in a different state. Because my father was quite possessive of her time, and she had a full life of her own, I didn't see her very much. Besides, her main job as my mom should have ended when I turned 18, but I still wanted more from her. I felt I had a big hole in my heart, and I desperately wanted my mom to fill it. I ached constantly.

One day, wandering around a local bookstore, the book, *Circle of Stones* by Judith Duerk literally jumped off the shelf into my hands. At home, I eagerly devoured every word. Judith honored my aching desire for more "mothering" from my mom. She voiced my longing to relate to other women in supportive, multi-generational ritual settings.

After reading the book, I decided to set my mother free from my unreal and frustrating expectations. At the same time, I began to gather in the love and "mothering" actions of various women friends, filling my "mother-less" hole with their love. Over time, this method not only freed me from resenting my mom's absence but allowed me to be totally grateful for whatever precious time I did spend with her.

2. Become the very person you are seeking to find.

This next practice is more radical, that is, it goes deeper to heal the roots of your empty or broken heart. Let me give you an example.

About fifteen years ago, again I felt the panic of abandonment accompanied by a huge surge of longing to be mothered. I no longer looked to my biological mother to fill those gaps, but I still felt somewhat un-nurtured. I hungered to be held, rocked and cuddled. True, I was in the middle of the grueling process of getting my Ph.D. That can drive anyone to infantile regression!

So I signed up for a workshop on healing with Korean shaman, Hiah Park. During one part of the weekend in a Chicago hotel, Hiah invited all two hundred conferees to lie down in the semi-darkness and imagine we were infants. She told us she would come around and walk on our chests (she was light as a feather and quick as a bird), massage out the pain and longing, and help us to heal. I eagerly lay down on the hotel ballroom floor in the darkened room, waiting with expectancy. I just knew she would heal my mother-wound.

Soon, I was shocked to hear howls of pain and sobs of sadness breaking out around the room. I watched out of the corner of my eye as Hiah stepped over some bodies in order to choose someone's chest to climb on. After massaging them with her bare feet, she knelt and held them, often rocking them in her petite arms until their sobbing subsided. Then she moved on to the next person. I couldn't wait for her to come to me.

As I lay there with baited breath, Hiah stumbled right over me to get to a man just beyond me. As she tried to balance lightly on the man's chest, my heart sank as I realized that she was holding out her hand, motioning for me to steady her. Now I had a tough decision to make. I had come to the workshop expressly to have her heal *me*. Yet I could see she really wanted me to help her heal *others*.

I made a quick, self-sacrificing decision. Reaching out to take her hand, we became partners in healing. For the next hour, I accompanied her, responding swiftly to every silent motion she made to steady her balance, to add pressure on the chest or to offer soothing strokes to her "patient." Amidst the wailings in the hotel room turned shamanic healing circle, sometimes I knelt down myself to cradle a weeping person in my arms.

When the healing session was over, Hiah and the rest of us gathered in a big circle on the floor to share what we had experienced. After a few deep breaths, I looked into my heart to process the event. Lo and behold—to my utter amazement, my mother-hole had been filled! The longing was gone. Miraculously, through my mothering of others, I had become the very mother I so desperately sought.

3. Change your self-talk from negative to positive.

We have an opportunity every day to re-train ourselves in our self-talk: how we talk to ourselves in private, in the silence of our minds. In the "old days," we used to call this process "changing the tapes," referring to audiotapes. For example, whenever you start to hear a nagging voice in the back of your head telling you that you're stupid, or selfish, or not worthy; whenever you feel you're being judged by an invisible tyrant who pronounces, "You don't deserve to be happy," "You will never find someone who really loves you," "You will never succeed at anything"—just nip that voice in the bud.

You know what you would say to a little child if they had been ridiculed or bullied by someone. Say those kind words to yourself. "I am worthy of love," "I will succeed at whatever I try," "I can make a difference in the world." So I say to you—change your CD! Change your *ipod*! Play only those tunes which remind you of your precious self-worth.

When you practice, scientists have proven that you are truly reprogramming your brain. The negative thoughts travel along ruts or grooves between certain neuro-synapses. Your negative thoughts love these tracks or ruts. But over time, with persistent repetition, your new thoughts will create new pathways. Retraining your critical voice is hard work, but there's nothing more important that raising your SLQ: your Self-Love Quotient. You *can* get a new "groove on" and dance to the music of self-appreciation.

4. Try visualization.

Visualization is another technique you can use to change negative self-talk into positive affirmations. Years ago, I attended a workshop on how to transform self-defeating behaviors. After a day of self-observance and self-inquiry, we were instructed to lie down on the rug and get comfortable. Then the instructor asked us to close our eyes and imagine that our negative voice was coming to attack us. *What image came to mind? Where were we? What did we feel?*

Can you close your eyes and imagine the answers to these questions? Perhaps you want to write them down in your journal.

At first, I found myself imagining that my negative voices came from a mean old witch inside of me, so I prepared for her to emerge. But what leapt out at me was a dragon—a huge dragon, roaring and breathing out tongues of fire, and chasing me down cobblestone streets. It was gaining quickly on me, intent on utterly destroying me.

In the nick of time, the instructor cried out, "Now turn around and *kill* whatever is trying to destroy you!"

Well, that directive hit me a bit harshly since I considered myself a pacifist. I'm the one who, as a child, always cheered for the underdog—*King Kong, the Creature of the Black Lagoon.* I just couldn't kill this dragon. However, feeling the dragon's breath hot upon me and quaking in my boots (was I some sort of medieval knight or peasant?), I scrambled atop a cobblestone roof. I realized I had to do something and *quick.* Summoning up all my courage, I turned around and yelled at the dragon with all my might, "*Drop dead!*"

To my astonishment, the dragon screeched to a grinding halt, disbelief in its red-hot eyes. My command totally deflated him. He turned and slunk away to his cave to lick his wounds. I was stunned by his response. Then, lying on the rug, it hit me that the dragon had the power to belittle and destroy me only because I had *given* him my power. Once I took my power back, he was a sorry sight indeed. I am still working with these practices, but my negative thoughts have rarely reached dragon proportions again. So there's hope for each one of us.

5. Last but not least, see yourself through God's eyes.

We set loose a mighty healing power when we turn to God, or Jesus, or another Spiritual Being, to save us from our lack of self-worth. In seminary over twenty-five years ago, I had recently gone through a devastating divorce. I was filled with low self-esteem, self-doubt and self-loathing. I thought, "Oh, my God, I've broken my life-long vows and let you down, Jesus. You will never forgive me. I'm a worthless person."

Around this time, my professor Ann Ulanov (again) was lecturing on identity formation. As she talked about the damaging role of low self-esteem in the formation of a positive identity, several of us nodded our heads in acknowledgement. She asserted that our low evaluation of ourselves was not really humility.

"No way!" I bristled inside myself. "I'm humble; I'm unworthy. I accept that."

Ann persisted in maintaining that our low self-image was *arrogant.*

"Arrogant? How so?" I questioned.

Because, she responded, we were putting our own (low) opinion of ourselves before God's high opinion of us. I felt like she had thrown a bucket of cold water on my face. From that day on, though I sometimes fell back into a low opinion of myself, I was no longer able to clap myself on the back in congratulations for my "arrogant low self-esteem."

Dearest, please keep up the effort to get to know the Divine, the one who created you and who loves you beyond belief. In my experience, there's nothing that makes life more bearable, or more beautiful, than a love affair with God. The Divine will appear, not always on demand, but the Divine will reveal itself in amazing ways. How do I know?

It was one of the darkest times of my life. My husband was in a mental hospital for his bi-polar disorder that raged out of control. My two young daughters were terrified to go to school and leave me. I was trying to finish my dissertation so that all the years of pain and sacrifice my family had endured would not be wasted. Also, during those excruciating months, I had resolved to keep my morning meditation time no matter what.

Sitting in the quiet on my living room floor, I felt that God had totally abandoned me. On top of that, I feared I was losing my family, maybe even my sanity. Truly I must be a worthless human being for causing such heartache to those I so deeply cherished. I closed my eyes, expecting to experience only the silence of despair, the emptiness of abandonment, my constant companions.

Suddenly, in my mind's eye, I found myself sitting at the bottom of a dark, damp well.

"Doesn't surprise me," I muttered under my breath.

I hunched over, shivering in the cold-seeping wetness. Numb, but ever the dutiful daughter of God the Father, I made myself pray with words that rang hollow, bereft of the slightest connection to God.

No response. Big deal. I hadn't really expected one, since none had been forthcoming for weeks.

But then, some tiny movement caught the corner of my eye. Astonished, I looked closer. From the dark brick wall, a tiny pink bud emerged on a fragile stem, radiating out its love to me. I blinked in disbelief, as its soft warmth penetrated my heart.

"Jesus?" I blinked, tears springing up. "Is that you? I'm not really alone, even in this God-forsaken place?"

The answer came clearly yet delicately as a rose petal.

"I am here, Pam. You are not alone. You mean the world to me. I am with you everywhere. I will never leave you alone. You matter."

Now, some of you *SoulQuesters* may have found this book jumping off the bookstore shelf into your hands, whispering enticingly: "Take me home with you. Let's travel together a while, as Holy Companions on a quest." Many times in my life when I've been lost, whirling or stunned, somehow I had the presence of mind to ask—even beg—the Universe for help. In response, trail guides, both divine and human, have magically and mysteriously appeared to me—sharing their wisdom, offering a helping hand, identifying the dangers, pointing out the pitfalls and most important of all, unquestionably accepting me for the person God created me to be. They kept me focused, if not on the stars, then at least on the horizon of my inner quest. They convinced me that I mattered.

So, my sweet companions, I'm here to tell you that *you matter*. Whether your parents planned your conception, or you were a complete surprise, even unwanted, whether you were a problem child or a troubled teen (who wasn't?), you matter. You matter in the most serious, earth-shattering, life-giving way. There is something special about you that can make all those you meet more happy, more wise, or just plain more alive.

You matter. If the deepening of the tiniest mitochondria matters to our physical bodies, then each of us matters to the great cosmos. Like Meg, we are called to name and love the darkness and hate that threaten to destroy our planet and ourselves. You can and must offer your gifts to the world, again and again and again, because

You matter.

THREE

Gender Matters:

The *Feminine Mystique* and the Feminist Critique

From the *Virginian-Pilot* newspaper article, "Female winners of the Nobel Prize," October 18, 2007:

Every October, the Nobel Foundation announces the new crop of Nobel Prize winners. Of the total 777 individual winners since 1901, in which field have women received the most Nobel Prizes?
A. Literature
B. Physics and chemistry
C. Peace
D. Physiology or medicine

A. Literature is not correct. Beginning in 1909, 11 women from nine different countries have won the Nobel Prize in literature.

B. Physics and chemistry are not correct. Four different women have won the prize in this field, beginning with the chemist Madam Curie in 1903, and again in 1911, the first woman to ever win the Nobel Prize twice.

D. Physiology or medicine is not correct. It took 46 years for a woman to win the Nobel Prize in this field. All told, only seven women have been winners, all of whom are from either the United States or Western Europe.

C. Right! Peace is correct. Twelve women from nine different countries have won the Nobel Peace Prize. In this field, the nationalities are diverse, including Mother Teresa of India and Aung San Suu Kyi of Burma.

These statistics (see www.nobelprize.org) mean that roughly once every decade, a woman has been awarded the prize. The shocking truth is that, in all, women account for 34 – or **4 percent** – of the 777 prizes awarded to individuals." (my emphasis)

Now I ask you, sisters of spirit, does this record present a true account of women's cultural contributions to the global community? A mere 4 %? Or do these statistics offer a false assessment of women's possible or actual achievements?

Not only are women as half the human race not achieving their potential, their well-being and their very lives are at risk *because of their gender*.

Here are some more shocking statistics.

Women as Victims of Violence

Global Trafficking

According to the U.S. State Department's *Trafficking in Persons Report* (June, 2005), of the estimated 600,000 to 800,000 persons to be victims of international trafficking (kidnapping, coercion, exploitation, especially for sexual purposes), approximately 80% are women and girls. *The Global Fund for Women* reports that one in three women will be raped, beaten or coerced into sex in her lifetime. Rape as a weapon of war is an increasing feature of global conflicts from the Sudan to Iraq and beyond.

In the United States

Even in our country, women are far from safe. For example, the *National Women's Study*, a three-year study done by the Institute of Justice for the Department of Justice (2000) revealed that of the over 4,000 women from ages 18 to 50, 13% of adult women have been victims of completed rape during their lifetime, 22% by strangers but the majority by fathers, relatives or friends.

The Department of Justice issued another study in 2005, showing that teenage girls are really at risk. For example, while 13-24 year-olds comprised only 11.7% of the population between 1998 and 2002, they accounted for 42% of the victims of violence committed by a boyfriend or girlfriend.

In addition, between those same four years, 84% of spouse abuse victims were women, and 86% of date rape or abuse crimes were women. Some organizations insist that only 60% of such violent crimes are even reported, making the actual number even higher. Shamefully, the United States has the highest percentage of all those countries who track and report rape.

Is it in "women's nature" to be abused, oppressed, overworked and underpaid, illiterate or under-represented like this? Is it in "men's nature" to rule over women? How did women end up at such risk around the globe, just because of their gender? Though there is no simple answer, a brief summary of the history of Western patriarchy may be helpful.

The Ancient World of Patriarchy

2,000 years B.C.E. up to the late 19th century

Rosemary Radford Ruether is a pioneer in Christian feminist theology that greatly influenced my generation. In her now-classic work, *Sexism and God-Talk: Toward a Feminist Theology*, she defines patriarchy as "the rule of the fathers." It is a form of social organization in which the father is the supreme authority in the family, clan, or tribe, and descent is reckoned in the male line, with the children belonging to the father's clan or tribe. All rights—political, economic, and social—belong to the father and are passed down through the father to the son(s). Furthermore, Ruether defines "androcentrism" as the cultural practice of valuing the white, propertied, free male as the norm for being human—physically, emotionally, morally, intellectually and spiritually—while women (and non-white males) are below normal. Actually, an androcentric culture views woman as defective human beings.

One day in our "Feminist Theology" class, Ruether suggested that the Christian tradition, strongly shaped by and colluding with an androcentric cultural tradition, has stereotyped woman as "being created second and sinning first—not a very good track record for us women!" She made us all laugh, even as we winced at the painful observation. Sexism—the practice of prejudice or discrimination based on sex, *especially* discrimination against women while valuing white, propertied males as the norm—has corrupted the Christian-based image of women made in the image of the Creator as stated in Genesis 1:27: "So God created them in His own image. Male and female created He them." (I know. "His" image. I told you it wasn't simple.) For millennia, patriarchal Christianity has marginalized and demeaned women, using them as scapegoats for the sins of "men."

Great chain of being

  Christianity—indeed all of our Western culture—has been influenced by the "Great Chain of Being" concept espoused by Greek philosophers around the time of Christ. Here it is, showing who rules over whom, according to their "God-given" nature:

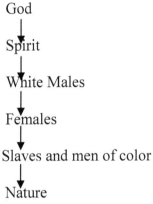

Deadly Dualisms

  Androcentrism distorts not only the male-female relationship, but all other important dialectical relationships when they are hierarchically ordered. The top line expresses what has been valued in our culture for the past two thousand years, the bottom line what is devalued.

God   *male*   spirit/soul intellect culture good grace reason
Nature *female* body   feelings   nature   evil works emotion

  Throughout the past two millennia, males have been identified with orthodoxy, that is, "right thinking," whereas women have been identified with heresy, "wrong thinking," like witchcraft. Remember learning about the Inquisition in Europe or the Salem witch trials on our own continent? Ruether demands that feminist theology reject the above dualisms and revaluate their worth *independent* of gender linking.

  Furthermore, in the Christian tradition,

- God is always referred to as male, i.e., "Father," "He," "Son";
- God intends it in the nature of things for superior males to rule inferior females; and
- God intends that human beings subdue nature and have dominion over the earth.

Ruether argues, and I agree, that this worldview is not God-ordained, but <u>man</u>-made (pun intended). Neither are the social, political, economic, educational and legal systems that support patriarchy ordained by a God, Christian or otherwise. The good news is that if these institutions are human-made, we humans can re-create them to express different values.

Now back to our mini-history lesson.

The Modern Period

Late 19th to 20th century
in Europe and the United States

Modernism was a trend of thought that affirmed the power of human beings to create, improve, and reshape their environment with the aid of scientific knowledge, technology and practical experimentation. Modernism encouraged the re-examination of every aspect of existence, from commerce to philosophy, to determine what was inhibiting progress, and then replacing those with innovative and improved ways to reach the same goals. In essence, the modernist movement argued that the new realities of the industrial and mechanized age were permanent and imminent, and that people should adapt this world view in order to succeed in the world.

Embracing change, modernism encompassed the works of thinkers who rebelled against nineteenth century academic and historicist traditions. Believing that the "traditional" forms of art, architecture, literature, religious faith, social organization and daily life were outdated, they directly confronted the new economic, social and political aspects of an emerging, fully industrialized world.

The modern world-view also held that, through application of the scientific method, the one and only reality would eventually be known, and all the laws of nature discovered and harnessed for human progress. Truth was considered "objective," that is, ultimately verifiable by everyone, not just scientists. Because science was viewed as the new and ultimate God, there would no longer be a need for belief in a divine creator. One last corollary: woman's nature was still viewed as largely inferior to man's.

World War II started to change the culture's stereotypes of women, however. Because a high percentage of males served in the war effort, many women left their homes to perform jobs in the public sector. Like "Rosie the Riveter," famous for repairing war planes, many women were astonished to discover that they were just as capable as their male counterparts in many public sectors. They began to discover talents they didn't know they possessed. Women also got a taste of life outside the home, many experiencing for the first time their power and personal freedom by supporting themselves. However, when the war ended and men returned home to take up their former jobs, women were sent back to their literal home front.

The Feminine Mystique

A few years before the war ended, a graduate student at the prestigious Smith College, Betty Friedan, sent a questionnaire to the women in her 1942 graduating class. The women who responded indicated a general unease with their lives, even though they were privileged in class and race and education. Based on her findings, Friedan hypothesized that women were victims of a false belief system that required women—mostly upper and middle class suburban women, no matter how talented or educated—to find identity and meaning in their lives solely through serving the needs of their husbands and children.

Based on this research, Friedan wrote the blockbuster *The Feminine Mystique* in 1963. Her book attacked the popular notion that modern American women could only find fulfillment through childbearing and home-making. In Friedan's obituary in 2006, *The New York Times* noted that her book "is widely regarded as one of the most influential nonfiction books of the 20th century;" "it ignited the contemporary women's movement and, consequently, permanently transformed the social fabric of the United States and countries around the world." Quite high praise!

The Feminist Critique

Readers, you may not know this, but the first-wave of feminism refers to a period of feminist activity during the nineteenth century and early twentieth century in the United Kingdom and the United States that focused primarily on gaining the vote for women. The term "first-wave" was coined, of course, only *after* the term *second-wave* feminism occurred. Second-wave feminism described a subsequent feminist movement that focused more on fighting social and cultural inequalities than on furthering political equalities.

Second-wave feminism began in the early 1960s and continues to coexist with what some people call *third wave* feminism. Second-wave feminism saw cultural and political inequalities as inextricably linked. The movement encouraged women to understand aspects of their own personal lives as deeply politicized, and reflective of a sexist structure of power. It urged the end to all kinds of discrimination against women.

During the 1970s or the second wave, I helped form a small but passionate women's consciousness-raising group in Virginia Beach. There were about ten of us, ranging from twenty to sixty years old. The 60-year-old was way ahead of her time in consciousness. We truly believed we were ushering in a new phase of history, one in which women would be equal to men in all ways: equal pay, equal access to education and to formerly all-male professions. We would finally be freed from millennia of cultural conditioning making women subservient to men, especially men in authority positions. We would be liberated from loathing ourselves *just because we were female.* Our husbands, banned from our meetings, were understandably anxious when we returned home from our women's lib group because we were all pumped up with our new-found female power.

Here's my summary of the second-wave movement.

> *Wait a minute, men! We refuse to allow you white privileged males to speak for our women's experience! No longer will the term "he" include the unnamed, invisible "she." No. We want equal air and press time. We demand equal pay and equal rights. We want to be visible and named. We will publicly burn our bras as a symbol of our defiance of sexism in our struggle for equality.*

Later in the movement, many of us feminists, including myself, realized that our agenda needed to change. Realizing that men as well as women are damaged by the stereotypes of patriarchy (i.e., real men don't cry), we no longer wanted to achieve equality in a *man's* world:

we wanted a whole *new* world. Hoping to challenge the systems of power along with violence and greed, we intended to transform economic and political institutions that governed our public life.

Third-wave feminism arose in the early 1990s as a response to perceived failures of the second wave, as well as a response to the backlash against initiatives created by the second wave. For example, third-wave feminism seeks to challenge or avoid the second wave's "essentialist" definitions of femininity, which often over-emphasize the experiences of upper middle-class, white women while under-valuing or excluding women of color and lower class women.

Before we start rocking wildly on all these waves of feminism, let's steady ourselves by examining three ways of viewing "woman's nature":

1. Essentialist or universalist: women are essentially the same the world over.
2. Evolutionist: women are evolving. Women evolve from a primitive state or culture into more civilized Western ways of being women.
3. Social Constructionist: a society totally constructs, that is, shapes, a woman's nature. Cultural diversity means everything. More about this position in a moment.

The universalist position on human nature

Perhaps you are a universalist. I was for many years. My parents believed in a universal human nature. They taught me that each person, no matter what religion, race or culture, was a child of God, deserving full human rights. They were early and avid students of Carl Jung, Swiss depth psychologist and former student of Sigmund Freud, the father of psychoanalysis. I am greatly simplifying Jung's great body of complex thought, but I want to use him as an example of a prominent universalist or essentialist. I urge you to do your own research into Jung's thought if you are thus inclined.

Because Jung viewed cultural trappings as incidental or inconsequential to the core of human nature, he was able to propose universal patterns or "archetypes" that exist in every person's psyche, no matter their race or gender. He developed some intriguing archetypes: the Child, the Hero, the Great Mother, the Wise Old Man, The Trickster, and the Eternal Boy.

Jung also developed his concepts of *anima*—the female aspect within a man, and *animus*—the male aspect within a woman. If you were a woman, dreams were the vehicle by which you could come to know and integrate your masculine side. Same with a male. Jung also invented the notion of the "shadow": that part of the psyche that holds aspects of ourselves that we either fear or don't want or like. In dreams, the shadow would show up as a black person.

I do think there's a lot of value in the concept of the shadow. However, since I first heard of Jung's concept of shadow, I wondered, "Does a black person dream of his shadow as a white person? What about a Chinese person? What nationality is their shadow?" Can you see the (white) essentialism here that is projected upon the whole, multi-colored human race?

Raised as a Christian, Jung came to believe that the Trinity was out of balance as a power symbol of the Godhead because there was no feminine element. I greatly appreciated his view. However, while Jung did women a great service in the Western world by lifting up the missing "feminine" element, both in psychoanalysis and Christianity, Jung was also a product of his sexist culture (as we all are). For example, in one of his writings, he claimed that a woman who used her brains was going *against* her feminine nature. I was not happy about that statement.

Still, as a young adult, I was proud and secure in my universalist position on human nature in general and women's nature in particular. For instance, I assumed that *all* women—black, white, or Chinese—held the same feminist agenda I did.

Evolutionary position on human nature

Now what about the evolutionary position? Maybe you're thinking: "Well, I do believe evolution is true. Native peoples aren't as advanced as we Westerners are. I'm sure that after we've taught them all we know, they'll catch up with us." I believed this, having been taught well by my culture and my parents. But this position is based, like essentialism, on gross generalizations. We can be more nuanced than that, can't we?

What's Social Construction, Anyway?

That was my question as I sat in my first doctoral class in 1993. I was surprised to learn that we no longer lived in the "modern world" but in the *"post-modern"* world, a concept I had never even heard before. Feeling stupid when the students nodded their heads each time the professor used the term, I didn't have the courage to ask what a "post-modern world" meant. The lecture was studded with strange words like "de-construction," and mixed with foreign French names, like Jacques Derrida.

"Who cares?" I can hear you young women groaning. "This is all academic gobbledy-gook. I'm living just fine in my so-called 'modern world.'"

"Well," I reply, "there has been a major shift in consciousness that can help us to view life less ethno-centrically and more fairly and accurately. This shift can help us increase our understanding of diverse cultures, promoting peace in place of misunderstanding and conflict."

"Prove it!" you demand.

OK, I'll try.

The post-modern period challenges the worldview and assumptions of the modern period by claiming that we human beings don't just experience the same world differently. Rather, *we live in multiple worlds*, often vastly different worlds. In this approach, there is no one universally-accepted version of reality or truth—only myriad versions of it, each with its own assumptions and truth claims, and each equally valid.

The goal in the post-modern paradigm is to be able to "de-center" yourself, to get out of the spotlight and put another in the light to listen to *her* version of reality. This approach leads to relativism, roughly equivalent to "I'm okay, you're okay" or "everything goes."

I was shocked when it finally sunk through my brain that throughout my whole adult life, what I had accepted as "truth," truth for *everyone*, I now saw as my own self-centered, ethnocentric version of truth. It was true enough for *me* but only in my specific gender/race/class context.

"Hey, wait, hold on!" you're crying out. "I disagree. We human beings *are* basically the same. The differences are minor. We should just ignore them, or at least minimize them. Let's just focus on our common human nature." (Do I hear essentialism raising its voice?)

The problem with that approach, dear sisters, is—who gets to define our "human nature" or our "female nature"? You, or me, or—God forbid—someone who hates women?

Did God intend one universal human language?

There's one more compelling argument against the universalist position. Legend has it (and perhaps it's true, if not fact) that there was a Pope in the Middle Ages who was terribly frustrated with all the wars and fighting going on in his kingdom. He believed that the different languages and dialects were fueling the fire of his people's misunderstanding and hatred. He proposed a solution.

The Pope ordered some nuns to lock an orphaned infant in a tower where they would care for its every need. But the nuns were forbidden to speak to the infant. That way, once the child spoke, the one true language that God had always intended human beings to speak would finally be revealed.

The nuns did as they were bidden, tending to the infant's every need and speaking nary a word. The Pope waited expectantly.

And guess what language the child finally spoke?

You guessed it. None!

There *is* no one language which God or nature intends all human beings to speak—because you can't be a human being *in general*. You can only be a human being *in particular*. Each one of us speaks a particular language handed down to us by our parents, extended family, teachers and culture. Conditioned from birth by the larger society and its institutions (education, law, economics, etc.) and by many smaller groups (ethnic, religious, etc.), we human beings are taught specific symbols and values which give us a specific worldview and mold us the distinct persons we are: hence, we are socially constructed.

Furthermore, each society constructs its concept of human nature to fit its environmental and philosophical needs and desires. Cultural anthropologist Richard Shweder in his book, *Thinking Through Cultures: Expeditions in Cultural Psychology*, provides the intriguing metaphor of human nature as a piano keyboard. That is, all human beings share a common human potential (the keys), but in every culture, some specific keys get played while others don't. Why is that?

Anthropologists don't really know why and Shweder says it's not their job to know. Their job is to pay careful attention to the embodied experiences of the people they observe in diverse cultures. Only after painstaking work of sifting through the differences, should one look for clues to *shared* human experience, our "common humanity."

I'm sure you've guessed by now that I believe that social construction accounts for much of what Americans call "human nature" or "woman's nature" ordained by a Creator. No longer can I easily or glibly discern the "essence" of human nature. After my anthropological studies, I have come to honor the particularity, distinctiveness and amazing creativity with which different cultures define "female nature." For example, I now see vast differences in how a woman experiences being a "mother" in suburban America, the Lakota nation, the Brazilian jungle Kayapo tribe, or the !Kung tribe in the Kalahari desert in southern Africa.

Human beings are diverse from birth. And that's actually a good thing, because once we admit that we are largely culture-bound and basically ethnocentric, we possess the possibility of opening ourselves to another person's culture or worldview.

However, at the same time that I deeply honor cultural differences, I admit that I cling to my essentialist belief that all human beings share *some common human nature*—something that makes us all laugh or cry, some quality that causes us to care for our babies or our loved ones. No matter our tribe, we desire to fulfill our basic needs; we yearn for peace and safety for our families; we hope to contribute to our families and to the wider world.

This would be a great time to journal. How do you view human nature: as an essentialist, an evolutionist, or a social constructionist? Maybe a combination? How do you view "woman's" nature?

Crossing the Great Gender Divide

I'm sure we all know both women and men who are our best friends as well as advocates for us on our quest for self-hood. Many of you men, especially those under thirty, are sharing housework and childcare with your wives, and making wonderful partners and dads. In 1985, the roles of husband and wife began to shift from women in the home as care-givers and men in the workplace. Many women started to work for the first time or go back to school. Equality between the sexes seemed within grasp. Unfortunately, while women took on new demands of a job, many working husbands didn't respond by contributing to household or childcare tasks. Too many women found themselves working *two* jobs instead of one.

I was fortunate. My husband John made tremendous sacrifices to help me reach my dreams. For instance, when I was a young mother and a college instructor, he sold his van to pay for my two week dream trip to China, taking care of our toddler, Chelsea, while I was gone, and working his lawn-care business. Over two decades, John broke a record for sharing childcare and housework, and with a glad heart at that, while we both worked full-time outside the home.

When I yearned to get my doctorate in far-off Chicago, John sold his landscaping business and started a new job to support the family. During the seven long years I struggled to finish my doctoral program, he'd bring me a cup of steaming coffee in the morning. He'd leave little post-it notes of encouragement around my study. When I finally earned my doctorate in 1999 and subsequently secured a pastoral position at Yale University, we packed up the U-Haul, drove to New Haven, and John started his landscaping business all over again. As a male, John is more of a feminist than many women I've met in my life.

Over twenty-five years, John and I have had our fair share of trials, and we are re-evaluating our relationship as I write. No matter what the outcome, John has helped me accomplish many of my dreams and has been a wonderful partner. I know of no other man who has blessed his wife more than John has blessed me. And I pray I've been an invaluable support to him and his major talents throughout the years of our marriage.

Another powerful example of a man who supports radical spiritual growth in both women and men is the Rev. Dr. Otis Moss, III, formerly of Atlanta and currently pastor of the renowned Trinity Church in Chicago. A few years ago, Dr. Moss preached to several hundred of us—ministers, laypeople, social workers, youth workers—under a large tent at the Children's Defense Fund gathering at Haley Farm in Tennessee. Preaching on the necessity of reclaiming one's self-esteem, he proclaimed:

> There are people who have been trying to write a period on our lives and our children's lives. They actually believe stereotypes: for example, that if you are a strong athlete, you can't do physics—you're not capable of it.
>
> And if you are a woman—women are still, in many churches, not allowed to preach because they are not worthy.
>
> So, if you think you have a period next to your name, you will never be able to rise to who God calls you to be! We have to

let people know—*no one has the right to put a period on your life.*

Dr. Moss then shared his own life story. As an African-American growing up in the South, he was given many standardized tests, tests designed by white males in a white privileged culture. When he continued to fail them miserably, year after year, Otis' teachers informed his parents that he was retarded. When he was about to graduate from high school, the white guidance counselor called him into his office and announced,

"Otis, you shouldn't even *think* about college. Your test scores put a *period* after your name."

Otis paid him no mind. Instead, he listened to his father who continually preached the liberating news of the Gospel: "Never place a period where God has put a comma." With this confident attitude, Otis not only went on to college but graduated with a Master's degree from Yale Divinity School. He easily obtained a job as a young pastor in Atlanta.

Then one day, Otis found himself having lunch in a restaurant near his old high school. He told us,

"I recognized my high school counselor. I was *eating* lunch, and my high school counselor was *serving* me lunch. And I asked him,

"Do you remember me?
Look what the Lord has done for me.
For I went to Morehouse College, *comma,*
and then I went on to Yale Divinity School, *comma,*
and God isn't finished with me yet, *comma!*"

We all cheered!

At the end of our time together at Haley, several young people stood up before the group to share how Otis' sermon and affectionate actions with them throughout the past week had touched them. One, a tall, black 26-year-old man from the Bronx, tears streaming down his face, declared: "Before I came here, I thought I was a period. But now I know I'm a comma!"

We cheered again. Then a young Hispanic woman stood up, tears of gratitude streaming down her face, as she announced, "I have received more love and attention here, especially from Dr. Moss, than I've gotten in seventeen years of living with my father."

After hugging and thanking the young people, Dr. Moss looked right at all of us, with a glint in his eye and powerful conviction in his voice:

> When anyone tells you you can't achieve what God is calling you to do, you tell them, '*Comma!*'
>
> If they tell you you're a woman and you can't do what God is calling you to do, you tell them, '*Comma!*'
>
> If you are a person of color, if you are disabled, if you're gay and they say you can't do what God wants you to do, you say, '*Comma! Comma! Comma!*'

By this time, in a frenzy of delight, we shouted right along with him, "*Comma, comma, comma!*"

So, dear readers, don't ever let anyone turn you back when you believe you are doing work you feel destined to do. When you hear a "No!" from anyone in your life, when someone tries to place a period after your name, just call out, "Comma, comma, comma!" Amen, Brother Otis, comma,

A Paradigm for the New Millennium—

P A R T N E R S H I P

Years ago, waking up from a chilling nightmare, I heard my own voice scream out, "*The price of pleasing the Father is too high! Too high!*" Given the status of women at risk and our planet in peril, it is high time we women and men create a new world order *together*. Today, we are moving into a new paradigm—a consciousness shift—that happens to the human race every 2000 years or so.

The currently evolving paradigm has two outstanding characteristics. First, "either/or" thinking will be replaced by "both/and" thinking, a more mature and more difficult stance to maintain. We will be able to hold previously polarized and antagonistic opposites, such as freedom and responsibility, emotion and intellect, nature and culture, in creative tension because we realize that both qualities are valid and necessary to express our full humanity.

Second, in many families, communities and institutions, hierarchy will finally give way to mutuality. The "win/lose" model of competition will be replaced more and more by the "win/win" model. Competition will yield to cooperation and collaboration. Mutual respect between genders, races and classes, and those of varying sexual orientation, is imperative. No one will feel privileged above another. Women and men will work together, sharing their talents and being equally compensated. Those of you in the Gen-Xer's, Gen-Y's and Z's understand this already. We in the previous generations are the ones who need to get with the program. Now is the time to join together in synergy to change our little part of the world. We can have a ball doing it, too.

That leads us right into the topic of sisterhood on our quest. (Any of you men from Mars, you can learn a lot of esoteric Venus knowledge in the next chapter!)

Ever done a sweat lodge?

FOUR

Sisterhood Matters:

Purifying Ourselves in the Sweat Lodge

In our increasingly isolated, individualistic world, sisterhood—warm feelings of connection, mutual support and admiration—matters, now more than ever. Does sisterhood exist between women of various races,[2] or might it be important to look at the impact race has had upon relationships between white and black women?

"Slow down!" I can hear you younger women sighing. "Don't make a mountain out of a molehill. We've come very far since the slave days and the Civil Rights Movement. Enlightened white and black women agree today that we are 'sisters.'"

You think so? At least one prominent black woman writer, Audre Lorde, has challenged white women's notion that a connection exists between all women *just because they are women*. She claims that such sisterhood does not exist in reality; it's just a pretense. As the old saying goes, "History not learned is doomed to repeat itself."

The Womanist Critique

I'd like to share with you the most important facts I learned during my second semester of studies in 1994. Because I had already taken a course on "Feminist Theology and Ethics," I thought it would be interesting to hear an African-American perspective on women's issues. So I enrolled in a course called "Womanist Theology and Ethics" at a sister seminary. A womanist is a black feminist. I went into the course with two assumptions. First, as a "good liberal feminist" (sic), I assumed that there was a common, universal female nature which formed an invisible but strong bond between all women, regardless of our racial backgrounds. Second, I assumed that because we black and white students were all Christian, we would desire to get to know each other and to care for each other's well-being. I was in for a shock.

---

[2] Class and sexual orientation matter, too, but are out of the scope of this trail guide.

First, I learned that Audre Lorde's 1979 essay, "The Master's Tools Will Never Dismantle the Master's House," was a critical turning point for white feminism. Lorde argued that just as white, privileged males had obliterated difference between males and females by projecting its white male face upon all humanity, white feminists have continued that oppression by presuming that in their white, middle-class experience, they can speak for *all* women.

Lorde asserted that no magic impulse was going to arise from within the white female "oppressor" to make her critique a social caste system from which she is benefiting, merely by the accident of her birth.

Me, an "oppressor"—good-hearted, fair-minded me?

"No way," I spoke up. Other white female students began to protest, too.

My African-American female professor calmed us down, and then challenged us to examine our racial and class privilege before we started to look for our desired "sisterhood" between the races.

"OK," I thought. "I'm a good student. I'll play along."

First, my daughters, I learned about slavery. Of course, I knew that slavery—an economic and political system designed to benefit the agriculture system in the South—was the most obvious and destructive dynamic that pitted black women against white. Violence against black slave women was legion. For example, so many white men raped black women throughout those years that one sociologist considered those rape acts "institutionalized crime."

But what I wasn't prepared to learn was the painful historical fact that many white women, *Christian* women at that, participated in the violence against black women and children (even if compelled sometimes by their husbands' threats). For example, whipping was one form of sexual terrorism. White mistresses would send a female slave, including a pregnant woman or nursing mother, to be publicly stripped and then flogged for the slightest offense, like burning the breakfast toast. Christian women did that?

"No wonder some black women detest white women to this day," I thought.

The difficult history lesson continued. The Abolitionist suffragettes, white women who sought to abolish slavery and get the vote, or suffrage, for women, believed that the purpose of the Civil War was not to free the slaves but to help the increasingly industrialized North gain economic superiority over the agricultural South.

In the decades following the end of the Civil War, it became clear that white men were not going to help black men build better economic and social lives. However, the Fifteenth Amendment passed on February 3, 1880, provided that state governments could not prevent a citizen from voting because of his race, color or former slave status. Black female activists rejoiced at the passage of this amendment. Ironically, most of the white Suffragettes supported black men getting the vote rather than women of any color obtaining that right. Leaders like Elizabeth Cady Stanton and the Grimke sisters argued that more similarity existed between white women and black men than between white and black women. Upon learning this, my conviction that sisterhood existed between white and black women took another dive.

A fatal blow between the Suffragettes and activist black women occurred at the first Women's Rights Convention in 1848 at Seneca Falls, New York. The white Abolitionist women withdrew their support for black women getting the vote because they did not want to offend their wealthy, Southern white sisters. In so doing, the Suffragettes betrayed their black "sisters."

I began to realize that I had also been naïve to think that the abolition of slavery improved black women's lives, even in the North. As industrialization expanded, many black women migrated north to find that the only source of employment open to them was *domestic work*, resembling their subservient position under white women in the South. I was fascinated yet appalled to learn about the "Cult of True Womanhood" that arose in Britain and New England in the 1800s, created and supported mainly by upper and middle-class white males, especially ministers and physicians. Its goal was to idealize white women for their work in their homes in so-called "cottage industries" while simultaneously excluding women from the use of power in the public marketplace. The cult's definition of white womanhood as privileged and home-centered clashed with the experiences of black women engaged in oppressive domestic work, alienating the two races of women even further.

With the emergence of the Civil Rights movement in the 1960s, black and white women again found some common ground for social justice. I know. I was part of that movement during my college years.

However, the union was short-lived. After white resistance to integration grew and Dr. Martin Luther King, Jr., the leader of the Civil Rights movement, was assassinated, the Black Power movement arose, promoting self-esteem for African-Americans with such slogans as "Black is beautiful!" In response, those white women who had been working with their black women friends felt it wise to leave the Civil Rights Movement. They began to focus on gaining on their own "freedom" from white male systems of oppression.

After several months in that class, dear readers, I began to understand why the black women students distrusted us white students, especially if we called ourselves feminists. Even though I had told them I had marched with Dr. King and was active as a college student in the Civil Rights Movement, and most of the black students hadn't even been born then, my words fell on deaf ears. When I brought up the subject of Jesus' teachings on the importance of forgiveness, I received cold silence and even sneers from some of the black women. I was beginning to see my supposedly black "sisters" through different eyes. Week after week, the tension between us mounted.

Next, we read Alice Walker's definition of "womanist." I was the first to admit that this definition would empower and liberate black women.

1. "A black feminist....usually referring to outrageous, audacious, courageous or *willful* behavior. Wanting to know more and in greater depth that is considered "good" for one.... Responsible.

2. *Also*: a woman who loves other women...their culture.... emotional flexibility....strength. Sometimes loves individual men....Committed to survival and wholeness of entire people, male and female....

3. *Loves music*. Loves dance. Loves the moon. *Loves* the Spirit. Loves love and food and....struggles. Loves the folk. *Loves* herself. *Regardless.*

4. Womanist is to feminist as purple is to lavender.

At the same time, I began to wonder if Walker's definition of womanist was a covert claim to black women's *superiority* over white women. I mean, purple is the *elemental* color while lavender is the *derivative*—purple mixed with white, purple diluted, purple watered down.

As I reflected upon Walker's definition, I admitted I was mainly lavender. Still, I believed I possessed several of the "purple" qualities, too, like "love of community, music, dance." Also, I had worked hard for years to be capable of some of the other traits she offered, such as "Loves herself. Regardless." So I was the color *purple*, too! I even knew a few black students in the class whom I considered lavender. Therefore, if Walker intended her definition *exclusively* for black women, I strongly disagreed with her, and was offended by her seemingly reverse racism. By the semester's end, we white and black students never found a way toward racial reconciliation or even understanding each other, let alone my coveted notion of "sisterhood."

Since that powder keg of a class, friends, I have embraced a few womanist values to complement my feminist ones, for which I'm thankful to the womanist students and professor. For example, in addition to working to obtain woman's individual access to male rights in predominantly male arenas, I now seek the welfare of the whole community. Whereas traditional feminists historically placed little emphasis on children's welfare, I now place a strong emphasis on children's welfare, having been influenced by the advocacy work of Marian Wright Edelman, African-American visionary and child activist. Finally, while feminists have often sought to overcome or even reject their family history, womanists seek to honor their extended families as well as their cultural and educational history. Now I do, too.

My strategy for transforming social institutions has also widened as a result of learning about womanist thought. Before the class, I was a reconciler, seeking unity and harmony between the races, but afterwards I adopted the womanist stance of being bluntly honest with the goal of "speaking the truth in love." At times, I find myself courageous enough to be disliked for my views—not an easy stance for a white girl well-trained in keeping the peace and pleasing others at all costs.

These days, when I engage in dialogue with women and men of other races or religions, I start by honoring our diversity and particularities, then only slowly and carefully work towards some common ground between us. I apply this approach in workshops on cultural diversity sensitivity training.

Since the 1990s, most feminists and womanists have been eager to include the voices and viewpoints of women from many other cultures, like *mujerista* (Spanish), Chinese, Korean, and Mayan women in Chiapas, Mexico. The list continues to grow. We need to hear from women of *all* races and ethnic groups to gain a more complete understanding of "woman's nature."

I wonder if reading about the history of race relations between white and black women has challenged or affirmed your understanding of "sisterhood." Do you find yourself resonating with the feminist or the womanist values, or perhaps other cultural values?

Soul friends (dare I say "soul sisters"?), one final point. It's important for whites to be aware that racism, both as an emotional and an economic reality, is actually on the rise in our country, despite the momentous election of a bi-racial president. Sadly, forty years after the War on Poverty and the Civil Rights Act, white and black Americans still live in two largely unequal worlds. For example, before the Civil Rights Act, African-Americans earned about 54 cents on the dollar compared to whites. Today, blacks earn less than 60 cents on the dollar. There is still much work to do.

Happily, groups of women sitting around coffee tables at Starbucks or at global corporate tables are daily growing more diverse. In our divided and competitive world, women of all colors desperately need solid sisterhood. But mistrust still exists between white women and women of color. The womanist writer bell hooks asserts that it is

> only when we confront the realities of sex, race and class, the ways they divide us, make us different, stand us in opposition, and work to reconcile and resolve these issues will we be able to participate in the....transformation of the world.

How might we begin to heal the alienation between women of different races?

As a white woman of privilege, I realize I can only speak from my racial context. We white folks can begin by acknowledging our privilege and our unconscious or inherited prejudices. While we may initially feel guilt over white women's participation in slavery, for example, guilt is not helpful because it leads to paralysis and inaction.

With the realization that racism and classism distort *all* women and men, we would do better to connect with our righteous indignation. Anger can provide the energy we need to bring justice to bear in our multi-racial relationships.

Second, we must redefine and redesign our analytical tools. Race must be one lens we use. In the 1960s, one day as I swam in the beautiful waters of the Atlantic Ocean in Virginia Beach, I asked my Southern friends why black people weren't allowed to swim with us whites. They told me that blacks were unable to learn how to swim. Therefore, the "law" was really protecting their safety. In response, I shut up and accepted that "truth." Today, I would make a big fuss.

Third, too many of us have been "seduced" into using psychology as the *only* tool to analyze human nature and culture. Incorporating the use of sociology and history, for example, we can and must perform analyses of gender, class and race, whether we're reading sacred texts or news articles on the Internet. Last but not least, we need to listen—really listen—to people whose experiences differ from ours in terms of race, culture, class and ethnicity.

I have learned from some women of color that the possibility of experiencing racial discrimination is never far from their minds, whether they admit it or not. Race *is* an issue all of us must continue to be sensitive to.

A black woman once asked *Latina* theologian Ada Maria Isasi-Diaz, "Given our history, how can women of color ever trust white women?" Isasi-Diaz replied that you can learn to trust those women who will "cover your back." This goes for men, too. And of course, there is reverse racism, as well. So let's just start with ourselves.

We can cover each other's backs in several ways. We can stand up for each other in public or private situations when we see discrimination happening. We can tell people to stop when they start to tell racist jokes. We can work for equality of the races in the marketplace. As we face the ways we dominate or are dominated by our racial make-up, let's use tough love to communicate more honestly yet thoughtfully. Women of all colors must keep imagining what true sisterhood looks like, and then share these dreams with each other. Brothers, we need your help, too!

Sisterhood is important and worth fighting for.

I've learned more about the reality of sisterhood from my sisters of color than I have from my own feminist colleagues. I shall be forever grateful to several Lakota Indian women in the frigid spring of 1995, as I recorded in my journal.

> It was a cold Sunday in March. For many long months, we in the Cross-Cultural Ministry class at Catholic Theological Union in Chicago, some twenty students, all Catholic except three of us—the professor and I were both ordained Protestant clergy—had studied and prayed and prepared hard for the field trip to learn from the Lakota Indians. We would stay with and interview both Christian and traditional Indians at the Rose Bud and Pine Ridge Reservations in South Dakota.
>
> I had worked and dreamed for months about worshipping with the Lakota Christians. The day had finally arrived. We prepared to go to Mass at the nearest Catholic Church in Mission. Since the relationship between the Lakota and the Catholic community was still rather fragile, even after twelve years of our professor's work of reconciliation, our professor asked if any of the Catholic students had misgivings about their Protestant peers receiving the elements of bread and wine during Mass.
>
> To my utter shock, one Catholic student half my age, a woman I had considered a "sister in the faith" the past few months, announced that she felt all Protestants should abstain, since our partaking would *profane* the body of Christ.
>
> I felt such shock and sorrow. The pain and agony of being excluded from the Lord's table by a fellow Christian—oh, Jesus! I burst into tears in the silence of my motel room. While several students voted to stay in the motel and celebrate an alternative worship service, I went with a few others to the Mass to protest in silent solidarity.
>
> Somehow I made it through that day's activities, though bewildered and numbed by this experience of arrogant exclusion.

(Weeks later, after much reflection, I would transform this experience into a small but important point of empathy with how Lakota people must have felt when proselytizing missionaries and the U.S. government kept them from performing their most holy rituals—the sweat lodge and the Sun Dance—by threatening imprisonment. It would not be until 1978 with the passage of the American Indian Religious Freedoms Act that they would be allowed to perform their rituals without fear of arrest. How ironic in a land founded on the very freedom of religion.)

That evening, eight of us women prepared to take our first sweat lodge purification in a domed, four-foot high, earthen-made structure, with woven mats covering the hard frozen earth. We had learned in class that, during the sweat lodge handed down from White Buffalo Calf Woman centuries earlier in a ceremony the Lakota held sacred, the leader would pour water over the rocks, causing steam to rise. The steam would then carry the participants' prayers skyward to *Wakan Tanka*, the *Great Spirit*, to heal and renew the Lakota community.

Our professor had cautioned us that our Lakota women hosts would share with us only as much of their ceremony as they felt we deserved by how they witnessed our treatment of one another. Because of the schism earlier in the day around Eucharist, I felt we were a communal failure already.

It was snowing lightly, crispy cold, dark with a crescent moon. The fire crackled warmly outside the tent-like structure, sending tiny sparks into the frosty air. In preparation for the ritual, I had removed even my contacts, which made me feel especially vulnerable since I had very poor vision. After we huddled self-consciously around the fire, we peeled off our clothes, layer by layer, down to T-shirts in the below-zero cold. I felt like I was dying to my old self, peeling off all the dead layers. I was *ganz nakt*—completely naked—down to my soul.

Then I crawled into the lodge on all fours, humbly, close to the ground, our dear Mother Earth. Like all the others who entered before and after me, I uttered reverently the ancient prayer, *"Mitakuye oyasin,* "All my relatives," which included not only human beings but all of earth's creatures, rocks and trees and all the cosmos.

Inside the pitch black dome, the steam rose from the water sizzling on the heated rocks. We huddled together as Lakota women have huddled for hundreds if not thousands of years in exactly the same way, chanting similar songs.

"Focus, pray, offer thanks to the four Grandfathers, *Tunkashila,"* urged the Holy Woman. "They will come and heed our uplifted voices."

As beads of sweat trickled down my whole body, I listened in amazement as one student prayed the *Lord's Prayer* in Swedish, the tongue of my ancestors, in this Lakota holy place.

At one point, the heat was so intense, I didn't think I could stand it. I wanted to burst right through the closed tent flap to gasp for cool air. As I felt my anxiety rise, I decided to do a Buddhist practice I had recently learned. Instead of resisting the heat, I ordered myself to 'eat' the heat. I breathed it in slowly and gratefully, with its pungent fragrance of sweet grass and sage. The Holy Woman's manner was so calm and caring that I began to believe I would come through this all right. Her language and tone of voice soothed me. I needed the purification so desperately.

"Create in me a clean heart, O God," I silently pleaded.

Then a miracle happened. The Holy Woman brought out her sacred peace pipe and shared it with us in the holiest of Lakota rituals. She announced, "We are all women, somehow bonded together beyond our differences." As a Christian woman, I felt included and honored by her.

Grace from on high pouring down on me on the very day when a Catholic woman had refused to share Eucharist—a

Christian's most holy meal—with me.   How ironic and humbling.

We couldn't keep the pipe lit, there was so much steam. We laughed and cried together, passing it around, relighting it, holding the bowl in the left hand and the stem in the right. When it was my turn, I drew in a breath of husky smoke. It was over too quickly.

My first Sweat Lodge. I endured! I was radiant, glowing, from within and without. When I crawled out on all fours, sweaty, wet and pink-skinned, again praying, *"Mitakuye oyasin,"* I literally felt like a newborn babe.

My journal entry concludes:

I want to honor and thank you, Sacred Pipe, gift of White Buffalo Calf Woman. The Holy Womb of the Lodge enclosed us all—Lakota, Protestant, Catholic, Swedish, French, American—as we prayed together. Truly, the reality of Lakota women inviting white Christian women to pray with them in their sweat lodge is like Jews inviting Nazis into their Temple's "Holy of Holies" to worship together.

The sweat lodge at Rose Bud stands amidst the beauty, garbage and brokenness of backyards. But there in the brokenness, for one shining moment, we were one with each other—true sisters.

Throughout the past chapters, dear daughters and sons, I have offered you instruments to help provide soul food for you and your companions on the journey. I have provided you with sharp tools to assess and confront any wilderness situation, whether personal or global. You can ask the crucial questions: who has the power and how are they using it? Who doesn't have power? Is race involved? If so, how? Who is suffering? What might be done? What might *you* do? Put up a shelter? Offer a cup of cold water? Share a sweat lodge?

Now on to the final task of preparation for the quest—setting up camp.

FIVE

Setting Up Camp

and Setting Your Sights

We're almost ready to hit the trail (figuratively speaking). But first, everyone needs a place to call their own, a small piece of earth and a dwelling to call "home." Your home is even better if it's a place of beauty and significance: a sanctuary, a resting place, a dreaming place. Ideally, we leave our base camp in the morning eager to start the day, and we return at night to that safe harbor, to collapse, to chill, to renew. Trekking on a path can be more fun when the travelers know that their tailor-made base camp awaits them at day's end.

Choose a safe place and time.

It is of utmost importance, daughters, that you establish your camp in a location that is private. It's important to feel safe so you can ponder, dream, reflect, make resolutions, test, experiment, push boundaries, spread wings or grow new roots. If you don't have your own study, you can use a corner of a bedroom or living room, even a bathroom.

Everyone needs some private time, as well. When my daughters were little, I never took a shower without their chatty, lovely presence in the bathroom. I loved every minute of it. But now I realize I should have stolen a few more moments of solitude somehow. A mere fifteen to twenty minutes will do wonders to help you recharge your batteries.

Build a personal altar.

Building a personal altar adorned with your special objects has become popular in many circles, and I find it personally satisfying. First, create a space for your altar. It doesn't have to be large. I have several in my bedroom: on my window ledge, on a dresser top. Then, use your creativity to decorate your altar with favorite photos or sacred objects, like a statue of a saint or goddess. Maybe you'll want to add objects from nature like flowers, seashells, stones or feathers you have found.

On one of my altars, I have a Celtic leather cross, stained and stitched by a dear friend, two tiger's eyes, one pink quartz crystal, a

Mexican beaded necklace of many colors given to me by two dear friends who scoured the markets in a tiny Mexican village to find just the right one. Another altar holds photos of my two daughters, a little dish, a tiny angel, a shaman's bird feather, another gift from a friend.

I also recommend placing a candle on your altar—a lovely one whose color, shape and fragrance please you. My favorite candle scents include orange and rose oil. Lavender is good too, and I've just discovered Meditation scent. As I light the candle, I might pray aloud or silently my intention for the quiet time. For example, "May I be honest with myself" or "Please, God, I'm so confused. Light my way in the darkness today." Finally, the ritual of lighting a candle reminds me of the old saying that it's better to light a candle than to curse the darkness. The altar provides a focus, a grounding or centering place for you to sit.

Play special music.

Another way to help create a safe and welcoming place for yourself is to play music. Though silence is its own kind of music, I like recorded music to center me: the St. Olaf College Choir singing sacred hymns in its lyrical *a capella* style, Lakota flute music, Celtic tunes or Gregorian chants. I've recently found some blissful music sung by Snatam Kaur on her CD entitled *"Grace."* My favorite healing chant right now is *"Ra Ma Da Sa."* I had the wonderful opportunity to chant with her in person in Virginia Beach while she was on her World Peace Tour. Experiment! Have fun! Find some music that inspires you, revs your motor, or calms you.

Then there's the practice of drumming. Drums of many kinds are widely available today. Drumming can help to clear out bad vibes in a room after a fight. It can help to build up your *chi* or energy if you've been depleted. Or if you've given your inner power away to some one (again), drumming can help you to re-claim it. A good tip: be sure you're alone or have permission from your housemates. After many years, my family is finally used to my drumming, although my cats still run for cover.

These aids and others, like meditation and yoga, which I highly recommend, can focus your intention and delight your senses. They will help to put you in an altered state of mind where you can be open and receptive to the Divine Presence or your higher self, ready to be renewed in your precious sanctuary.

Practices for Base Camp

1. Keep a journal.

Keeping a journal is an excellent way to get in touch with one's inner self. You can record your feelings, fears or desires or just reflect and daydream. Sometimes you'll need to do the hard work of discernment which can include, as you know, making lists, prioritizing items, weighing pros and cons in a decision, etc. A journal can be your best friend—totally accepting of you, and totally available to help you explore your life, with absolutely no judgment.

Journal types abound these days: lined or unlined, large or small, illustrated pages or pages filled with inspirational quotes. Be sure the cover art is attractive to you so that you won't be able to resist its voice when it whispers, "Come write in me!" Keep your journal in a safe place where only *you* will read it (unless, of course, you choose to share portions of it with a trusted friend or mate).

Now, what should you write about in your journal? Everything. No topic is unworthy of your exploration or attention. Everything matters as you struggle with or celebrate your life's unfolding. Accomplished journal writers recommend writing every day at the same time, if possible, programming your psyche to be receptive to inspiration. It's a good idea to wait a few days before you read over what you've written to glean additional insights into specific dreams, fears, etc. I'm often surprised to find fore-shadowings of future events in my journal, or bits of wisdom that on re-reading jump right out at me. My basic rule of thumb for journal writing is, "Whatever works, do it!" Carve at least fifteen minutes of time out for yourself every day if possible.

2. Study your dreams.

I've met many people over the years who claim they don't dream. But did you know that everyone dreams every night? Studies have shown that if a person is not allowed to dream, that is, if a scientist interrupts a person's REM (Rapid Eye Movement) periods in which dreaming activity occurs, within the short time of two weeks, the participant will begin to hallucinate, hear voices, and literally "go crazy."

Thus, the process of dreaming is crucial to our psychological and emotional well-being. Dreaming apparently helps our brains process the day's activities (though scientists still don't agree on how or why).

Dreams give feedback on our lives. Once in a while, they might even provide guidance or, in rare instances, forecast the future. Your "inner" subconscious life wants to connect with and contribute to your "outer" conscious life.

Even though scary dreams and nightmares are tough to examine, they can provide helpful insight, too. One night, during a particularly difficult time in my life when I thought I had finally made some gains in my self-esteem, I had a terrible nightmare. When I awoke, I was badly shaken, fearing that all my hard work had been in vain. In fact, my psyche had betrayed me rather than support me. I asked my mom, a Jungian-based therapist, why my subconscious had "ambushed" me while in my dream state. She told me that it is *only* when our psyche is feeling strong enough that our subconscious will even dare to present "scary" material for us to deal with. How reassuring!

My dad also valued nightmares. He believed that if you faced and analyzed your nightmare, you were bound to find a golden nugget somewhere. So, friends, don't shy away from working with a particularly upsetting dream. Pay attention to your dreams.

I know; I know. First you have to *remember* your dreams! Here are some tips:

- Keep a pad of paper and pencil right by your bed within easy reach in the morning so you won't jar your memory too much. (Some people even use a tape recorder.) This concrete action informs your sub-conscious that you are serious about remembering your elusive dreams.
- Write down any snippet you remember. Often other pieces of the dream will re-surface.
- Write in the present tense, not the past tense.
- Draw an image or two from the dream if you feel like it.
- Finally, share the dream with someone you trust. Often while sharing, you will remember more details or glean further insights.

Just as a foreign language takes months or years to learn, it may take a while to get really good at decoding your own dream symbols. Each person's subconscious has a symbolic language and images (even puns) all its own. But you can start picking up important clues right away, and it really can be fun. You may want to join a dream group or consult a good book on dream analysis. However, don't take a dictionary of dream symbols and automatically plug those meanings into your dream symbols. Rather, take the time to ask yourself what the symbol means specifically *to you* in light of your own lived experiences.

There are at least three levels of dream interpretation: personal, interpersonal (about others), and prophetic. I recommend starting your dream interpretation with the *personal* level. What might this dream be saying about *you* in your current life situation? Consider the characters as acting out parts of yourself. Let's say your best friend appears in your dream. What qualities do you associate with her or him? Are they judgmental or tolerant? Stingy or generous? Sometimes I speak to the characters, asking them what they are trying to tell me. For example, what trait do I need to change? What talent am I ignoring that I should be using? How well or poorly am I relating to a specific person in my life?

Let's say you have a dream about someone driving your car and you are the passenger, a fairly common dream theme. You might ask yourself, why did your subconscious pick that specific person to be the driver, the one who is steering your life? What are the characteristics you associate with that person? Is that person rude or considerate? A go-getter or someone who easily gets swayed by others' opinions? You may be displaying some of those qualities as the car's driver. Your subconscious is using those particular dream symbols to give you some honest and concrete feedback. Then you can work on taking back the wheel.

Here are two examples from my own dream work to illustrate the process of dream interpretation. As a teenager and young woman, I had recurring nightmares of darkly clad men chasing me and trying to kill me. Usually they fired shots at me, but a few times they pursued me with knives. I always woke up in terror, followed by sheer relief that it had only been a dream. When I told these nightmares to my dad, he suggested that these men stood for my masculine side that was trying to "shoot me down," to tell me that I would never amount to anything. It was discouraging to think that my inner male self was sabotaging me.

Over the ensuing years, I worked hard to build up my self-esteem. Then one night, I dreamed that a man was standing over me in my bed, a knife in one hand, ready to slit my throat. I thought to myself, "I'm sick of these attacks. Enough is enough!" With jaw clenched, I grabbed his wrist, slowly turning the knife away from me and pointing it towards his *own* throat. I woke up, shaken but proud that I had broken my pattern of victimization by defending myself. A few similar dreams occurred in the next months, but finally the nightmares stopped, never to return again.

The second dream sample occurred several years ago while I was going through a rough time in my marriage. I dreamed of a cruise ship sinking into the deep ocean, going down not once but three times. The first time it sank, I felt sad. Then I watched in surprise as it resurfaced. As it sank again, I thought, "It will never bob back up!" Amazingly, it did. The third time this Titanic-like ship went under, I muttered, "Now it will never re-surface. It's doomed for sure." Astonished, I watched it resurface for a third time. Standing on the deck, in trim rows, stood uniformed sailors, alert but "at ease."

Having worked with my dream symbols for decades, I interpreted the dream in the following way.

First of all, I reflected upon the past few months of my life—my context. Did this dream have to do with my vocation or my marriage? My marriage. The stress of our family's move from New Haven to Virginia Beach had taken a toll on everyone. My husband worked valiantly in his new job to keep us financially *afloat;* hence, the ship and sea metaphor made sense. My husband's stress triggered the manic phase of his bi-polar disorder, and he began to suffer fits of rage, at life, and sometimes at me. Things got so rough that I began to wonder if our marriage would survive. Indeed there were several months during which I feared that our marriage, just like the ship in the dream, was indeed "sunk."

Back to the dream. What else might the ship symbolize to me? A ship is a vessel, a vehicle that takes people from one place to another. The ship symbolized my life and the dangerous high seas represented my world, especially how my family was being impacted by the rough seas of emotion around us. I noted, too, that my unconscious had chosen a particular kind of ship, a "cruise" ship, rather than a rowboat or a submarine. Why a cruise ship?

When our family made the decision in 2005 to move back to Virginia Beach, I imagined that our life would become more fun than it had been for a long time, kind of like a "cruise." Also, since my husband had landed a high-paying job with excellent prospects, I felt that we would finally be able to "cruise" along, enjoying financial stability. John Lennon's song lyrics came into mind: "Life is what happens when you're planning something else" and life sure took a turn for the worse. Under the strain of flipping houses for his demanding boss in a market gone haywire, my husband lost his temper, then lost his job, while I lost my will to finish this book, and our daughters were traumatized by the whole thing.

After four months of struggle to regain our equilibrium, we found good family therapy, as well as medication for my husband that seemed to help. Family and friends kept praying for us. Thus, my dream concluded with the visual image that our marriage status had changed from "We're sinking! Abandon ship!" to the "At-ease!" but alert stance of the seamen whose job it was to maintain the marriage on the rough seas of life. My dream symbols were Pam-specific, poignant and helpful in reflecting to me my journey during those tumultuous months.

Dreams don't only reflect our current situation. They can also provide guidance, sometimes far into the future.

Here's a case in point. Twenty-five years ago, I was a month away from graduating from Divinity School, and I wasn't at all sure what I was going to do afterward. No matter how much I prayed for direction, I had not received any clear guidance. I had spent three years, thousands of dollars, and worked very hard to get several "Credits with Distinction." Where did God want me to use all that expensive, hard-earned knowledge? Was God going to use me after all that work or, in some sort of bad cosmic joke, was God going to abandon me?

Then I had a dream in full-blown color that marked me forever. I was a passenger flying in a futuristic type of airplane, with large windows on all sides. I could see everything below, especially the thickly forested land covered with snow. The beautiful wilderness was clear, crisp and virgin. As we started our landing approach, all of a sudden the plane turned into a bus (dreams are good at this type of shape-shifting). We drove around a tiny obstacle and up into a church driveway. In the front yard stood a Jewish woman wearing a stunning necklace made of a golden cross and silver Star of David (Jewish symbol) with other jewels shaped in symbols of faiths which I didn't even recognize.

Waking up in amazement at the beauty of this dream, I eagerly began to interpret it. First, the airplane symbolized the vehicle of my career, while the sky stood for the world of Spirit or the heavenly realm. Second, although in my waking life I couldn't "see" my next employment opportunity, the airplane in my dream had lots of windows, representing many options. Too, the plane was futuristic with a brand-new design, symbolizing my future spiritual vocation which would include "renewing" and "re-visioning" church worship and spiritual community in the years to come.

I continued my analysis. The pure, virgin landscape indicated to me that I would cover new ground, new territory in my professional role as a spiritual leader of my people. As were my grandmother and mother before me, I would be some kind of pioneer.

The airplane turning into a bus represented yet another aspect or future stage of my vocation life. Like the airplane, the "bus" represented *public* transportation as opposed to private, which foreshadowed the fact that my vocation would take me into in the *public* arena. This dream was very accurate in its forecasting, for I've been involved in building spiritual communities for almost thirty years now.

The bus drove around "a tiny obstacle," symbolizing my current situation of having no specific job in hand, and into a church driveway. What did the church driveway symbolize? I would only learn this in retrospect. The year following my ordination, I figuratively "drove into" and started a little house church in Virginia Beach, fashioned upon the early Christian house church model.

The Jewish woman in the yard in my dream represented my passion for Jewish-Christian dialog, as well as my love of the Jewish people. The stunning necklace of cross/star/holy symbols reflected my growing passion for interfaith dialogue, also to unfold years later. The expensive jewels symbolized the "precious" nature of my spiritual quest. Whenever I've doubted my calling over the years, this dream has been an inspiring touchstone for me.

So keep a record of your dreams when possible and review them when able. You'll be surprised, even gratified.

3. Pray.

Prayer, any kind of request or petition or expression to the Divine, is the third practice I've consistently used to transform and heal my inner self. There are an infinite number of written formal prayers collected into texts. *The Lord's Prayer* and the *23rd Psalm* are two of my favorite prayers from the Christian tradition. My Old Testament professor loved to claim that there was a psalm to help a person pray under any human circumstance. There are wonderful prayer anthologies of prayer as well. My favorite is entitled: *Prayers for a Thousand Years: Blessings and Expressions of Hope for the New Millennium*, a collection drawing upon many spiritual traditions. Another is called *Laughter, Silence & Shouting: An Anthology of Women's Prayers*, by Kathy Keay.

While written and formal prayers can be powerful and beautiful in word and image, there is something special I find about a spontaneous prayer uttered straight from the heart, right, friends? These days I pray right to Jesus, sometimes calling him affectionately "J.C.", or to Mary, or Spirit, just as I would address a best friend. In a centuries-old text, Brother Lawrence called this activity "the practice of the presence of God." Sometimes, I imagine talking to Jesus in the most unlikely places: while he guides the dentist's hand as he drills into my tooth, or while Jesus walks with the realtor and me to search for my perfect home. Sometimes, I even invite Jesus or Mary to jump into the car seat next to me when I'm driving and we catch up on things.

Prayers can also provide wonderful guidance. Several years ago, one of my daughters was having a serious physical and emotional crisis. Her condition was worsening, but I could not get her pediatrician to cooperate with her treatment. We were brand new to the area, having recently moved one thousand miles. This pediatrician had come with a friend's high recommendation. But as I watched my daughter grow more and more depressed, my heart broke. Frantic, I thought, "I've got to find another doctor, the right one." But how?

I finally decided: "OK. I'm going to pray. And God, I'm going to invite you into my heart to lead me. I know *you* can find the right doctor for my daughter."

I began searching the *Yellow Pages*, running through a daunting list of hundreds of doctors in four nearby cities. As I combed through the names, I wondered how I was ever going to choose the best one. Then one name jumped out at me: Marguerite. I thought to myself: "That's an uncommon name. My grandmother was named Margueritte. Maybe that's God's sign."

I immediately called the doctor's office to set up an appointment for my daughter. In my decades of experience, pediatricians always have a long waiting list for appointments, sometimes weeks or months, but the doctor's secretary said they could see my daughter the next day! I brought my daughter in, and the doctor, kind and cheerful, immediately began working to create the right treatment program for her.

What an answer to prayer!

But the story doesn't end here.

A few weeks later, my husband and I were walking around a hardware store, when we bumped into the new doctor with her two daughters. After exchanging pleasantries, she started to walk away, then hesitated, and turned around to inquire of me, "Can I ask you something?"

"Yes."

"Since your last name is Bro, do you know any of the Bros who live in the Chicago area?"

Puzzled, I answered, "Yes," wondering where this was going.

"Do you know Margueritte Bro?"

Even more surprised, I answered, "Yes. She died twenty years ago, but yes, she was my dear grandmother."

With undisguised wonder in her voice, the doctor confided, "Well, your grandmother and grandfather worked with my parents in the 1950s for the State Department in Korea and Indonesia. When I was born, my parents named me Marguerite after *your grandmother.*"

"Oh, my God!" I gasped. And we became fast friends from that day on. Fifty years later and a thousand miles away, God answered my prayer to help heal my little girl.

What miracles might be awaiting you if you experiment with prayer?

4. Use medicine cards.

Remember the old joke:

> *"Do you have trouble making up your mind?"*
> *"Well, yes and no."*

Perhaps you're at a crossroads in life: deciding between two different career tracks or discerning whether to leave or stay in a long-term relationship. Maybe you need to make a smaller decision. Life is full of such events. One last base camp practice to help with discernment or guidance is the use of a card deck. These decks are based on the original Tarot cards which their French creator Etteilla and others used in the late 1700s to forecast the occult future. Tarot cards may be too bizarre for some of you to experiment with right now. I admit they spooked me when I first dared look through a deck in my twenties, especially when I drew the hanged man card symbolizing death. No young person wants to get a message, symbolic or not, of death!

Today, however, there are decks using all kinds of cultural, literary and spiritual themes, embellished with beautiful artwork. For example, in the early 1990s, when "inner child work" was popular in the New Age culture, I began experimenting with the *Inner Child* card deck by Isha and Mark Lerner. Drawing on myths, fairytales and Jungian archetypes, these colorful cards can lead you into places dark or light, cold or sunny, to reflect your inner process and suggest some possible steps to take towards more wholeness and joy. (When my girls were little, they loved to spy on me when I used my inner child cards, and mocked me in fun in their spookiest voices, "Inner grown-up, inner grown-up!")

When I began my field work with the Lakota Indians, I was drawn to *The Medicine Woman Inner Guidebook: A Woman's Guide to Her Unique Power* by Carol Bridges. The wisdom in her beautifully decorated cards continues to teach me about my life choices. Last but not least, I use a deck for guidance by Jamie Sams called *Sacred Path Cards: The Discovery of Self Through Native Teachings*. Sams shares her personal initiations with her grandmothers, as well as native traditions, which can truly enrich any *Quester's* life.

Just remember that a deck is just a tool, not the word of God written on stone tablets. Always check in with your brain, heart and intuition, since you are the best authority on your own life.

Joseph Campbell, the wise philosopher, offered what is now considered classic wisdom: "Follow your bliss." Another spiritual teacher advises: "Follow your bliss and the money will follow." Finally, Protestant theologian and poet, Frederick Buechner, offers a lovely guideline for discerning your life's work: "The place God calls you to is the place where your deep gladness and the world's deep hunger meet."

For spiritual guidance and growth, I can't recommend the above practices highly enough. They can provide you with invaluable insight and compassionate wisdom about your past, your present and even your destiny. Hopefully, after reading this chapter, you will experiment with creating your own specialized base camp routines.

Choose Holy Companions on Your Quest

Every day, you are walking through life with significant others—parents, spouse or partner, children, friends, co-workers, bosses, employees. The best advice I can offer is to choose wisely the people you hang out with, let alone build your life with—your trekking buddies, so to speak. As you know, it's vitally important that you choose friends that like and respect you, who believe in you and your gifts, who want you to be happy and contribute to this world. Choose companions who are loyal and true and share your deepest values. Oh, and they're honest. They won't lie to you and they try not to lie to themselves. (I'm just applauding the wise choices you're already making).

I'm sure you ask yourself how much you *enjoy* your friends. Do they make you laugh? Do you feel better about yourself and your goals when you are with them? Do you feel "seen" or better "understood?" How much do they support the real 'you' or the "you" you intend to become? Here's another guideline. Remember that old camp song, "Make new friends, but keep the old. One is silver and the other gold"? It's so true. My daughter Chelsea wrote her own version when she was five: *"Make new friends, but keep the old. One is hairy and the other bald."* Now that I'm over sixty, those lines really ring true.

Since we learn so much about building good relationships through trial and error, it's important to keep risking. In my twenties, I dated a lot of men, looking for that special someone to marry. (No smirking! Most women my age held that goal.) The relationship would break up for some reason, and I'd cry and cry. However, within a short time, I'd be dating again, passionate about my latest boyfriend. My youngest sister, Alison, once asked, "Pam, your heart was just broken. How can you be dating and in love again so soon? Why even keep trying?"

"I don't know," I replied. "I guess the joy and promise of loving just makes it worth all the risk and pain."

As I keep reflecting upon and learning from my choices, especially my choice of male friends, each "failure" has taught me a lot about myself and others.

Choose a Spiritual Teacher

Choose a spiritual teacher wisely, dear ones. Listen to the words they speak, which can reveal a person's motivations, attitudes and values. More importantly, look to their fruits. Is the leader joyful, compassionate and kind? Is he or she devoted to the welfare of not just their own community but of all persons? Or are they motivated by greed, power, sex or egotism? As you know from history, it's easy to get taken in by a leader's charisma and charm. So, look to their fruits.

Of course, there will be times in our lives when we find ourselves wandering the wilderness alone. We feel cut loose, out of synch with our family or out of touch with a meaningful spiritual community. Such isolation can be an integral part of the spiritual quest. I've found myself in such a place several times in my life.

For instance, while getting my M. Div. degree from Union Theological Seminary in New York City, I was a member of Riverside Church for five years (1978-1983). The senior pastor then was the dynamic, Holy Spirit-filled, William Sloane Coffin. He had made a worldwide reputation during his fifteen years as Chaplain of Yale University—marching with Dr. Martin Luther King, Jr. for civil rights, and working ardently to stop the war in Vietnam. To be sure, he caused some uproar with Yale's president and Board of Directors, having been jailed several times for his social justice work. But in the last half century, most people I know who ever heard Bill preach thought he was the most inspiring Protestant preacher alive. He "walked the talk" of his Christian faith eloquently, boldly, and full of grace and humor. I not only revered him; I loved him.

After graduating from seminary, I left New York City, Riverside Church and my beloved pastor/mentor/friend, Bill. I got married, had two daughters, started a church and served it as pastor for seven years, taught college, and finally moved to Chicago to get my Ph.D. That process took seven years, not the three years I had originally anticipated. After a family member's illness caused us to lose our home, our jobs, indeed almost everything but each other, I didn't think I had the willpower to finish my doctorate. However, since my husband and children had already sacrificed so much for my dream, I dreaded letting them down by not completing it. So with incredible support from my family, friends, and spiritual community, in 1999, I finally received my doctorate.

Having experienced so much cut-throat competition in my graduate school, I made the gut-wrenching decision *not* to apply for my former "dream job": teaching in academia. Rather, I decided to go back to work in the church world. While seeking a pastorate, I worked as a secretary for a law firm, a church, and then a synagogue, just to keep food on our table. After putting out resume after resume to churches across the mid-West and East coast, but receiving no job offers, I found myself falling into despair about my future, and more importantly, my family's future.

Then I found out that Bill Coffin was coming to Chicago to celebrate his 75th birthday. For years, my husband had heard me rave about Bill's powerful influence on my faith life. In my preaching at Christpoint Community Church, I had often quoted from Bill's stirring sermons at Riverside Church. So my husband and I bought tickets for the dinner to be held in his honor.

A month later, there we were, sitting at round tables with 600 others whose lives Bill had touched or transformed. Listening to his friends catalog his life-long contributions to peace, justice, and the faith, while watching the amazing outpouring of love towards him, a realization dawned on me, slow and warm as the rays of the sun.

I leaned over to John and in a tone tinged with awe, whispered: "John, God wouldn't have brought me to Riverside Church and Union Theological Seminary and given me all those opportunities just to abandon me here in Chicago to work as a file clerk. I see now who I am, and *these are my people*."

After the party, I proudly introduced John to Bill. Then I hugged Bill, thanking him for being such an inspiring role model. After I bragged a little about earning my doctorate, Bill teased: "You know, Pam, don't you, that education kills by degrees!"

God, or "Divine Mischief" as my friend Sandi nicknames God, surely has a sense of humor. Six months after Bill's party, although several Chicago churches had finally offered me a position, I accepted the most thrilling offer: to become Associate Pastor for the Church of Christ in Yale University. For several years, I preached with pride from Bill's very pulpit!

Join a Spiritual Community

We human beings and other creatures appear to be separate, distinct entities, yet some quantum physicists insist that we are intimately interconnected. For example, have you heard of the "butterfly effect"—the scientific theory that the breaking of a butterfly wing here on earth can affect life on a planet thousands of light years away? Another illustration is the verifiable phenomenon that occurs in every classroom: within fifteen minutes' time, students and teacher are actually breathing in each other's water vapor. At least one physicist has surmised that the atoms of the very air that Jesus once breathed now permeate every molecule on our planet. Friends, we are not as isolated and separated as we would like to believe. Native Peoples wisely remind us that we human beings are bound together within the whole web of creation.

At the same time that we recognize our "interbeing" (Thich Nhat Hanh's word), I believe it's beneficial for each person to sink roots into the fertile soil of a *specific* spiritual community. My anthropological training and field experience has taught me that we are wired, biologically and emotionally, for community. What do I mean?

In his book, *The Scent of Love,* Keith Miller proposes the reason why the early Christians were such "phenomenally successful evangelists." It wasn't because of their gifts, such as speaking in tongues, and it certainly wasn't because Christianity was such an easy doctrine to swallow, because it wasn't. They were successful because they had discovered the secret of *community.*

As a rule, Miller claims, the early Christians didn't have to lift a finger to evangelize or to get new folks to join them. Rather, he muses:

> Someone would be walking down a back alley in Corinth or Ephesus and would see a group of people sitting together, talking about the strangest things: something about a man, and a tree, and an execution and an empty tomb. What they were talking about made no sense to the onlooker, but there was something about the way they spoke to one another, about the way they looked at one another, about the way they cried together, the way they laughed together, about the way they touched one another, that was strangely appealing. It gave off the *scent of love.*

> The onlooker would start to drift further on down the alley, only to be called back to this little group like a bee to a flower. He would listen some more, still not understanding, and start to drift away. But again he would be pulled back, thinking, "I

don't have the slightest idea what these people are talking about, but whatever it is, I want to be part of it."

Miller insists, and I agree, that this is not just a romantic envisioning of what the early Jesus movement was like. This is what happened and can still happen to any community of people committed to growth in love of God and neighbor. *We are wired for spiritual community*—to share our deepest lives, our more intimate thoughts and feelings, fears and desires, with others. And we will grow in the Spirit, especially if our community includes study, self-examination, spiritual practices such as prayer and fasting, and service to others.

Friends, you might take some time to reflect upon the spiritual community you currently belong to. What qualities of the leader inspire you? What is it about the community that you love? How are you supported and challenged to become the best "you" you can be?

If you are not currently part of an intentional spiritual community, shop around. Observe the folks. Ask questions. Give them some time to reveal their truest selves and motives. Then trust your intuition. Once you have found a good match, you will most likely give off that precious scent of love.

Setting Your Sights

Now that you've consciously designed and set up your base camp, it's time to set your sights. Where are you headed in your quest for self and Spirit? The Internet offers infinite resources, whether detailed road maps or the calming British voice on the car's GPS. In the old days, mariners used only a compass and the stars to navigate the treacherous high seas. Today, spiritually speaking, using a star—or in this case a spiritual ideal—to guide you to your destination is a wise practice.

Set your spiritual ideals.

Note I said "spiritual" ideals. You may have in mind an ideal of your perfect job, husband or home, but I'm focusing here on your soul. What qualities of character do you hope to build, what goals of spiritual growth do you wish to attain? How can you start today, now? When I was young, my dad's preaching made Jesus come so alive that I could picture him healing the sick and the mentally anguished, or scooping the children up onto his lap, or speaking to marginalized women. So one of my earliest ideals was to grow in love, especially loving "the least of these."

Though we can hold several ideals at once, our primary spiritual ideal will certainly shift as our life situation changes. So it's wise to re-assess your spiritual ideals every once and awhile. New times require new stars.

> A Hasidic tale recounts that an old Rabbi once asked his pupils how they could tell when the night had ended and the day had begun.
>
> "Could it be," asked one of the students, "when you can see an animal in the distance and tell whether it's a sheep or a dog?"
>
> "No," answered the Rabbi.
>
> Another asked, "Is it when you can look at a tree in the distance and tell whether it's a fig tree or a peach tree?"
>
> "No," answered the Rabbi.
>
> "Then when is it?" the pupils demanded.
>
> "It is when you can look on the face of any woman or man and see that it is your sister or brother. Because if you cannot see this, it is still night."

After reading this story, I decided to experiment with an ideal which would cause me to recognize and honor God in each person I met.

What is your primary spiritual ideal at this time in your life?

Caution: Choose an ideal that is authentic to you: it is yours, not what you think someone else would want you to choose.

Set your goals.

Your goals become easier to define once you have written down your ideals. Why bother to set goals at all? Because you are now taking total responsibility for your life. You're using your creativity and imagination. You're focusing your energy on what you want to accomplish in your life, tomorrow, next month, or next year.

While I've always made a list of my daily goals, I've often done it half-heartedly. Though I have attained some of my larger life goals, I've often been fuzzy about imagining them or timid in claiming them. I'd think things like, "OK, God, you just pick out which _____ (job, man, income) you think would be good for me, and I'll accept it." The truth is that I was afraid to commit myself, hesitant to voice my heart's desires.

Recently, God handed me a wake-up call in a line in the wonderful spiritual autobiography, *Eat, Pray, Love* by Elizabeth Gilbert. Liz's friend Richard questions her gently in an ashram in India.

"Liz, why do you have a wishbone where your backbone should be?"

Ouch! I winced when I read those words. I realize I'd always had that anatomical problem. But now I am grateful to Richard for naming my tendency to (pretend to) be a goody good Christian girl, so that God would reward me with the things I badly wanted but felt unworthy to receive. I'd been a "wishin' and a hopin' Christian" or a "wishin' and a hopin' partner" rather than focusing sharply and intently on my goal with a strong backbone to support me.

For months now, I have been consciously working on replacing my wishbone with my backbone, boldly setting goals and acting on them. It feels so good. For example, here are some of my current goals:

- Ride a horse by July 1.
- Plant flowers and mulch the yard by July 15.
- Redo my website by August 1.
- Have a fun-filled two-week vacation from August 18th to the 30th.

How do you set your goals? Are you a list maker like I am? Abundance author Edwene Gaines recommends making a list of your top twelve goals and prioritizing them. Cross them off when they've been reached so that you can add new goals. She even urges keeping a goal notebook. Be as specific as you can, she urges: detail, detail, detail.

Not only should you picture the details in your mind's eye (*visualize*), it's better if you can actually *feel* the thrill of possessing or obtaining your goal *right now*. Picture your hands on that new Jeep steering wheel; feel the leather saddle creaking beneath you on your noble steed; breathe in that heady fragrance of your new boyfriend's aftershave. Mind is the builder and the physical is the result, but heart and imagination build our reality, too.

For each goal, Edwene suggests stating a completion date, a *reasonable* date, that is, or the universe may get stumped. After listing each one of my major goals, I always add the phrase "or better," meaning, "Universe, you're welcome to show me a better goal or a more reasonable completion date." Making this statement keeps me humble yet open to Divine possibilities and timing.

So, time travelers, what are your twelve current goals?

An example of goal setting

In my twenties, my number one goal—based on my spiritual ideal to become more loving—was to find a smart, wonderful and loving husband who would also make a great father for any children we might have. However, my first attempt at marriage at age 26 broke down after two years. My husband and I had been deeply in love. What had happened? In desperation, we went to a local pastor for counseling who did not know us from Adam (or Eve). After listening to our problems, the pastor sided with my ex-husband. When I shared my concerns, he even laughed at me, suggesting I should have married a church organist rather than a fast car-racing businessman. That session with him put the final nail in our marital coffin. With great sadness, we gave up on reconciliation and filed for divorce.

After the divorce, my self-esteem plummeted. I gave up imagining my ideal mate. I felt that since I had broken my marriage vow, God would never find me worthy to have a mate again. I went through a lot of soul searching, read a lot of books on building healthy relationships, and talked at length with both married and single girlfriends to garner their wisdom. My best friend at the time, Betsy, and I decided we were tired of judging ourselves as "losers at love," so we began to laugh at ourselves. We even came up with a name for our condition: "Desperate Lady Syndrome." The power of naming ourselves felt good.

Through the next few years, we worked on ourselves, and guess what? We began to rely on our own strength and appreciate our loving natures. More and more, each of us became our "own woman." In honor of this progress, we re-dubbed our condition, "Shaky Lady Syndrome." That felt even better.

The best advice we ever read, however, suggested that we make a list of the qualities we desired in a mate, and then, rather than *trying to find* that ideal mate, we worked on *becoming* that mate. Instead of having antennae out to trap a husband, we focused on improving ourselves. I worked hard on building up in myself the loving, playful, and smart qualities that I desired in my ideal mate. During this time, the old demon "doubt" would rear her ugly head. I feared I would never marry again.

One day as I sat in my living room deeply discouraged, my sister ran out of her room, cheeks flushed, heart racing. She burst out that while in meditation, she had been praying for me, and she had glimpsed the legs of my future husband. Cute legs, too! Whenever self-doubt crept into my mind, I would remember her "vision." That boosted my spirits for a long time. After several more years of working to become my own ideal mate, my husband-to-be and I found each other. Or, as the 13th century Persian poet Rumi so beautifully puts it, "Lovers don't just discover one another. They are in each other all along."

Shape a Vision.

Questers, now is a perfect time to gather up your goals into one overarching vision for your life. What do you spend your time daydreaming about? When you scour magazines or roam malls, what are you hoping to find? Reflect upon these questions, and then sum it all up in a vision of your own. My overall vision for my life right now is *to be transformed from an anxiety-filled, poverty-ridden worry-wart to a woman of stalwart and exuberant trust in her own gifts and in the abundant goodness of the Universe.*

You artistic readers might like to create a vision-board on a large poster board, covering it with images and words symbolizing elements of the life you desire. Even those of you who are artistically challenged can make a colorful, eye-popping collage from magazine pictures and photos to inspire you.

Write your mission statement.

For those of you who are left-brained, another option is to write your mission statement—your life's purpose—on a sheet of paper and tack it up where you can see it everyday: on your closet door, your bathroom mirror or your fridge. Make sure that you put it in a safe

84

place where no one will tease you about it. Though written years ago, this mission statement still inspires me to be my true self when I feel lost or down.

> **I am**   *Healer*   *Teacher*
>   *Romancer* *Preacher*
>   *Lover*
>   *Praise singer* *Beauty bringer*
>   *Listener*   *Story-teller*
>   *Bridge builder*
>   *Honorer of bodies--creatures & earth*
>   *Circle maker* *Myth shaper*
>   *Heart dancer with*
>   *My family, My community, & My cosmos.*

Someone once said, "What you are is God's gift to you. What you make of yourself is your gift to God."

So be creative. Make a collage, a painting, a poem. Dance, sing, drum and shout. Have fun! Use that backbone, my dears, to sail the schooner of your life under the star-studded skies.

Attitudes to stash
in your back-packed soul

We're almost ready to begin your intentional quest of your life. Here are a few suggestions on what attitudes to pack.

l. Be determined.

There once was a whole group of frogs making their way through the forest to their new home. Two elderly, frail frogs weren't paying attention and fell into a large, deep hole. They started to jump frantically up and down in order to get out and save themselves. Their friends above looked down at them, realized how old they were, and started yelling down to them,

"Save your energy. Just give up and die. You'll never make it back up here. You're too old. Stop struggling!"

The two older frogs kept jumping and jumping, but made no progress. Finally, one of them gave up, lay down, and— croaked. *(Sorry.)*

The frogs above kept yelling and gesturing to the remaining frog, "Give up already! You're never going to get out of that deep hole. Just give up!"

To their astonishment, the frog in the hole began to jump harder and harder still, more determined than ever. Lo and behold, on his final jump he made it back up to the surface.

The other frogs, stunned and amazed, gathered around him, asking him how he did it. The frog made some signs with his hands, explaining that he was deaf. The whole time the frogs were yelling at him to give up and die, he thought they were cheering him on!

We need the *chutzpah*, the guts and good spirits, of this old frog as we journey through life. No matter what, we need to "keep on keeping on." Be like that frog in your sheer determination to survive and thrive.

2. Use humor.

Here's a valuable practice from Benjamin and Rosamund Zanders' insightful and clever book, *The Art of Possibility: Transforming Personal and Profession Life*. "Remember Rule #6."

Two prime ministers are sitting in a room discussing affairs of state. Suddenly a man bursts in, apoplectic with fury, shouting and stamping and banging his fist on the desk. The resident prime minister admonishes him: "Peter," he says, "kindly remember Rule Number 6," whereupon Peter is instantly restored to complete calm, apologizes, and withdraws.

The politicians return to their conversation, only to be interrupted yet again twenty minutes later by a hysterical woman gesticulating wildly, her hair flying. Again the intruder is greeted with the words: "Marie, please remember Rule

Number 6." Complete calm descends once more, and she too withdraws with a bow and an apology.

When the scene is repeated for a third time, the visiting prime minister addresses his colleague: "My dear friend, I've seen many things in my life, but never anything as remarkable as this. Would you be willing to share with me the secret of Rule Number 6?"

"Very simple," replies the resident prime minister. "Rule Number 6 is 'Don't take yourself so goddamned seriously."
"Ah," says his visitor, "that is a fine rule."

After a moment of pondering, he inquires, "And what, may I ask, are the other rules?"

"There aren't any."

3. Take risks—and be willing to fail.

Another crucial attitude to bring on your journey is your willingness to risk and your readiness to make mistakes. Have any of you struggled with the deadly DNA of perfectionism? It's often passed down from generation to generation. My father and grandmother modeled it, if unconsciously, for me and I adopted it, whole-hog. For instance, if I wasn't perfect, which for me meant getting A pluses in my high school and college work, then I felt worthless. I was driven to excel, and whatever I couldn't excel at (like drawing), I dropped from my life. Caught between the two extremes of Miss Perfect or Miss Failure, I could find no safe middle ground. As my workaholic behavior grew and my suffering deepened, I realized I needed a new attitude, one that would allow me not only to try new things but even to fail.

I love the slogan I once saw on a poster: "Behold the humble turtle who only gets ahead by sticking his neck out!" However, I needed something more than a slogan to confront the suffocating snake of perfectionism that coiled around my psyche, threatening to strangle me. Learning something new *always* involves the possibility of making mistakes, doesn't it? In fact, sometimes we learn more by failing in a project or relationship than by succeeding. So how was I to proceed?

The Zanders suggest that whenever you make a mistake, instead of beating yourself up by saying things like "You stupid so and so," you throw your hands up in the air and proclaim, *Isn't that fascinating?"* Then, take a few deep breaths and proceed to reflect on what could have been done differently, or how you want to proceed after learning from your mistake. You might even take some time to refocus on your ideal. This technique can also be applied to your treatment of others when they make a mistake.

This is a powerful spiritual discipline, one that I'm still practicing. For example, after I told my teen-aged daughter Kaitlyn about my newly discovered spiritual discipline, whenever she made a (rare) mistake, I would look at her, and before I could open my mouth to criticize her, I would pause, throw up my hands and say, "Isn't that fascinating?" I did the same with my own mistakes. She tells me I'm improving but still have a long way to go. So, under my breath, I whisper to myself: "Isn't that fascinating!"

One more thing. This light-hearted, non-blaming approach to failure might leave you wondering what happens to standards of excellence for our behavior. Ben Zander acknowledges that no one facing surgery wants it performed by an unskilled surgeon. High standards of performance are important. However, it's critical to make a distinction between excellence and perfectionism. Having an ideal and striving for excellence doesn't mean that you are trying to be perfect. Thank God. Working towards excellence is not something to live *up to* as much as something to live *into*.

I learned another practice for healing my deadly strain of perfectionism during one of my seminary classes. I gleaned a pearl of wisdom from the work of child psychologist, D.W. Winnicott. In the 1950s, when children exhibited mental and emotional problems, psychologists usually blamed the children's mothers. Challenging this diagnosis, Winnicott maintained that a mother need not try to be "perfect" in order to raise a well-adjusted child. All she needed to do was to be *"good-enough,"* which included responding readily to the infant's cries, feeding and changing the baby to make it comfortable, and so on. She did not have to be (nor can any one ever be) perfect. What a liberating gift to those besieged mothers.

While studying Winnicott's "good-enough" approach to mothering, I realized I might apply it to my tyrannical trait of perfectionism. So whenever I heard my inner critic start to chastise me with comments like, "You're not perfect, girl; you're a big failure. Who do you think you are, anyway? Just give up on getting a good husband or a great job," I replaced my usual response of "You're so right," with, "Well, maybe I'm not perfect, but I'm definitely 'good enough.'" That shut her up.

We can continue to strive for excellence, encouraging ourselves to develop our talents and skills. At the same time, we can reassure ourselves as often as necessary that, as a therapist, dancer, CEO or social worker, we are already *good enough*.

4. Show extraordinary respect for yourself and others.

The following story, *The Rabbi's Gift*, eloquently expresses this important attitude.

> The monastery had fallen on hard times. It was once part of a great order which, as a result of religious persecution in the seventeenth and eighteenth centuries, lost all its branches. It was decimated to the extent that there were only five monks left in the mother house: the Abbot and four others, all of whom were over seventy. Clearly it was a dying order.
>
> Deep in the woods surrounding the monastery was a little hut that the Rabbi from a nearby town occasionally used for a hermitage. One day, it occurred to the Abbot to visit the hermitage to see if the Rabbi could offer any advice that might save the monastery.
>
> The Rabbi welcomed the Abbot and commiserated. "I know how it is," he said, "the spirit has gone out of people. Almost no one comes to the synagogue anymore." So the old Rabbi and the old Abbot wept together, and they read parts of the Torah and spoke quietly of deep things.
>
> The time came when the Abbot had to leave. They embraced. "It has been wonderful being with you," said the Abbot, "but I have failed in my purpose for coming. Have you no piece of advice that might save the monastery?

"No, I am sorry," the Rabbi responded. "I have no advice to give. The only thing I can tell you is that the Messiah is *one of you.*"

When the other monks heard the Rabbi's words, they wondered what possible significance they might have. "The Messiah is one of us? One of us, here at the monastery? Do you suppose he meant the Abbot? Of course—it must be the Abbot, who has been our leader for so long. On the other hand, he might have meant Brother Thomas, who is undoubtedly a holy man. Certainly he couldn't have meant Brother Elrod—he's so crotchety. But then Elrod is very wise. Surely, he could not have meant Brother Phillip—he's too passive. But then, magically, he's always there when you need him.

"Of course, he didn't mean me—yet supposing he did? Oh, Lord, not me! I couldn't mean that much to you, could I?"

As they contemplated in this manner, the old monks began to treat each other with extraordinary respect, on the off chance that one of them might be the Messiah. And on the off *off* chance that each monk himself might be the Messiah, they began to treat themselves with extraordinary respect.

Because the forest in which it was situated was beautiful, people occasionally came to visit the monastery, to picnic or to wander along the old paths, most of which led to the dilapidated chapel. They sensed the aura of extraordinary respect that surrounded the five old monks, permeating the atmosphere. They began to come more frequently, bringing their friends, and their friends brought friends. Some of the younger men who came to visit began to engage in conversation with the monks. After a while, one asked if he might join, then another and another. Within a few years, the monastery became once again a thriving order, and—thanks to the Rabbi's gift—a vibrant, authentic community of light and love for the whole realm.

5. Nurture an attitude of expectancy.

Just like the distinction between perfection and excellence, I urge you to make a distinction between expectancy and expectation. Expectancy is important. Without it, hope and vitality can go out of life. I do my best to expect good things to happen to me every day. However, I also know that I can sometimes sabotage myself by holding unreasonable expectations of myself or others. Then I must remind myself to lower the expectations but hold onto the expectancy. Admittedly, this is difficult to learn, but I've found a clue. Perfectionism and unreal expectations seek to trip you up, to make you fall flat on your face, while excellence and expectancy only want to dance with you.

6. Express gratitude and joy.

Finally, sons and daughters, I hope you can maintain "an attitude of gratitude" on your quest. The medieval mystic Meister Eckhart of Germany believed that if the only prayer a human being offered throughout their whole life was, "Thank you, God," that would be enough to be soul-enlightened.

"What about joy?" you ask. "What about our constitutional right to 'the pursuit of happiness?' What's so special about joy?"

Well, happiness is great when it happens. You could almost call it "happen-ness." Since happiness depends on external circumstances, it can't be controlled. In contrast, joy emerges from a deeper place in the soul. Joy may spread through you quietly, like rays of a sunrise caressing the dark but expectant horizon. Or joy can be tears of gratitude welling up in your eyes when your sweetheart forgives you, or when your boss points out your good intentions even though your business project failed.

Joy is also magical because it multiplies when shared with another. The old saying is true if not mathematically correct: "A burden shared is halved, and a joy shared is doubled." Quiet deep joy can be nurtured, though not controlled. It's a gift that I've seen my daughters express while making bread pudding together for the first time, sipping a little rum while pouring it into the doughy mixture, all three of us growing warmer in body and spirit. Or joy can be the bubbly, leaping-and-prancing-around type of emotion—the type when you pull your clenched fist down towards you with a jubilant "Yes!"

We can't control what life brings us, but we can determine our response to life. No matter what our circumstances, choosing to be joyous can be liberating. My dad loved to tell the following parable almost as much as I loved hearing him tell it.

> The Buddha was walking through the lush forest with some of his disciples. They came upon a man, a Brahmin, of the highest priestly caste in India. He asked the Buddha, "How many lifetimes do I have left before I attain *nirvana?*"
>
> The Buddha looked into him deeply and proclaimed, "Only one."
>
> The man walked away, thoughtful and sad.
>
> Further along the path, the Buddha and friends came upon an Untouchable, a man of the lowest and most despised caste. He inquired of the Buddha, "How many lifetimes do I have left until I attain *nirvana?*"
>
> With infinite compassion, the Buddha replied, "You, my son? Do you see that large tree over there? As many lifetimes as leaves upon that tree."
>
> To which the man responded, "Oh joy, rapture!"
>
> And in that instant, he attained *nirvana*.

So, my dear ones, grab your backpack, sling it over your shoulder, set your star-sights and program your spiritual GPS. The wilderness is calling.

SIX

———

Befriending Your Body:

Your Sidekick on the Trail

The Church says: The body is a sin.
Science says: The body is a machine.
Advertising says: The body is a business.
The body says: I am a fiesta.
—Eduardo Galeano

*Guys, the first part of this chapter aims mainly at women, but the rest includes you, too!

Sidekicks make remarkable traveling partners through the maze of life. They are our best friends. They make us laugh, sometimes even at our expense. They come to our rescue. A classic example from my mother's generation is that of Bing Crosby and Bob Hope. If you want to howl with laughter, I highly recommend their "On the Road" movies. From my Sixties generation, there's Pat Brady in his old Jeep played sidekick to the elegant, crooning cowboy, Roy Rogers. Of course, almost everyone, no matter their age, seems to know the laughable Lucy with her faithful side-kick, Ethel. Side-kicks these days seem to come in groups, not pairs: think of the women in *Sex and the City*, or both men and women in the popular television series, *Friends*.

How do you feel about your body? Do you regard it as a sidekick? A bother, a burden? Can you see your body, like Galeano suggests, as a *fiesta*, a celebration of your amazing senses? A wild and joyous party of smelling, sight, touching, tasting, hearing, singing and dancing? If you are female, how do you feel about your body as *female*: i.e., menstruation, making love, being pregnant, giving birth, nursing a baby? If you're over thirty, do you feel the same way about your body that you did when you were a girl, a teenager or a young woman? If not, what has changed?

In our country alone, nearly ten million women (and one million men) suffer from an eating disorder. One percent of all teenaged girls will be anorexic, and 15% of those will die of complications. This is heartbreaking. *Top Sante*, a U.K. community health magazine, surveyed 2,000 women in their forties, and reported the following data in their August, 2005 issue:

- Over 50% have a disordered way of eating, such as missing breakfast, snacking instead of eating lunch, eating chocolates and drinking wine instead of having their evening meal.
- Most find losing weight much harder after 40.
- 70% have made serious attempts to diet during the last 12 months.
- Most want to weigh less than they did when they were 20 and at least 20% less than they currently weigh.
- Over 30% are regularly on one diet or another.
- Over 30% take slimming pills or laxatives.
- Over half have had cosmetic surgery or would consider it.
- Almost all of them envy women of their age who have nice bodies.
- The vast majority are unhappy with their bodies.
- Most hate their middle, hips, thighs and upper arms.
- Most rated their bodies at 7 out of 10 when they were young, but now rate them at 3.5 out of 10.

Many of us treat our bodies as objects to conquer. We manage our bodies, subduing their unwanted urges. We try to control our appetites as best we can. (OK, some of us cave in pretty easily. Homemade chocolate chip cookies are my downfall.) Perhaps we even view our bodies as weak because they are susceptible to illness and injury. In extreme cases, such as in eating disorders, we may perceive our body as enemy, or else feel totally disconnected from it. We may feel that others view us as a temptress, using our bodies to manipulate them; perhaps we even see ourselves that way.

Our culture insists that a woman is attractive only if she is young, slim (even dangerously skinny), and sexy. Through ads on TV and in magazines, women are encouraged to resist the process of aging or to camouflage it: with hair dyes, Botox, eye creams with wrinkle removers, as well as more extreme measures like face lifts and tummy tucks.

In addition to the media's distorted portrayal of femininity and female bodies, there's another mainly negative cultural influence upon a woman's body image—Christianity. While trends show we are rapidly becoming a pluralistic society, many Christians still believe that America is a "Christian" nation. Whether or not you are Christian, you might be surprised how much influence the Christian tradition covertly exerts upon your perception of a female body. Our broader culture has assimilated many of the Roman Catholic Church's views on women, flesh and sin, and passed them down to you. So how, in general, has Christianity shaped the Western female body image, which may affect you and me today?

Some Christian Scriptures and Traditions
Devalue the Body

The story of Paul's conversion in the *Book of Acts* (found in the New Testament immediately after the *Gospel of John*) is quite fascinating. Saul (circa 5-67 C.E.) was a devout Jew who engaged in persecuting the early Christians, even helping to stone some of them to death. While riding his horse to Damascus to participate in what we would call a "hate crime," stoning Christians, he was blinded by a brilliant light, knocked off his horse and questioned by the voice of Jesus: "Saul, Saul! Why do you persecute me?"

Ultimately, Saul, renamed Paul, became a Christian, and started Christian churches in Rome, the capital of the Empire, as well as much of Asia Minor.

Because Paul's fourteen letters to the early churches are included in the canon of the New Testament, Paul's teachings (or those attributed to him) have strongly influenced Christian communities over the past two thousand years, specifically in the West. On one hand, Paul's concept of the human body as a temple of the living God is quite beautiful. In his *First Letter* to the church in Corinth, 6:19-20, Paul chastised some members of the church who were flirting with sexuality in potentially dangerous ways:

> Do you not know that your body is a temple of the Holy Spirit, who is in you, whom you have received from God? You are not your own; you were bought at a price. Therefore honor God with your body.

Paul elevated the concept of the body to a high level of respect when he made the comparison that fledgling Gentile converts were equal with Jews in the body of Christ. In *Ephesians 3:6*, he wrote:

"This mystery is that through the gospel the Gentiles are heirs together with Israel, members together of one body, and sharers together in the promise in Christ Jesus." In *Colossians 3:15*: "Let the peace of Christ rule in your hearts, since as members of one body you were called to peace. And be thankful."

Paul's most creative use of body image is found in his description of how members in a congregation should relate to each other in *1st Corinthians* 12:12, 15-17, 25-26:

> The body is a unit, though it is made up of many parts; and though all its parts are many, they form one body. So it is with Christ.
>
> If the foot should say, "Because I am not a hand, I do not belong to the body," it would not for that reason cease to be part of the body.
>
> And if the ear should say, "Because I am not an eye, I do not belong to the body," it would not for that reason cease to be part of the body.
>
> If the whole body were an eye, where would the sense of hearing be? If the whole body were an ear, where would the sense of smell be?
>
> There should be no division in the body, but its parts should have equal concern for each other. If one part suffers, every part suffers with it; if one part is honored, every part rejoices with it.
>
> Now you are the body of Christ,
> and each one of you is a part of it.

Too, Paul's letters often aimed at bringing conflicting groups together across the dividing lines of race, gender and class—a worthwhile goal, wouldn't you agree? For example, this famous statement is found in *Galatians* 3:28: "There is neither Jew nor Greek, slave nor free, male nor female, for you are all one in Christ Jesus."

At the same time, although Paul could appreciate the body in these important ways, he often wrote of his great mistrust of the body, especially its sexual urges. And he detested human flesh for its susceptibility to sin. For example, *Romans 8:10* says: "But if Christ is in you, your body is dead because of sin, yet your spirit is alive because of righteousness."

Furthermore, in his letters, Paul often stated that the body/flesh is sinful, thus causing the person to sin. For example, *Romans* 8:3, 6, states:

> For God has done what the law, weakened by the flesh, could not do: sending his own Son in the likeness of sinful flesh and for sin, he condemned sin in the flesh….to set the mind on the flesh is *death*, but to set the mind on the Spirit is life and peace….
> (my emphasis)

After Paul's death, many male church leaders continued to teach that the human body is a distraction, or worse, a hindrance, to the growth of the soul. Hence, the body's desires and needs were to be ignored or chastised.

I've already mentioned the abysmal track record Christian tradition assigns to females: "Woman was created second and sinned first." Paul continued this misogyny. For example, in *Second Corinthians* 11:3, Paul denigrated women's status: "But I am afraid that just as Eve was deceived by the serpent's cunning, your minds may somehow be led astray from your sincere and pure devotion to Christ." In *First Corinthians* 11:7, Paul advised: "A man ought not to cover his head, since he is the image and glory of God; but the woman is the glory of man." Why isn't she, too, the glory of God?

Paul also discouraged women from becoming leaders in the new churches through admonitions like the following in *First Corinthians* 14:33-35.

> As in all the congregations of the saints, women should remain silent in the churches. They are not allowed to speak, but must be in submission, as the Law says. If they want to inquire about something, they should ask their own husbands at home; for it is *disgraceful for a woman to speak in the church.* (my emphasis)

Several times in my early years of ministry, angry men who had just heard me preach spit this passage right into my face, calling me a disgrace to the Christian faith.

For two millennia, the dominant Christian view of relations between men and women has been based primarily on Paul's writings (or writings ascribed to him). Check out this passage in *First Corinthians* 7:1-4.

> Now concerning the matters about which you wrote. It is well for a man not to touch a woman. But because of the temptation to immorality, each man should have his own wife and each wife her own husband. ...for the wife does not rule over her own body, but the husband does; likewise, the husband does not rule over his own body, but the wife does.

In theory, Paul's advice sounds fair to both sexes, yet in reality, for nearly 2,000 years, the Roman Catholic Church has ignored the clause allowing the wife to "rule over [her husband's] body." Besides, wouldn't most of us today challenge the idea of *anyone* ruling over someone else's body? Shouldn't each person "rule" over his or her own body?

In addition, highly respected church fathers, like the prolific Tertullian (155-230 C.E.) made denigrating comments about women. Tertullian claimed that "Woman is the devil's gateway" through which sin entered the world. St. Augustine (354-430 C.E.), another influential historian, theologian, and respected church father (who also coined the concept "original sin," big surprise) observed:

> What is the difference whether it is a wife or mother; it is still Eve the temptress that we must be aware of in any woman....I fail to see what use woman can be to man, if one excludes the function of bearing children.

In other words, much of Christian tradition viewed women as useless, *except* for birthing children. Because theologians taught that women caused men to lust and thus to sin, men were totally left off the accountability hook for their own "sinful" actions.

Not only did many church fathers blame women through Eve's actions for causing sin to enter the world, but they also regarded females as imperfect human beings compared to males. For instance, twelfth century church theologian, Thomas Aquinas, considered one of the greatest in the Catholic Church observed: "Woman is defective and misbegotten." The Catholic Church still refuses to ordain women as priests because they don't image Jesus *in their anatomy*.

Throughout the centuries, and especially in the Middle Ages in Europe, thousands of Christian women suffered from these church teachings, internalizing the hatred toward their own female bodies. During the Middle Ages, Catherine of Siena, Italy (1347-1380 C.E.) is a case in point. A brilliant Scholastic philosopher and theologian, she worked to bring the Papacy back to Rome from its displacement in France, and helped to establish peace among the Italian city-states. More than three hundred of her letters have survived. They make fascinating reading. Considered one of the great authors of early Tuscan literature, Catherine is one of my heroes.

However, despite all her bravery and accomplishments as a woman, Catherine was one of many female medieval mystics who hated her body—to the extreme. She constantly admonished her body. She practically starved it for years, eating only communion wafers for weeks at a time. At one point, she even forced herself to drink the pus she had collected in a bowl from her plague patients. In one of her letters, Catherine was adamant about treating her body with "a sweet and holy vengeance"—not exactly a loving attitude toward the flesh. Take a look at Rudolph's Bell's fascinating study, *Holy Anorexia*, if you're interested in learning more about medieval women mystics and their eating practices.

I hope this brief and admittedly grossly oversimplified survey gives you a taste of how Western Christian religious authorities have belittled and shamed women and their bodies *just because they're female*. There is hope, however. Many Catholic and Protestant women are courageously and creatively reforming these traditions.

Even some men are contributing to this effort. Brian Wren, a prolific British hymn writer, is counteracting Christianity's body-demeaning tradition. In his book *What Language Can I Borrow? God-Talk in Worship: A Male Response to Feminist Theology*, Wren shares the process of his consciousness-raising. One day, his sister, a faithful Christian all her life, informed him she could no longer worship in a church service that made her feel invisible *because she was a woman*.

Thinking she was being ridiculous, Wren agreed to research the two hundred or so hymns in their British hymnal. He was shocked to find that indeed almost all references to God and to human beings were male in gender: Father, Son, King, Lord, etc. Deeply affected by his discovery, Wren began to write new hymns that expanded images of God to include the female as well as other images. He has also affirmed the innate goodness of the human body in Christian terms in the following celebrative poem, *Good is the Flesh.*

> Good is the flesh that the Word has become,
>> good is the birthing, the milk in the breast,
>> good is the feeding, caressing and rest,
>> good is the body for knowing the world,
> Good is the flesh that the Word has become.
>
> Good is the body for knowing the world,
>> sensing the sunlight, the tug of the ground,
>> feeling, perceiving, within and around,
>> good is the body, from cradle to grave,
> Good is the flesh that the Word has become.
>
> Good is the body, from cradle to grave,
>> growing and aging, arousing, impaired,
>> happy in clothing, or lovingly bared,
>> good is the pleasure of God in our flesh,
> Good is the flesh that the Word has become.
>
> Good is the pleasure of God in our flesh,
>> longing in all, as in Jesus, to dwell,
>> glad of embracing, and tasting, and smell,
>> good is the body, for good and for God,
> Good is the flesh that the Word has become.

"But really," I hear you younger women asking, "who *cares* if you love your body? Why is that so important?"

Karly Randolph Pitman, writer, speaker, and mother of four, answers:

These are good questions. After all, loving your body isn't on par with feeding the hungry, sheltering the homeless, or fostering orphans. It's not like we're ending violence against women.

Or are we?

When we beat ourselves up for not being physically "perfect," however we define it, we are committing violence: violence against ourselves. And because we're all connected, we are also committing violence against other women: our peers, our daughters, and our granddaughters....

So what will prevent my girls from pursuing their dreams? If they buy the lie that they have to be super thin and youthful to be beautiful, that they have to loathe and control and try to shape their female form into something unnaturally unattainable, *that* will hold them back. The other freedoms won't matter, if they aren't free in their mind: free to love and accept themselves.

I have the power to change that. You do, too. That is why, as a woman, loving your body is some of the most important work that you can do....

In loving your body, you release love into the world. You release courage. You release forgiveness. You release compassion. You release acceptance.

That sounds like important work to me. Love your body; love yourself. Love your body; change the world. Love your body: it matters.

My anorexia began at age thirteen, on Christmas Eve. Of course, no one called it anorexia in the late Fifties. At that time, we lived in Syracuse, New York. My dad, three sisters and I had packed up our car to deliver Christmas gifts. I began to feel queasy, sick to my stomach. Since I hadn't thrown up since I was an infant, I didn't realize what was happening to me. Back at home, my fever mounted. Around midnight, I ran to the bathroom, trying to keep myself from gagging. I didn't know what was happening to me. Finally, I threw up—no way to stop it.

I became irrationally terrified of the feelings of nausea and the gagging, as well as the acrid aftertaste in my mouth. I especially feared the loss of control over my body.

That evening after I vomited, my mom cleaned me up and comforted me. Still, the next day I made up my mind. I was *never* going to experience those awful feelings again. The problem was how to guarantee that.

"I know," I reveled in my cold reason. "I'll never eat again."

I began starving myself that very day.

As the weeks went by, I was curiously calm while my parents grew concerned and then alarmed at my irrational decision. My mother begged me to eat something, so I agreed to eat some *Wheat Thins* and drink some water, but nothing else. A month went by. I lost more and more weight, and I was skinny to begin with. I don't remember my folks taking me to a doctor, although Mom claims they did. There was nothing to be done. I refused to eat anything but crackers, Tigers Milk bars, and some beef juice my mother carefully and anxiously prepared.

As my immune system weakened, I contracted the mumps. I ended up dropping out of school for a whole semester, and shrinking to a near skeleton. After five months, I referred to myself as the white Biafran, after the Biafran tribe in Africa that was starving at the time. (I cringe now at my comparison, because their starvation was not self-inflicted as mine was. But I was only twelve and didn't know better.)

That summer, my father decided to take a job at a university in northern Wisconsin. We packed up and moved to a tiny town up north. There I met a girl my age who attended the same Methodist church our family did. One day before school started, she invited me over to play.

"Aren't you embarrassed to be seen with someone as skinny as me?" I asked.

"No," she cheerily replied.

From that day on, I began to eat again.

I'm forever grateful to my dear friend "Jewel" for her unconditional acceptance of me during that time of suffering.

Over the years, I have worked hard on my emotional baggage, especially my relationship with my dad. He was a wonderfully gifted and talented man and father, yet his episodes of unpredictable rage, sometimes aimed at me, terrorized me. When I learned from Dad's sister that he had suffered physical violence as a boy, compassion welled up within me. I began to forgive him for his bad treatment of me, and when a new traumatic memory arises, I forgive him again. Of course, healing takes time. I continue to give thanks for all the teasing, goodness, spiritual wisdom and passion for choral music that he shared with me throughout the years, and that helps the healing along.

I *know* I am one of the lucky ones, for I never struggled with anorexia again. If you have an eating disorder, please seek professional help immediately. You're worth it. Through the process of strengthening your body image and reclaiming your self-worth, you *can* heal. In the meantime...

Daughters and sons of both Spirit and Flesh, of the sacred Mother and spiritual Father, how might we love our bodies more?

First, let's recognize the gains our culture has made throughout the past fifty years.

Cultural Advances towards Women's Bodies

Menstruation—*moontime*

I assume most women in our culture, at least the last two generations, view menstruation as a natural though inconvenient and even painful monthly event. What an improvement from my youth. In 1960 when I was 13, I remember everyone referring to menstruation as "the Curse," that is, God's punishment to women for being offspring of the "temptress," Eve, in the Garden of Eden.

I'm also excited about the recent, though ancient, view that a woman's body is a holy, sacred vessel able to conceive and bring forth new life. This view is popular in some circles of Wiccan/pagan women and New Age authors like Vicki Noble in her book, *Shakti Woman*. I met some Native American women on the reservations that held this view, as well.

Some Lakota women I've met have renamed the menstrual cycle "moon-time." I like that term much better than the non-descript, unimaginative term, "period." I mean, what are we women— sentences? Excited about this new consciousness and poetic yet scientifically accurate term, I once urged my teen-aged daughters to use the phrase "moontime" in place of "period." They thought I was crazy. Though changes in consciousness come slowly, we elders must share with our young women the attitude that menstruation is not a curse but a holy event. Let's take back the "power of the period."

The body image of a pregnant woman

In my mother's day, pregnant women literally had to "hide" in their homes. Going out in public was kept to a minimum. In my youth, pregnant women were beginning to come "out of the closet," I mean "the home." They began to feel pride in their ballooning, blossoming bellies. Nowadays, our culture seems to accept if not celebrate the fact that a pregnant woman is beautiful. Some stores even provide designer clothes for the expectant mother. I get such a kick out of watching pregnant women as they strut around the mall, proud of the new life growing within them, some with pierced rings in their bulging navels. Quite a change from women hiding under tent-like dresses. And husbands, no one can make your wife feel more sexy than you!

Giving Birth and Birthing Centers

From time immemorial, women have given birth at home, assisted by female family members or midwives. Only in the past century have male doctors taken over the process, placing expectant moms in the hospital with sick people, ostensibly to "protect" the mother and infant, but also implying that giving birth is a "sickness" rather than a natural and healthy process.

You've probably heard how women in the 1950s were over-drugged and rendered unconscious primarily to make the doctor's job easier. Research continues on the negative effects of these practices on the mothers and the newborns. The women's movement in the 1970s and 1980s did much to foster the training and use of midwives to assist in home births. While that practice seems to be waning, most hospitals now offer specially designed "birthing centers" resembling a bedroom rather than a hospital environment—a welcome advancement. It's ironic that many people still view the process of giving birth as a medical procedure rather than as a natural event.

While on the Pine Ridge and Rosebud reservations in South Dakota, I talked with several Lakota men who told me they would not allow a woman to perform the Lakota's most holy yearly ritual, the Sundance. In this ritual, men pierce their bare chests with bone skewers tied to rawhide strings which are then tied to a sacred tree around which they dance for three days without food or rest, as they attempted to pull the skewers out of their chests. During this intense time of pain, the men offer themselves to *Wakan Tanka*, the Creator, in a sacrifice of thanksgiving for specific answers to prayer the year before.

My first response upon hearing these men was that they were being macho, even sexist. But then the men added that they exclude women from the Sundance not because women aren't strong enough to bear the pain but because the women already honor the Creator by enduring the painful act of child-birth. Sheepishly, one man admitted he would never want to go through *that* pain.

So if a man starts to give you grief, daughters, over your "bitchy" PMS behavior, you can set him straight quickly. Ask what he does that can compare to the physical pain and emotional joy of bringing a baby into the world?

Breastfeeding
Although the act of breast-feeding in public is still against the law in some states, (can you believe it?), many women now feel comfortable discreetly nursing their infant in public places. Studies have shown that the nutrition in breast milk far outweighs the nutrition of bottled milk. As a new mom, it's exhilarating to realize that your very own body is completely supplying what your baby needs to keep it alive and thriving. Furthermore, some studies have shown that mothers are protected from some serious diseases later in life because they breastfed their infants.

Last but not least, breast-feeding can be an incredible bonding experience for mother and infant alike, though there are exceptions: illness, discomfort with one's breasts, etc. I encourage you to breast-feed your baby if you get the opportunity. Give it a try, at least. Their little fingers curled around yours will melt your heart, bonding you with your precious bundle. And the rewards of those warm fuzzies will get you through many nights of sleep deprivation.

Befriending Your Body

Imagine yourself in Flora Slosson Wuellner's shoes, bra and pants suit. In her 1989 book, *Prayer and Our Bodies*, Wuellner, a therapist and Christian retreat leader, relates that a retreat member complained that Wuellner's guided meditations left him feeling ungrounded.

When she returned home, Wuellner sat down in prayer to confront her beliefs about her body. She began,

"*What* is my body?"

An answer of sure and gentle strength seemed to rise from a deep place…"You are asking the wrong question." …

"All right, then," I responded. "*Who* is my body?"

Again I sensed a gentle, and now amused, response into my conscious thoughts: "Why don't you ask your body that question?"
…
I focused on my bodily self, sitting so quietly in the chair: "Who are you?"

Responses rose so swiftly and urgently into my conscious mind that I was almost overwhelmed….

> "I am your friend and closest partner.
> Sometimes I am your mother and father.
> Sometimes I am your child.
> Always I am your lover and spouse.
>
> I am the truth-teller. I witness to you your unknown self… the stored wisdom and hurts of the ages and generations before you….
>
> I am your partner in stress and pain. I carry much of your suffering, so your spirit does not need to carry it all alone….
>
> I am the visible means by which you relate and unite with others.
>
> I am one of the major ways by which God abides with you, speaks to you, touches you, unites with you.
>
> Far from separating you from your spiritual life, I open it to you.

You can pray with me, for me, through me. I can pray also, in my way, when you cannot.

I am always in embrace with you, though sometimes you ignore me or even hate and try to harm me.... I will never leave you.... Together, in passionate unity, we will become the fully alive human being."

Wuellner was stunned by her body's revelation. She realized she could never go back to seeing her body as

a prison of my spirit, a beast of burden to be driven... a slave for my habits, or an instrument to be possessed. God was revealing to me the hidden but deeply responsive companion of my life's spiritual journey....

After reading this passage, I, too, sat stunned. Like Wuellner, I had undervalued or even ignored my body's well-being. As her body's message sank in, I began to feel that it made a lot of sense. I decided to explore a new relationship with my body. I began to talk to it, listen to it, pray for and thank it. Through the coming months, I began to respect my body in new ways. Our relationship continues to grow. I now see my body as my intimate, beloved companion. It teaches me so much; that is, when I take the time to listen.

After twenty years of learning to befriend my body, I am convinced that every person's body is waiting to make their acquaintance. Your body is eager to enter into a purposeful, intentional relationship with you. Now is the time to start treating your body as your *best friend.*

Prize your sexuality.

I'm sure many of you readers already prize your sexuality, fiercely guarding your sexual intimacy as you would a precious treasure. Of course, you're aware of the very real danger of contracting STDs or HIV/AIDS. But your physical safety isn't the only thing at stake. Emotionally, a woman is more vulnerable than a man during and after the act of sexual intercourse. During the sex act, a woman opens her body, anatomically, to receive her partner. In contrast, a man typically stands out, puts out and then withdraws, his emotions mirroring his anatomy.

I learned about female sexual vulnerability the hard way. Maybe all women do, men, too. During the sexual revolution of the 1960s, *for the first time in human history,* women were free to have sex without worrying about becoming pregnant—we were liberated from our anatomy. I began to experiment with the new found freedom the Pill afforded.

During those radical days, my dad warned me to be careful about choosing a respectful and loving man as a sexual partner. I assumed Dad was just being "a male chauvinist," but to my consternation, I soon realized he had a point. For after making love with my boyfriend, I began to feel an intense physical bond with him that he didn't seem to feel towards me. Biologically, my nesting desires started to kick in as well, despite my valiant attempts to resist them with my sexually "liberated" mind.

From the '60s to the '80s, protecting my virginity was not my goal. Experimentation was.

Then, to my surprise, early in the 1980s, I was courted by a movie star!

Fritz, a friend from Virginia Beach, had traveled to New York City on a hot July weekend to rescue me from my convent-like existence in seminary. He took me to the Hotel Carlyle to see his favorite jazz pianist, Bobby Short. Since we were early for the show, we walked around the magnificent lobby. I marveled at the ornately gilded mirror on the wall facing the elevators. As my eyes roamed from the ceiling down to shoulder level, I began to exclaim, "Fritz! Look at this...."

My voice trailed off as my eyes rested on a pair of eyes staring directly into mine, eyes belonging to one of my favorite male movie stars (comparable today to Brad Pitt or Leonardo DiCaprio). All eyes, including Fritz's, were upon the two of us as I slowly pivoted to face this ruggedly handsome, Oscar-winning actor.

"Are you W.B.?" I asked sheepishly. I knew darn well who he was. He shyly nodded.

"I would tell you that you are a wonderful actor, but that would sound corny, wouldn't it?" I babbled. (Who was my script writer, anyway?)

Again, he nodded. The elevator bell rang, announcing its arrival. The doors opened. Our eyes were literally locked as he backed into the elevator. (Yes, backed in. I admit I did look rather hot that night, my white blouse showing off my tan, my slit black skirt revealing my shapely legs.) The doors closed. W.B. was gone.

I was stunned by the unexpected encounter. All through the evening, Fritz kept saying he thought the movie star was smitten with me. Preposterous. Nevertheless, after some (minimal) reflection, the next day I decided to write him a note stating that each of us hoped to be married one day and settle down. And though I was in seminary, if he ever needed a friend, I was available. (Sounds terribly naïve to me now.)

Then I forgot all about the meeting.

A week or more passed. I was in my dorm room around midnight when the phone rang. A man's soft and low, extremely sexy voice inquired,

"Is this Pamela Bro?"

"Yes."

"The one who goes to seminary?"

"Yes. Who are you?"

Silence.

"Who are you?" I repeated, starting to get irritated.

The previous semester, I had worked at a phone crisis line in downtown New York City, handling more than my fair share of calls from potential suicides, lonely men and not a few sex fiends.

"Who are you?" I demanded. "If you don't tell me right now, I'm going to hang up!"

"Aha-a-a," he drawled, smooth and slow. "I get it. You can't talk now. There's someone in the room with you. Shall I call back tomorrow night?"

"Alright, but only if you tell me who you are, buster!" I threatened, slamming down the receiver.

A tiny inkling of familiarity with that voice on the phone arose inside me.

"Oh, my God!" I gasped, turning to face my suite-mate. "I just hung up on W.B.!"

At midnight the following evening, six of my friends and I huddled in my room waiting for the phone to ring. It did, and it was W.B. During the next three days, we talked and talked for hours. He was in town in the process of editing his new movie about an American journalist who becomes involved with the Communist revolution in Russia and seeks to bring its idealistic spirit to the United States. He wrote, starred and directed this film. Pretty darn talented man. You can see why I was attracted to him. (OK, he was sexy, too.)

I was so excited when he called me and we talked, that I couldn't sleep or eat for three days. I felt like a princess.

At one point, I told him that I admired his acting ability. He seemed genuinely touched.

"No woman ever tells me that," he confided. "They always tell me how sexy I am. And you don't even make it sound corny." Now *I* was touched.

W.B. often complained how tired he was from overwork. I was so fatigued and star struck after three days of his calling me to talk that I finally offered to give him a back rub to relax him. He agreed. The next night, which happened to be hot and sultry, he sent a taxi for me. I arrived, shy and excited, at the door of his penthouse suite. He met me at the door, scantily clad in only expensive shirt tails. You'll have to use your imagination to finish the rest of the scene.

When I left the next morning, I warned W.B. that I didn't want to be just one more notch on his already considerably notched (by encounters with his famous female co-stars) belt. He promised me I wouldn't be. But he never called me again.

Months later, on a cold, rainy night in November, I went to see W.B.'s movie. Sitting by myself in the darkened theater, I felt unreal. My mind just could not fathom that I had been intimate with the gorgeous man up there on the big screen. Yet I don't regret my encounter with W.B. at all. We had some great talks, even spiritual ones. I remember now that when his movie *Shampoo* came out, my husband and I went to see it. I was so saddened and sickened by W.B.'s character's lack of depth that at one point on the drive home, I burst into tears—almost like he was already a dear friend of mine who was going down the wrong path. My husband thought I was crazy. After all, it was just a movie. Still, I think W.B. and I are kindred spirits in some way.

Because both W.B. and I had had quite a few intimate partners over the years, I was lucky we met before the onset of the AIDS epidemic.

So, dear daughters, don't be like me. Be wise. Practice safe sex and protect not only your most intimate body parts, but your *heart.* Honor your body as the special creature it is, allowing you to share ecstasy with another human being through the holy act of love-making. And sons, respect your sexuality as well! Your bodies and hearts are precious, too.

Thank your body.

Think about a time when you stubbed your pinkie toe. Where does all your attention go? On your next date or your next deadline? No. All you can think of is your throbbing toe. Not only does pain constrict our consciousness, but we tend to get angry at a body part that gets injured, don't we? When I broke my ankle, forcing me to hobble around on crutches for months, I was furious at my ankle for being so vulnerable. It was months before I realized that my ankle seemed to be the weakest part of my body, but it was really the strongest because it bore the brunt of my frantic, rushed lifestyle that contributed to my accident.

Many spiritual teachers recommend that we thank our body parts once in a while. Thich Nhat Hanh offers a wonderful meditation in which he introduces listeners to all of their body parts, having them smile to each one: "I smile to my liver. I smile to my lungs."

Praying for the health and wellbeing of your body is also a good idea. In 1976, I flew out to Chicago to visit my grandmother who had been diagnosed with terminal liver cancer. Tears in her eyes, she confided to me that she felt betrayed by her organs, since she had been praying for them intentionally for seventeen years *every day*. We cried together.

When I returned home to Virginia Beach, I mentioned this to a good friend, often wise beyond his years. He mused, "Maybe she's got it wrong. Maybe she lived seventeen years *longer* just because she prayed for her organs."

"Good point," I thought. And though I'll never know the truth, I prefer to believe his version.

Reclaim your body's wild nature.

In her ground-breaking book, *Women Who Run with the Wolves*, psychoanalyst and storyteller Clarissa Pinkola Estes invites us women to seek and claim the Wild Woman within us—the instinctual feminine nature that so many of us have lost touch with. In the introduction, Estes invites us to rejoin Wild Woman:

> So, ...whether you are possessed of a simple heart or the ambitions of an Amazon, whether you are trying to make it to

the top or just make it through tomorrow, whether you be spicy or somber, regal or roughshod—the Wild Woman belongs to you. She belongs to all women.

To find the Wild Woman, it is necessary for women to return to their instinctive lives, their deepest knowing. So let us push on now, and remember ourselves back to the Wild Woman soul. Let us sing her flesh back onto our bones.... Let us return now, wild women howling, laughing, singing up The One who loves us so.

For us the issue is simple. Without us, Wild Woman dies. Without Wild Woman, we die. *Para Vida,* for true life, both must live.

In a later chapter, Estes eloquently describes the power of the human body.

The body uses its skin...and flesh to record all that goes on around it. Like the Rosetta stone, for those who know how to read it, the body is a living record of life given, life taken, life hoped for, life healed....
The body remembers, the bones remembers...even the little finger remembers. Memory is lodged in pictures and feelings in the cells themselves. Like a sponge filled with water, anywhere the flesh is pressed, wrung, even touched lightly, a memory may flow out in a stream.

To confine the beauty and value of the body to anything less than this magnificence is to force the body to live without its rightful spirit, its rightful form, its right to...the natural joy that belongs to the wild nature.

Estes recommends that we claim the bodily traits, both desirable and deplorable, that we've inherited from our parents. On my mother's side, for example, I've inherited thin, baby-fine hair and terribly poor eyesight. At the same time, I've inherited her gifts: beautiful skin, radiant smile, health, perfect pitch, and her love of classical piano and sacred choral music.

Then what might we do to come to terms with our body image heritage, in order to heal our dislike of them?

First, Estes suggests that we gather together in a small group, bringing photographs of our mothers, aunts, sisters, mates, grandmothers, and other women who have been significant in our lives. After the participants line up the photos, each woman would repeat, "These are the women of my bloodline" or "These are the women from whom I inherited." Then, we would tell a story or secret about each photo. Tears of sorrow or gales of laughter that follow will cleanse the "dirty laundry" of our self-loathing, healing not only us but perhaps other members of our clan.

Second, Estes suggest we make a Scape-coat. (No, not a scape-*goat!*) What in the world is that?

> A scapecoat is a coat that details in painting, writing, and with all manner of things pinned and stitched to it all the name-calling a woman has endured in her life, all the insults, all the slurs, all the traumas, all the wounds, all the scars.
>
> It is her statement of her experience of being scape-*goated*. Sometimes it takes only a day or two to make such a coat; other times it takes months....
>
> At first, I made a scapecoat for myself. I had in mind...that I would disperse some of my old woundedness by burning the scapegoat. But you know, I kept the coat hung from the ceiling in the hallway and every time I walked near it, instead of feeling bad, I felt good. I found myself admiring the *ovaries* of the woman who could wear such a coat and still be walking foursquare, singing, creating, and wagging her tail. Other women felt the same.

Estes promises that Wild Woman will hold us in her symbolically strong arms while we experience all of our feelings, especially those of rage or grief. She assures us that "although there will be scars and plenty of them, it is good to remember that in tensile strength and ability to absorb pressure, a scar is stronger than skin." I love the gutsiness of Estes' next recommendation:

> It is also a good idea for women to count their ages, not by years, but by battle scars. "How old are you?" people sometimes ask me. "I am seventeen battle scars old," I say. Usually people don't flinch, and rather happily begin to count up their own battle scar ages accordingly.
>
> As the Lakota painted glyphs on animals hides to record the events of winter, and the Nahuatl, the Maya, and the Egyptians had their codices recording the great events of the tribe, the wars, the triumphs, women have their scapecoats, their battlecoats....
>
> Let there be no mistake about it, for you have earned it by the hard choices of your life. If you are asked your nationality, ethnic origin or bloodline, smile enigmatically. Say, "Scar Clan."

Working with Estes' ideas has convinced me that if we women are going to reform and transform our world into a more hospitable place for our challenging, mysterious, precious bodies, we must call back the Wild Woman in us. We must use our voices call forth our intuition, imagination, and bodily-based instincts. Estes counsels:

> ...Use your love *and* good instincts to know when to growl, to pounce, to take a swipe, when to kill, when to retreat, when to bay till dawn. We can all assert our membership in the ancient scar clan.... Let us not overspend our anger. Instead let us be empowered by it. Most of all, let us be cunning and use our feminine wits....
>
> So come out, come out wherever you are! ...What you do today influences your matrilineal lines in the future. The daughters of your daughters of your daughters are likely to remember you, and most importantly, follow in your tracks.

Yes, this is my prayer for you, daughters of my daughters—may you follow in whatever Wild Woman tracks I can leave you while I'm on this earth.

In my teens and twenties, I was meek and mild. Now I practice my Wolf Medicine whenever I can. Thank goodness, Estes provides a few helpful hints for the meeker ones among us. She writes:

> Over my lifetime as I've met wolves, I have tried to puzzle out how they live, for the most part, in such harmony. So, for peaceable purposes, I would suggest you begin right now with anything on this list. For those who are struggling, it may help greatly to begin with number ten.

General Wolf Rules for Life
1. Eat
2. Rest
3. Rove in between
4. Render loyalty
5. Love the children
6. Cavil in moonlight
7. Tune your ears
8. Attend to the bones
9. Make love
10. Howl often

Ow-oooooooh!

Pack questers, may we embrace our side-kick bodies, our *fiestas*, with grace and gratitude as we continue our quest. Now on to the next "leg" of the journey—(oops, seems we're still dealing with yummy body parts)—opening your heart.

SEVEN

Opening Your Heart:

Courage on the Quest

...The secret of love is in opening up your heart.
It's okay to feel afraid,
but don't let that stand in your way.
'Cause anyone knows that love is the only road.
And since we're only here for a while,
we might as well show some style.
Give us a smile!

Isn't it a lovely ride?
Sliding down,
gliding down.
Try not to try too hard.
It's just a lovely ride.   —James Taylor

While training as a hospital chaplain at Babies Hospital in New York City in the early 1980s, I had the surprise of my life. I had been visiting the children on my ward, including a child named B.T. I stepped into his room and there was James Taylor! Musician Carly Simon, then James' wife, was out entertaining the children on the floor with her delightful children's songs. James, an idol of mine for years, sat down on the hospital bed, motioned for me to sit across from him, and asked me in his quiet way, "Do you have a favorite song of mine that I could play for you?"

My mind raced through so many: "You've Got a Friend," "Fire and Rain," or "Shower the People You Love with Love." But what leapt to my lips was "The Secret o' Life." James sang the whole song right to me like a gentle troubadour, and I felt my shy heart blossom in response.

The origin of the word "courage" is French, meaning "large heart." A large heart, a wide, blooming, open heart, just as J.T. sang to me, is exactly what we need on our journey through life's wilderness: a heart

116

full of style, open to loving—smiling, gliding and sliding through life—giving us a lovely ride.

Having courage does *not* mean having no fear, sweet girls. It means proceeding with a large and vulnerable heart in the *face* of that fear. It means allowing our hearts to be loosened up and broken open to make room for more love and compassion to flow in. How might we become braver in matters of the heart, opening to life and to love and to courageous acts of Spirit?

Before we fill our hearts with courage, however, most of us need to empty them a bit. As we quest, sometimes we need to claw through the brush, briars and brambles of blame or shame, self-pity or self-doubt, our funky fears or our damaged dreams. We need to practice a "*Feng Shui* of the heart." *Feng Shui* (pronounced "fung shway") is the ancient Chinese practice of arranging home or work environments to promote health, happiness, and prosperity through aligning the *chi* or energy with spiritual forces. The first and primary goal of *Feng Shui* is the removal of all clutter in the environment. So how might we remove the clutter strewn around in our hearts?

Clear the Underbrush from Your Heart

We can and must forgive. The act of forgiveness can clear the underbrush from anyone's overcrowded, over-grown heart. In Jesus' day, Judaism taught that forgiving a person three times was a magnanimous gesture of good will. However, Jesus expanded that practice into "70 times 7;" in other words, one must never stop forgiving another. *(At the same time, you may need to clearly distance or protect yourself from someone's abusive behavior.)* Jesus himself practiced forgiveness, even while brutally nailed to a cross: "Father, forgive them, for they know not what they do."

Spiritual teachers from many traditions extol the liberating practice of forgiveness. Here's a powerful sampling:

> *"Every human being comes from the hand of God, and we all know something of God's love for us. Whatever our religion, we know that if we really want to love, we must first learn to forgive before anything else."* Mother Teresa of Calcutta (Catholic)

> *"Life is an adventure in forgiveness."* Author Norman Cousins

"If you want to see the brave, look at those who can forgive. If you want to see the heroic, look at those who can love in return for hatred." The Bhagavad Gita (Hindu Scripture)

"The practice of forgiveness is our most important contribution to the healing of the world." Marianne Williamson

"We witness by being a community of reconciliation, a forgiving community of the forgiven." Desmond Tutu, Former Anglican Archbishop of South Africa.

"Forgiveness is not an occasional act; it is a permanent attitude." Dr. Martin Luther King, Jr., African-American civil rights leader, prophet and preacher.

I can hear you fuming under your breath: "Why should I forgive him/her anyway? That S.O.B. or b-tch doesn't deserve to be forgiven! Isn't revenge wiser? Doesn't cursing them for the rest of my life have more integrity?"

In the popular book, *The Secret,* Joe Vitale paraphrases the South African spiritual leader Nelson Mandela by claiming, "Refusing to forgive someone is like taking poison and believing the other person will die."

I repeat: refusing to forgive is like taking poison and believing the other person will die.

That's right. While you might be feeling self-righteous about hating the *other* person's guts, the anger, hatred or ill feelings are actually poisoning *you,* not your enemy. So you and I must forgive the other person, not for their sake, but for *ours.*

Another effect forgiveness can have is to restore a broken relationship, to reconcile you with the person who's wronged you, or you've wronged. Ideally, when you tell a person how hurt or angry you are (using "I" language, not "You stupid ..."), the person will immediately repent and ask for your forgiveness, which you will graciously provide. Then you both have the opportunity to make amends and begin to restore your relationship.

However, as you know, life is not always ideal. You may ask to be forgiven, but the other person ignores you or refuses to make amends, and you end up feeling like the Lone Ranger. The good news is that it doesn't matter. It doesn't even matter if the person you want to forgive, or you want to forgive you, has died. The bottom line is that *you* forgive. *You* untie the tether binding you both. Then you will be free.

Now after doing some heart-cleaning, we are ready to expand our hearts.

Some Heart Openers

1. Crack open the door of your heart.

I learned this technique under duress. My new (first) husband and I had invited my mother-in-law over to our home for my birthday dinner party. She became increasingly insulting to me, making rude, unkind comments. Reduced to tears, I fled upstairs to the solace of my bedroom. I'd had it. I refused to go back down to dinner. That would teach the old witch.

My sister followed me upstairs and sat next to me on the bed.

"I know your feelings must be terribly hurt. And I honor your pain," she consoled me. "But she's a sad, lonely woman who's upset that you've won the heart of her only son and now she has to share him with you. Come on, Pam. You can forgive her."

"I'll never forgive her," I sniffled.

"You don't have to," she continued. "But you don't want to stay miserable like this and ruin your own party. Don't *you* forgive her. But open the door of your heart a tiny crack and let God push you through."

"No. God can't 'cause I won't," I snorted with conviction, wiping my runny nose.

After my sister left the room, I sat, pondering what to do next. Slowly and stubbornly, oh so stubbornly, I decided it couldn't hurt to open my heart a tiny crack—tiny, mind you. So I did. First, I imagined the door of my heart. Yes, there it was, shut up tight against my mother-in-law. Next, I imagined forcing it open a tiny crack. So far, so good. To my surprise, I felt a strong gust of Presence push me right through that heart door toward my mother-in-law's heart. A warm wave of compassion for her lonely, miserable life flooded through me. Surprised that I felt relief so quickly, I jumped off the bed and headed downstairs to continue the party, which, I must say, was a big success.

2. Imagine the presence of a holy teacher.

This next practice is more difficult and requires time and concentration. Find a quiet and safe place to close your eyes, take some deep breaths and relax. When ready, go back in time and space in your mind's eye to revisit the event of the trauma. When you have recreated the scene clearly in your mind, invite whoever is your holiest teacher—God or Jesus or the Holy Mother—to join you in the situation. Drawing upon their strength and wisdom, open your heart to what might transpire. Afterwards, thank the Holy One and slowly open your eyes.

When I was in my twenties, I admired an older woman who was renowned as a leader of prayer in our spiritual community. I considered us friends. One night I babysat her youngest daughter. When she returned, her teenaged daughter ran to her, complaining that I had left the child all alone for an hour while I hung out with my boyfriend. Shocked at this blatant lie, I looked at my friend, certain she'd believe me rather than her unreliable daughter. Instead, she launched into an attack, screaming that I was irresponsible and a whore at that. I fled her house in fury.

Over the next few days, I found myself growing more and more anxious that I would run into her because we worked for the same organization. Days dragged into weeks. By coincidence (or was it?), I attended a self-help workshop in which the teacher invited us to close our eyes, and imagine ourselves on a beach with a (perceived) "enemy." *That* choice was easy.

Next, the teacher suggested that we visualize ourselves walking calmly along the beach. I saw my former friend coming towards me across the sand. My heart began to beat rapidly. Then, the teacher told us to invite a holy figure to join us. Immediately, Jesus appeared, offering me his hand. Hesitantly, I reached for it. Then, as the woman approached us, I stood my ground, trembling with not a little self-righteous indignation. I watched Jesus carefully to see what he would do next. Would he protect me from her vile tongue? Would he reprimand her or even demand that she apologize to me? That would be sweet.

I watched in disbelief as he extended his empty hand to her. Before I could protest, I could feel Jesus transmuting the negative energy between the woman and me. As it dissipated, the woman and I looked into each other's eyes for a brief moment, and then she walked off down the beach. I became aware that my anger and hurt were disappearing like water into the sand. I no longer drank the poison of our relationship. I too walked on, cleansed and free. Although she and I never regained the closeness of our previous friendship, whenever I saw her after that, I was able to be polite to her and sometimes truly kind.

3. Visualize the person as an infant or little child.

I learned this practice from my dear Thây. I have resorted to this practice only in the hardest of situations in which I couldn't see one thing about that person that could redeem them as human. For instance, I've used this practice to help me pray for political leaders who have caused great suffering and even death to others (like Osama bin Laden, Hitler, or some of our former U.S. governmental leaders). I've tried using it to forgive a child molester or murderer or terrorist. Through this exercise, I've sometimes glimpsed a part of their pure soul. It is difficult work but worth a try.

Visualize the person you seek to forgive *as a little child.* If you have a photograph of the person as a young child to help you picture him or her, that's even better. See him playing happily, his whole being full of joy before life took its toll and he chose to respond by becoming bitter, rage-filled or murderous. If even this is difficult, imagine that person as a little *baby*—sweet and pure, full of wonder, her whole life before her. Keep praying for compassion. As you look deeply into their soul, you may find your heart widening to embrace them.

I remember a dear friend who practiced this technique fearlessly. She desperately wanted to forgive her father for molesting her as a little girl, but her anger was too great. After years of meditation and prayer, her father appeared to her in her meditation *as a little boy.* With shame in his eyes, he revealed he'd been sexually violated by one of his parents. When he approached her to violate her, seeing the terror in her eyes made him feel less alone with his own inner child's terror. Her grown father then told her he was terribly sorry for hurting her. My friend recently told me she has made some progress in replacing her anger with compassion for her dad's childhood torment, as well as for her own. Her heart was softly opening.

Fanning the Forest Fire of Anger

These techniques may work when you're angry with *people*. But what about the times when you're just plain **angry at God**?

Sometimes it's good to fan those flames of anger, though you fear your whole forested heart will be consumed. My Jewish friends have taught me that God can take our anger. In fact, God welcomes it because God knows we human beings only get mad at those we love. Otherwise, we'd just say, "What the hell?" and forget about them and get on with our lives.

Anger is a very important and healthy emotion, sisters. It signals us that something is wrong, that something needs attention; something in us or around us demands to be faced, acknowledged and usually changed. Too, anger can provide us with that energy, that passion, to get the job done or the transformation accomplished, like the alchemist's dream of melting the often selfish, human heart's common lead down into precious gold.

Here's a true story of such a conversion.

In my late thirties, I had just returned from a two week tour of China. My friend, popular Episcopalian priest, Michael Vermillion, had invited me to come to his rapidly growing church to present my slide show of the tour and lead a special communion I had designed using Chinese symbolism. I was excited. This event would kick off our new agreement: Michael would mentor me in his dynamic mode of preaching and engaging the congregation in dialog. I was already preparing to submit my request for a sabbatical year to the church I pastored, Christpoint Community Church.

The slide show and communion service were well received. Michael was very pleased.

A few days later, a friend called with the news: Michael had been riding with a colleague on his way to an Episcopalian retreat center when an on-coming car on the fast-moving interstate jumped the median and forced their car off the road. Michael hadn't been wearing his seat belt. He was thrown thirty feet beyond the car onto the highway. His neck was broken. He was now on life support at our local hospital.

I hung up the phone and sat down. At first I was stunned, but then I began to shake violently. How could this happen? How could God *let* this happen? Michael, though divorced, had a teenaged son and daughter and a congregation who adored him. He was doing God's work, for God's sake! How could he die in the prime of his life, now?

And what about my plans for Michael to be my mentor? Oh, I knew my thought was selfish, but I was furious at God for this tragic turn of events. As a Christian, I had been taught that death was my enemy, and Michael's potential death certainly was my enemy. Hadn't Jesus died to overcome death? Was the bread and wine I had served to Michael last Monday to be his last communion on this earth?

During the heart-sick days that followed, I alternated between ranting and raving at God for his cruelty and capriciousness, and praying frantically for Michael's survival and full recovery. That would take a miracle, the doctors said.

"You're pretty close to not being my God anymore," I fumed at Jesus' Father in heaven. "You've abandoned me, my hopes and dreams for the future, and you've surely abandoned Michael."

I cried myself to sleep the night before the day that Michael's family planned to remove his life support. Then I had a dream.

It was pitch black. Michael was standing in the middle of a huge, well-lit football field. Standing on the sidelines, I saw that one goal read "Life" and the other goal "Death." I heard a voice within me, tender yet firm, say,

"Your job, Pamela, is not to tell Michael which goal to run to. Your only job is to *cheer him on*."

I awoke, deeply shaken by the wisdom and tone of that voice. Rather than raging at God, I decided to light a candle and start cheering Michael on, regardless of the outcome.

"Go, Michael, go! Run, Michael, run!" I prayed and prayed.

That morning, his family removed the life support system and Michael died.

A large part of my self-centered ego died that day, too. Over the next months, whenever I found myself missing Michael or mourning his death, I would allow myself a few minutes to do so. Then I would recall that dream and picture myself—pompoms and all—cheering Michael on...in his new life with God.

Some More Heart Openers
for the Quest

What other practices might help open your precious, tender, brave heart?

4. Open your heart to infinite love.

Perhaps, like me, you'll need to face your fear that human love is a limited, even scarce, commodity. I bought into that myth for years until I discovered that nothing could be further from the truth.

After giving birth to my darling daughter, Chelsea, I awakened, literally, every morning with a song of joy in my heart, eager to see her sweet face again. When Chelsea was one and a half years old, I left her with John so I could tour China for two weeks. I took Chelsea's photo with me, her golden white hair glowing and soft blue eyes a-twinkle. When I showed her photo to the Chinese people I met, they beamed at her countenance, whispering, "Angel!" I knew exactly what they meant.

John, Chelsea and I spent four magical years together, dancing, singing, playing the piano, learning to ride a bike. She entertained us constantly.

One of my favorite memories was watching two-year-old Chelsea perk up around Christmas time when our little house church met for worship in our ranch-style home. Gathered in our living room, we sang carols that resounded with the line: *"Gloria in excelsis Deo."* A few years later, as Christmas rolled around again, Chelsea told me she thought we were singing just to her: *"Gloria in ex Chelsea's Day-oh!"*

One summer day, when she was three, Chelsea burst into a chant at the dining table: "Zippedee dolphins! Zippedee dolphins! We love you just forever!" Dolphins, I later discovered, were her power animal. Another time, she heard us discussing the Pope's upcoming visit to America. After choking on a bit on food one night at dinner, she swallowed and then piped up, grinning: "I guess that went down the wrong Pope!"

When Chelsea was a little over four years old, I learned that I was pregnant again. Though I shared the news with John and Chelsea joyously, inwardly I was scared to death. I was convinced I had given all the love I possessed to Chelsea, more love than I knew I was even capable of. How could I love a *second* child? Impossible.

How wrong I was. The moment I held tiny, strawberry-blonde Kaitlyn June in my arms, my fears fled as waves of love surged through me, widening the shores of my grateful heart even more.

"Oh, my God," I rejoiced. "Love *is* truly limitless!"

5. Open your heart to life's blessings.

In a song by the country group *Sugarland,* lead singer Jennifer belts out:

> *I ain't settlin' for just getting by.*
> *I've had enough so-so for the rest of my life.*
> *Tired of shooting too low, so raise the bar high.*
> *"Just enough" ain't enough this time.*
> *I ain't settlin' for anything less than everything.*

Sweet sisters of spirit, where in your life might you be settling? What might your life look like if you raised that bar?

Maybe you remember the movie *As Good As It Gets* with Jack Nicholson. Is your current life "as good as it gets?" Or do you see your life as a constant struggle—for money, friends, fame or fortune? The one important question, indeed the *only* question to ask yourself, is, "How good can I *stand* it?" In other words, what is your "Bliss Quotient?" How much happiness will you allow your heart to experience? How much beauty can you appreciate? How many and what kind of people do you allow your heart to enfold?

The point is not the quantity—it's the *quality.* The Universe can deliver to us only what we are willing and able to receive, a thimble full of blessings or a whole ocean. The choice is yours. The rewards may surprise you—delicious and sweet.

6. Swim in the pool of self-love.

Do you feel burned out, dry and depleted? Are you seeking respite from a desert storm of swirling, sand-stinging emotions? Take a vacation—right now, this moment. Close your eyes. Take a few deep breaths. Relax. Now start to lazily daydream. What do you see? Maybe you envision a wonderful island in the tropics, palm trees swaying in the breeze, you lounging beside an aqua pool, sipping salty margaritas. Sounds great!

Now I'm going to reroute your fantasy so that you find yourself floating on the aqua pool of self-love.

"Self-love?" you retort. "No way. There's too much ego in the world already. I'm not adding to that scum pool."

In my own life as well as in the lives of the women with whom I do spiritual life coaching, the same issue constantly emerges—our lack of self-love. Oh, we women are great at lavishing love on others: our spouse, partner, baby or best friend. But when it comes to loving ourselves, we scrimp and scrape the bottom of our heart barrel, if we pay attention to our needs at all. Remember the commandment, "Love your neighbor as yourself"? It's not "Love your neighbor and forget about your self."

The practice of loving yourself intentionally every day will enlarge your capacity to receive blessings from life, whether in your relationships or your recreation, in your worship or your work. Ironically, a healthy self-love reduces rather than feeds an unhealthy, self-centered ego. Since the love in your heart is connected to an ocean of Divine Love, just dive in. Make it a practice to immerse yourself often in those healing, balmy waters.

7. Act like a child.

Another way to foster your heart's spiritual growth is to act like a little child (if you ever did—some of us were adult children from Day 1.) My father once wrote: "The child's trustful turning to take an adult's hand [is] a model of the risk which everyone must take in choosing "the greater walk with God.'" Acting child-like is hard for a lot of grownups, intent as we are on being "responsible" and "mature." Paying attention to children at play can help us. We can learn many things: how to be spontaneous and playful, how to be hurt but immediately forgive the person, or how to trust another.

Children can remind us how important it is to live "in the present moment," to laugh at our "busyness" and our inflated self-importance. For example, when my daughter Kaitlyn was three, she wanted me to play with her. I assured her I would, but only after I cleaned the kitchen cabinets. Kaitlyn kept nagging at me to stop and play with her. Irritated, I barked at her: "Oh, hold your horses." She ran out of the kitchen, only to return a moment later, thrusting her purple plastic pony into my face.

"OK, Mommy, I'm holding my horse!" she beamed.

I immediately put down my sponge and joined her in play.

I remember when my Godson, Joshua, was a little tyke. Hearing his mother slip on the stairs and fall a few feet to the bottom landing, little Josh came running over to her, yelling: "Mommy, are you OK?"

Then he added, "My heart got to you before I did!"

Would that our adult hearts were so responsive.

8. Breathe.

Thây teaches breathing exercises to all his students, exercises which at first seem disarmingly simple. He insists that each breathing exercise be done at least *three* times. Why? Scientists have shown that our emotions run on specific neuro-pathways in our brains, created by our habitual emotional response of fear or anger, for example. However, when we do intentional breathing exercises, we cause our neurons to fire along *new* pathways—of peace, quiet, calm. The breathing sequence must be repeated at least three times in order to redirect and "en-groove" the new neuro-pathways.

The good news is that the following exercises can be done while you're waiting in line at a store, or in traffic, or in a doctor's office—literally anywhere. Within minutes, you should feel your pulse slow and your heart calm down. This is the most basic practice.

> *Breathing in, I know I'm breathing in.*
> *Breathing out, I know I'm breathing out.*

At first, I thought this exercise was so obvious that it was silly. After several years, (I admit I can be a little dense sometimes), I began to understand why this breathing exercise is a powerful tool for centering one's self or for preparing to meditate. What usually happens when I meditate is that while I slow down my breathing, my thoughts keep racing around, darting and swinging all over the place. No wonder some Buddhists call this "monkey mind." In Thây's breathing exercise, however, I unite my mind *with* my body. Focusing my scattered thoughts upon the slow, rhythmic pace of my breath and naming this, I live, at least briefly, in the present moment. I feel grounded and of one piece, body and mind. How sweet that is.

This next exercise is helpful when you are going into a situation where you need to feel strong and unshakable. First, picture a majestic mountain (real or imagined) right inside of you. Then repeat three times, "Breathing in, I am a mountain. Breathing out, I am solid." As you continue to practice, you can shorten these sentences to phrases, like "In, mountain. Out, solid." Almost immediately, I bet you will feel your energy become solid as a mountain's base within you.

To prepare for a situation in which you must be calm and clear-headed, you can picture a lovely, serene lake inside of you. Then repeat three times: "Breathing in, I am a lake. Breathing out, I am calm." "In, lake. Out, calm." Soon the water will become so still, you can see the pebbles on the lake bottom sparkling in the sunlight.

When you are exhausted but still have one more client to see or one more child to put to bed, this last practice is helpful (and it's one of my favorites.) Visualize your favorite flower: rose, daisy, or gardenia. Absorb its color, admire its petals; inhale its fragrance. Then repeat three times: "Breathing in, I am a flower. Breathing out, I am fresh." As you step out to greet the person, smile (even a half smile will do) and present yourself as a lovely bouquet.

9. Go for a walking meditation.

Whenever you are filled with unpleasant emotions—fear, anger— or have had a fight with someone, you can go for a walking meditation, preferably outside in nature. As you walk in silence, be conscious of each foot as you plant it carefully, intentionally, upon the earth. Be aware of the sun shining upon your face or the wind's chill caressing your cheeks. As you continue to walk, offer your emotions to Mother Earth. How lucky we are that she is strong enough to receive them and transform them without harming herself or others.

Then, as you (hopefully) calm down, reflect upon the cause of your emotional turmoil. Perhaps you will even be calm enough later to talk to the person with clarity and kindness. At the end of your walking meditation, be sure to thank Mother Earth. Thây recommends gazing back over the path you've traversed, and picturing a flower blooming in each of your footprints. I love that!

I've heard both Thây and his life-long female companion, Chang Không, confess how difficult it can be to transform upsetting emotions into positive ones. For example, in their youth, they fought to rescue Vietnamese Boat People who, fleeing to escape the violence of war-torn Vietnam, were drowning in make-shift, flimsy boats. Thây's and Chang's emotions ran so strong that they needed to walk for hours, even days, to be able to regain their centered selves. It was reassuring to discover that even such highly advanced teachers as they had to walk many hours to regain their equanimity. Thây is fond of reminding us that peace is not a future goal. "Peace is every step." Right here. Right now. Right under our feet.

10. Practice mindfulness.

Another practice of Thây's which I have found extremely helpful is the practice of mindfulness: complete and nonjudgmental attention to someone. Thây is adamant that you don't have to be a Buddhist to practice mindfulness. No matter which spiritual path you follow, or which religion you belong to, this practice will deepen your spiritual growth.

It's so easy, isn't it, to jump to judgment about someone else's behavior? We all do it, every day. The point of the practice of mindfulness is to train yourself to look deeply, with gently focused attention, into a specific person's heart (even your own). Certainly, this practice can take years, but you will eventually be able to tap into a person's suffering. When you do, you will find your judgment ceasing, your hard heart softening and perhaps even opening in compassion like a lovely lotus blossom.

A pastor was traveling on the subway in New York City one Sunday morning after church. It was a lovely spring day. People were reading their *New York Times,* quietly enjoying the ride. At one stop, a father and his three children boarded the train. Soon the quiet turned to *mayhem.* The children chased each other up and down the center aisle, bouncing into each other and knocking people's papers askew. People began to get annoyed. The pastor could feel the tension brewing.

Since he was sitting next to the father, he leaned over and quietly hinted: "Your children seem pretty rambunctious today. They seem a little out of control."

"Yes," replied the father. "We were just at the hospital where they watched their mother die. We're on our way home now."

"I'm so sorry," the pastor gulped. Slinking back into his seat, he offered up a silent prayer for the family. He thanked God that he had managed (barely) to hold back his irritation while opening up a tiny space for mindfulness. May this story be a wake-up call to each one of us.

11. Repair your leaky heart.

Do any of you suffer from what I now affectionately call "Leaky Heart Syndrome?" Participating in an empowerment workshop several years ago, I learned that I suffered from that very affliction without even knowing it. For instance, I was addicted to watching the evening World News on television, tears inevitably welling up as the world's pain and suffering paraded before my eyes. I actually believed I was offering my compassion to their suffering and doing some good. But the workshop leaders finally convinced me that what I was really doing was leaking out my heart power, rendering me totally unable to alleviate someone's real pain in my own circle of life.

The workshop leaders suggested that I monitor myself while watching the news. First, I should pay attention whenever I start to worry about the world's terrible condition. Worry is a big heart drainer. It's a strain on the body and it never leads to change. Second, every time I am tempted to open my heart to pour out my "love" for some cause or person, I should take a moment to ask myself: "Is this really *my* problem or someone else's?" It's especially crucial for those of us who are care-givers, mothers, pastors, teachers or social workers, for example, to remember that we are not the only actors in the universe. Others are just as, if not more, capable than we are to render new solutions to age-old problems, or to lend the needed helping hand.

So, "Leaky Heart Syndrome" sufferers, join me! Get into recovery. Whenever someone asks you to volunteer, even for a worthwhile cause (which admittedly is the hardest to refuse), or when you see a news story that breaks your heart, take several deep breaths, check with your heart, and ask if this is something you really want to "give your heart to." If not, say, "No, thanks." Let your heart vessel continue to fill up with its vital energy of caring. Then, when you do decide to say "Yes" to someone or some worthy project, you will have the necessary heart power to actually accomplish that work.

12. Cultivate a kind heart.

A few years back, a study was done in which 90-year-olds were asked what words of wisdom they would offer young people today. The researchers expected that the elders would advise things like "Work harder" or "Spend more time with your family." They were startled to hear that most of the elders, without hesitation or qualification, told them: "Be more *kind*."

Do you remember the popular bumper sticker a while back: "Do random acts of kindness and senseless acts of beauty?" The sticker challenged the hard-hearted worldview that expected others to do random acts of violence and senseless acts of cruelty. That bumper sticker movement raised my consciousness and propelled our family into practicing random acts of kindness for several years. For example, on road trips, we'd pay the toll for the car behind us. What an adventure to watch people's faces light up, first with confusion and then with gratitude.

Finally, holy companions, courage, take heart, especially in the hard times. Keep on keeping on! Everyone has their heart stomped on at some time. Everyone throws in the towel, crying "Uncle!" That's the nature of the human condition—guaranteed. The only choice you have is whether or not to get back up again, and again and again.

Singer/song writer Carly Simon puts it this way in a song to her jilting lover:

> "Don't mind if I fall apart;
> there's more room in a broken heart."

And we're back where we started this chapter, with an enlarged heart capable of receiving, holding and bestowing more love.

And, to aid you during those difficult times, you may be surprised to find yourself visited by a Holy One.

When our family was going through yet another turbulent period, I remember feeling so full of despair that I felt like a piece of lead. Exhausted by life, worn down by strategies that didn't change anything, prayers that didn't rise above my deadened heart, I walked like a zombie into yet another self-help lecture, grasping at my last spiritual straw.

Entering the cold, bare-walled auditorium, I felt my life force seeping out of me. After the lecture, the speaker invited us to meditate together. People uncrossed their legs and put down their note pads. The shuffling finally settled down. Sitting in the darkened room, I still felt restless. Peeking through squinted eyes, I saw that everyone else in the room had their eyes closed, and seemed to be calmly communing with God.

"Good for them," I muttered in the mildest sarcasm I could muster.

As my gaze wandered listlessly around the dreary hall, something caught my eye. There, in the upper right hand corner of the room, robed in blue and white, floated a vision of Mother Mary. A large tube ran down from her heart into my heart, transfusing it with her warm and vibrant blood. Almost instantly my chilled body began to warm; my spirits began to rise.

Startled, and always concerned about the welfare of others before my own, I whispered, "But, Mary, can you really afford to give me all this blood?"

With a twinkle in her eye, Mary replied: "Don't worry, dearest Pam. I'm hooked up in back to an infinite supply!"

Come on, courageous, open-hearted sisters—gliding down, sliding down—let's take that lovely ride that J.T. promises.

EIGHT

Using Your Brains:

A No-Brainer

My two adult daughters are still blondes. When they were young, they used to howl when they told "dumb blonde" jokes to each other, a luxury only a blonde should be allowed. Listen in. (It helps if you use a Valley Girl accent for this one.)

> When a blonde sat staring at a carton of orange juice for several hours, her roommate finally asked, "What in the world are you doing?"
>
> Defensively, she replied, "Well, it says, 'Concentrate.'"

I like this old joke: "That blonde was so dumb, it took her two hours to watch *Sixty Minutes*."

LOL!

Friends, go out and use those incredibly smart brains of yours, no matter what your hair color.

NINE

_____

Tithing on the Trek

"We as a human race have managed to build the internal combustion engine, eradicate polio and make TV dinners you can heat in just minutes in the microwave. But we have not yet learned one of the most important things of all: how to form a healthy attitude toward money.

"We have to learn to be masters of our money, and not let it be the master of us. We must realize that the power to bring about real and positive change in this world is not in gold bullion, stocks or bonds. Instead, the power is within us, as children of God, at the level of our spirituality.

"Money is a means to an end, not the end itself.... simply having money is not the goal. The goal is to use it to do whatever your heart leads you to do, and to do that which fulfills your divine purpose."
—Edwene Gaines

Remember Edwene Gaines, author of _The Four Spiritual Laws of Prosperity,_ from the Goals section in Chapter Five? To gain abundance of all kinds, in addition to setting goals, Gaines recommends that you practice forgiveness and that you cast a precise vision for your life. But when I first read her book a few years ago, it was her section on tithing—the practice of giving 10% of one's income to a person, organization or cause—that really got my attention. Let me re-introduce her to you in her own words.

"My name is Edwene Gaines, and I am a woman of power.

"This hasn't always been true. There was a time years ago when my days were filled with fear and deprivation. I had holes in my shoes. I was working two jobs, sixteen hours a day, and still I couldn't make ends meet. Sometimes I didn't even know how I was going to feed my hungry child.

"Then I asked God to help me turn my life around. After I did, some of the things I felt called to do seemed a little crazy, but I did them anyway. As a result, my life has been completely transformed. I now own a beautiful retreat center. I travel first class. I have fine clothes, jewelry, and a lovely home. If I want something, I simply buy it….

"Yes, I am a woman of power, and I am also a woman of passion: it's not enough for me that I now live in comfort and luxury. I have made a commitment that I would be responsible for changing the way that all people think about the potential for prosperity and abundance in their lives…. My mission is not complete until you, too, are living a life of true prosperity."

I thought, "What? You mean me, too, Edwene? Poor, struggling me? I'm all ears."

You see, all my life, I have *hated* money. My daughters, Chelsea and Kaitlyn, know that's true. I hated its stranglehold over my life: the anxiety and struggle to make ends meet, the hassle of balancing my bank account, or of doing taxes. I envied others who seemed to "have it all together" financially.

Growing up, I was influenced by my father's attitude towards money. As a preacher and theologian, Dad extolled the virtue of pursuing spiritual knowledge over earning a good income, probably based on Jesus' admonition to his disciples in *Matthew* 6: 24-25, 31-34.

No one can serve two masters. Either he will hate the one and love the other, or he will be devoted to the one and despise the other. You cannot serve both God and money….

Dad seemed to consider matters of money "beneath him." For example, one of his brothers had worked hard and was a self-made millionaire, but he wasn't big on "spiritual talk." Although Dad disdained wealth, he ended up devoting much of his time scrambling to make a living instead of a life. As a young person, I modeled my money beliefs and behaviors on Dad's and they stuck tight like Velcro.

When I turned sixty (yes, I'm a slow learner sometimes), I decided I wanted to change my attitude and my actions toward money. I longed to take pride in how I handled my financial affairs. My wealthy uncle had contributed generously to a northern Wisconsin college as well as helping to endow the Chicago Symphony Orchestra. I believed that he was the one in Dad's family who had gotten the wealth gene, whereas I would always be scrambling for financial security, like my dad. I could never be like my uncle. Or could I? Was the practice of tithing the missing link to my poverty-oriented life?

Gaines discovered her key to prosperity in a quote from the Old Testament Book of *Malachi,* chapter 3, verse 10. God commands the prophet:

> Bring all the tithes into the storehouse so there will be enough food in my Temple. If you do, says the Lord Almighty, I will open the windows of heaven for you. *I will pour out a blessing so great that you won't have enough room to take it in.* Try it! Let me prove it to you!   (my emphasis)

Gaines decided to call God's bluff, to make him prove his promise. As she worked with the law of tithing, she found out that it didn't even matter if she *believed* in it. Like the law of gravity, it "works" whether you believe it or not. As she tithed, amazing things began to happen in her financially-challenged life.

Gaines insists that the Law of Abundance requires you to tithe 10% of everything you earn, *right off the top.* And you must tithe it to any source that has given you spiritual food. What's spiritual food, you might ask? Gaines responds:

> That which inspires us, teaches us, reminds us of the Truth, and causes us to remember who we really are. It is the infilling of spiritual energy that reconnects us consciously to the awareness of our own innate divinity.

That means it could be a micro-banking organization that lends to women in developing countries, or an organization fighting breast cancer or rescuing abandoned dogs. It could be the kind waitress who sees your sad mood, and gently asks, "How ya doing, honey?" There's no limit to how you can define "spiritual good."

Now don't get me wrong. Before reading Gaines' book, I had heard the tithing pitch from preachers in their pulpits. I thought they were just trying to amass more wealth for themselves or their congregations. I even tried to tithe several times. I truly intended to pay God his 10%. The trouble was that each time I finished paying my bills, (I admit I never had enough faith to tithe off the top, as Gaines recommends), I never had money left over to tithe. Finally, I just gave up on tithing.

But a few years later, my life was about to change.

Severe health issues had caused me to cut down, almost eliminate, my national speaking engagements. When I felt a bit stronger, I took a $9 an hour job at a local spiritual bookstore. While I enjoyed the work and the people there, I was barely making enough to pay my bills. At least, I reassured myself, I had re-entered the work force and was rebuilding my health.

For six months, I worked at the bookstore during the day, and studied Gaines' principles and chanted her affirmations at night. I so badly wanted to transform my attitude toward money. Then I made a bold decision. I prayerfully, and somewhat anxiously, decided to quit my job—with no other offer in hand. I intended to "prove" God just the way Edwene had. I wanted to force him to make good on his promise in Malachi. Amazingly, I didn't worry obsessively as I have done in the past. Each morning when I awoke, I prayed for financial guidance, and worked Edwene's program of affirmations and vision-casting. Most importantly, I kept a little notebook to record my tithing—right off the top this time.

A few weeks after I'd left the bookstore job, a dear friend of mine invited me to dinner at her home. During the dessert course, she offered me a $1500 a month stipend for a year to research programs dedicated to empowering local at-risk youth—one of my passions.

At first, I was speechless at my friend's amazing offer. Was she the Universe's response to my new thought patterns about money? The promise of God fulfilled? I will never know for sure. But I do believe that if I hadn't read Edwene's book, and if I hadn't been working on boosting my self-worth and allowing myself to receive God's abundance, either my friend wouldn't have been moved to make the offer, or I wouldn't have allowed myself to accept it. Thank you, power woman, Edwene. And thank you, cherished benefactor and friend—you know who you are, and so does God.

Certainly, friends, there are times when all of this "abundance" stuff seems like fluff or fodder. Indeed, some of us may find ourselves on food stamps right now. Or perhaps after a serious illness or a devastating divorce, we have chosen to file bankruptcy and start all over. Keep loving yourself as you do.

For those of you who wish to delve deeper into the roots of your relationship with money, I highly recommend *The Energy of Money: A Spiritual Guide to Financial and Personal Fulfillment* by Maria Nemeth, Ph.D. If you're ready to be ruthlessly honest with yourself, you must complete her tough exercises, such as how you've cheated on your tax returns or cut corners at work. Nemeth suggests healthier alternatives.

Thanks to my life coach who recommended the book to me, I courageously tackled the book's exercises, and now, how do I feel about money?

I *love* it. It's my ally, my pal, a valued friend on my spiritual journey.

The lyrics from my friend Ricky Jans' magical children's musical, *Captain Marbles*, comes to mind. Millionaire Uncle Arnold loves his money, nicknaming his dollar bills "George" after George Washington's picture on them, even fondly kissing them on stage. Here, he extols the merits of money.

> *Money, what else could you find*
> *that's so legal and so tender?*
> *Money, could Fort Knox find*
> *a better reason to defend her?*
> *Money, it means a mint to me!*
> *And tell me what's more up-to-date*
> *than currency?*
> *Money, it's a priceless commodity*
> *that makes the day sunny!*

Get it? "Legal tender"? "A mint"? "Up to date" equals "currency"? Brilliant. Today, although I admit I'm still working with the practice of tithing, I'm steadily increasing my sense of abundance, and many of my days are more sunny.

So, my questers, don't wait as long as I did to experiment with tithing. Start a new trick on the trek of your life. Start tithing—not out of guilt or shame, but out of gratitude for the bounty and goodness of the Universe. Pay attention to where your spiritual food comes from and share some of your income—off the top—with that person or organization. And just watch those windows of heaven open up and pour out a blessing so great, you won't have enough shopping bags to contain it!

TEN

Sitting 'Round the Campfire:

The Power of Story

It was a dark and stormy night in the Ozarks. Three men were seated around the campfire. One of them said, "Joe, tell us a story!" And Joe began, "It was a dark and stormy night in the Ozarks. Three men were seated around the campfire. One of them said, "Joe, tell us a story!" And Joe began....

Remember those nights around a campfire when you were a girl—huddled together in the star-spangled darkness around a crackling fire, fingers sticky from eating S'mores off whittled branches, spines tingling as friends or family tried to outdo each other with ghost stories? As we trudged off to our tents, following bobbing flashlights, our minds reeled with the power of story—to scare, comfort, allure and amaze.

Language is a fascinating thing. Yes, yes, I know I've been an English teacher, but it's more than that. Do you remember the story of Babel in the Bible? (Now that's a tongue twister. See *Genesis* 11.) In ancient days, so the tale goes, the people were getting too uppity. They wanted to build a high tower—taller than any they had ever built—to reach up to heaven and to make a name for themselves. The people conspired together, they designed a great tower, worked hard to build it, and sure enough, they were ready to climb to heaven.

This made God angry. God's people are supposed to know they are within God and God is within them, but they are not supposed to think they don't need God. So God destroyed the tower, but he was still worried that the people would aspire to overreach their place. So God confounded them by scrambling their tongues so that, from then onward, each nation would speak its own language. Unable to communicate clearly, nations would unable to conspire together in their efforts to usurp God's power and position.

Judging from the shape of things today, with over forty armed conflicts around the globe, God may have cursed humanity more than

God intended. Of course, being unable to speak another's language is not the only source of global conflict, but it too often seems to prevent us from clearly understanding one another and building peaceful relations. What is the mysterious power language holds?

The power of language

The spoken word, though not perfect in expressing every nuance of thought or feeling, is the major vehicle of communication for all peoples: "I see a rose," "I feel happy," or "I think you're crazy." Remember the story about the Pope and the infant in the tower where we learned that there is no one universal human language? Each culture develops a language that serves its particular needs, to help it deal with the necessities of its common life.

For example, because we are a consumer culture, we have many different words for "garbage." Think about it: trash, litter, recyclables, refuse. Less consumer-oriented, or less wasteful, cultures have fewer words to express the concept of "garbage." Another example. We Americans have about three nouns to describe snow: snow, sleet and mush. Beyond that, our vocabulary won't allow us to distinguish with just one word. And we function just fine with those three. By contrast, Eskimos need to be very specific in their descriptions of difficult weather conditions in order to survive, so their language has almost twenty different words to describe "snow."

Linguists can now demonstrate that language allows us to actually *perceive* what we see. You could say that what we see *before* our eyes is first really seen *behind* our eyes—shaped by the expectations, worldviews and life experiences of our very culturally-conditioned brains. If we lack the belief system and the language to "see" something, we may not be able to "perceive" it at all. A classic example from the field of anthropology is that of the Aborigine tribe in Australia who, when shown photographs of themselves taken by the anthropologists. They could only "see" a flat piece of paper, not their three-dimensional body image upon it because their brains had not been culturally trained to "see" in that way.

Here's a true story that shows the ability of language and worldview to determine what is actually perceived. In his book, *Yuwipi: Vision and Experience in Oglala Ritual*, William K. Powers recounts the time a white psychiatrist attended a *yuwipi*, a Lakota (Sioux) healing ceremony performed by a shaman or medicine man, on the Plains in the western United States.

Upon entering a small, dark room in which all the windows had been covered, all participants—the Oglala Indians and the Western white psychiatrist—were instructed to empty out their pockets. Then they all gathered around the shaman who was sitting on the floor in the middle of the darkened room. Someone placed a blanket over the shaman's head and body, encircling him with rope and tying it securely around him. As the medicine man began the ceremony with chanting, flickers of light began to dance around the room, somewhat capriciously, accompanied by the sound of little clicking noises.

Hours later, when the healing was accomplished and the ceremony finished, the window drapes were removed. Sunlight flooded the room. The psychiatrist was shocked to see the shaman now sitting on *top* of the blanket, the rope all untied.

"What happened?" asked the psychiatrist.

The shaman told him that his little helpers, "the spirits," had joined him in the room, unbinding him and shining their tiny lights to help with the cure of the patient.

The psychiatrist had no worldview in which to place the existence of such "spirits." Even though he had witnessed all lighters being checked at the door, he insisted that the little lights had been made by the Native men, flicking their cigarette lighters on and off.

The power of the printed word

I had still more to learn about the power of language. In class at the University of Chicago on orality, the tradition and power of the *spoken* word, we began by examining the power of the *written* word. I myself have always been an avid reader. In fact, one reason my eyesight is poor now is that, when I was a child, I would sit for hours under my blanket at night, reading by flashlight to my heart's content. Novels like *Treasure Island* and *The Count of Monte Cristo* transported me out of my suburban, sometimes boring, environment into exotic worlds of boldness, bravery, cunning and daring.

The written word provides much more than entertainment. Books, magazines, newspapers, and the Internet offer abundant information on every topic imaginable, as well as many people's wisdom. Written texts easily cross the boundaries of space, allowing a text written in one geographical location to be read around the globe. Texts also erase the bounds of time constraints, outliving the relatively short life span of their author. A final benefit of the written word is that it can easily be read in solitude, anytime and anyplace—a marvelous freedom for the reader.

Finally, because the written text "freezes" the spoken word in space and time on that previously blank piece of parchment, it has the capacity to unite a community or nation with that single, authoritative text. For example, think of the first printed Bible translation by Gutenberg's press around 1440 C.E. All the people who could read were finally on the same page, literally.

Drawbacks of the printed word

Enthroning literacy has some drawbacks, however. Let's go back in history even farther.

Because of the "freezing" capability of a written text, those in religious or political power could stamp one specific printed version of the text as "true," i.e., "orthodox" or acceptable, while labeling any competing texts as "heretical," i.e., inaccurate, or worse—damned as falsehood.

When I was growing up, for example, Christians believed that there were four, and *only* four, Gospels in the New Testament. Since the discovery of the Nag Hammadi and Gnostic Gospels in the Middle East in the late 1940's, however, most Biblical scholars now agree that there were *dozens* if not hundreds of gospels floating around in the first centuries after Jesus. The fact is that all but four were destroyed, "deleted" as it were, by Roman Catholic Church leaders in order to consolidate, unite and more easily control common people throughout different countries. A lot of blood and ink was spilled in this endeavor. For an action-packed account of the historical process of canonization, (the formation of the Christian scriptures), read Elaine Pagels' book, *The Gnostic Gospels.*

Another potential drawback of the written text is that the reader may become socially isolated. I'm sure you're familiar with the phenomenon of computer addiction, accompanied by a lack of face-to-face contact with live human beings. An addicted reader might do the same, even inhabiting a fictional world. Yes, a character in a book or online can become our best friend: inspiring us, comforting us or whisking us away into dazzling worlds. But it's healthy to cultivate friendships with people we can see and touch, as well.

The Spoken Word Echoes
from Wall Street to Hollywood,
from Canyon to Cliff

We Americans value the written word so highly that we make literacy the benchmark of a highly-evolved civilization, dividing the world into literate and non-literate countries. Before taking my university's course on orality, I too believed that so-called "primitive" oral cultures were not as sophisticated as our literacy-based culture. Many Americans proudly claim that our use of the printed word in science and technology far exceeds that of most cultures, making us again superior.

I was in for a shock when my esteemed professor insisted that even though we *literati* look down on non- or pre-literate cultures, ironically, almost everything we experience in our own culture is *not* couched in scientific *facts* but in oral *story*. True, some students still read their textbooks, or some still read newspapers (though the numbers are declining), and using a computer demands at least minimal reading skills. However, the professor claimed that most of us *hear* rather than read our way through the day: through the news on TV or radio, through music on iPods, through sharing our gossip at the water cooler or the coffee bar, or through discussing and debating in the workplace or marketplace. I began to admit he was right.

My professor pressed on, arguing that even science uses more story than fact in its research and applications. His main illustration? The "big bang theory" explaining the origin of the universe, which, though based on scientific data, is still primarily a *story*. Indeed, except for pure mathematical equations, he maintained, we Westerners live more and more as our ancestors did—in the oral world of *stories,* not the written world of words.

"You still with me, readers?"

"Go on," you say.

Drawbacks of the spoken word

Certainly, oral tradition has its own set of requirements. For instance, all listeners must be in the same geographical area and time frame. They must share a common language. The social group must have a storyteller or clan leader who possesses a talent for storytelling and has been rigorously trained to be able to remember the group's stories for their accuracy and meaning.

The power of the spoken word

But the benefits to be gained from hearing the "simple" spoken word are many, as well as quite complex and sophisticated. First, hard-won ancient tribal wisdom, including its history, values and purpose, is passed down by word of mouth. From this process, a shared identity of the social group emerges and solidifies. Second, unlike reading a text in solitude, telling and hearing a story requires a communal setting. Thus, when listeners are face to face with the storyteller, a sense of intimacy and camaraderie is established. The storyteller must use body language and emotions to express the meaning of the tale, engaging the senses, hearts, minds and souls of those present. Last but not least, traditional oral cultures have complex symbol systems, just as literary texts do. The symbols are just not obvious to us literal left-brainers.

I encourage you to take an anthropology class on orality. I bet your eyes will be opened to this truth—*oral stories have power*. They have the power to connect us in community, to stir our blood, to open our hearts, to pry open our eyes and ears to undiscovered worlds, and to tell us Who and Whose we are. In other words, oral stories have the power to communicate, to entertain, and to transmit the meaning and mission of our individual and communal lives.

I've been rereading Dr. Rachel Naomi Remen's excellent book, *Kitchen Table Wisdom: Stories that Heal*. Dr. Remen has suffered for thirty-five years with Crohn's disease, a painful, debilitating colon illness requiring many difficult surgeries. Overcoming these battles, she became a physician, but not just an ordinary doctor—one with the heart of a rabbi, like her beloved grandfather.

Dr. Remen believes that stories fulfill a vital purpose beyond provoking our laughter or our tears. Indeed, the very act of sharing our stories helps us **to live**.

> *Hidden in all stories is the One story.* The more we listen, the clearer that Story becomes. Our true identity, who we are, why we are here, what sustains us, is in this story. The stories at every kitchen table are about the same things: stories of owning, having and losing, stories of sex, of power, of pain, of

wounding, of courage, hope and healing, of loneliness and the end of loneliness. Stories about God.

In telling [stories], we are telling each other the human story. Stories that touch us in this place of common humanness awaken us and weave us together as a family once again.

After the proverbial Tower of Babel fiasco, it's about time we share a common language and human bond again, don't you agree? Since I just mentioned the Big Bang theory, let's start with a creation story.

A New Creation Story?

An Archeological Dig for the Goddess

Imagine lying on a blanket at night with your camper friends, gazing up as shooting stars go whizzing by. Your mind begins to expand into the mysteries of creation. Perhaps a Christian scripture springs to mind, like the words of the psalmist:

> *O Lord, our Lord, how majestic is your name*
> *in all the earth!*
> *You have set your glory above the heavens. ...*
> *When I consider your heavens, the work of your fingers,*
> *the moon and the stars, which you have set in place,*
> *what is man that you are mindful of him,*
> *the son of man that you care for him?*

Looking up at the Milky Way, imagine yourself traveling back in time to the dawn of human history. Daughters, how do you picture the origin of the universe? Who appears as the Creator of this star-studded Universe—an elderly white man with a long beard, enthroned in the clouds, as I was taught "in my olden days?" How do you envision the earliest human communities?

The origin of the patriarchal age seems to coincide with the origin of the printed word. A *written* record of an early matriarchal society has yet to be discovered. Thus, lacking literary evidence, any conception of the earliest matriarchal cultures has to be deduced from non-literate forms, such as sculpture, art and architecture.

To further complicate matters, some feminist anthropologists, myself included, are quick to point out that almost all classical anthropological studies of "primitive" tribes were done by males, men who brought their largely if not completely unconscious patriarchal worldview to their observations. Because indigenous peoples are rapidly and tragically disappearing under the onslaught of globalization, accurate case studies of ancient tribal gender relations or ritual life may never be obtained.

Over thirty years ago, when I began to search for a new creation story, I was thrilled to come upon the work of Riane Eisler, cultural historian and evolutionary theorist. Princeton anthropologist Ashley Montague announced that her ground-breaking book, *The Chalice and the Blade: Our History, Our Future,* written in 1987, was "the most important book since *The Origin of the Species."*

Eisler offered two reasons why the earliest civilizations must have worshipped the Goddess rather than a male God. First, ancient peoples must have revered women because they were child-bearers, the obvious source of new human life. Second, early peoples must have been mystified by the occurrence that "woman bleeds monthly but does not die." These two factors must have caused ancient peoples to conceive of their deity as "Mother," a divine female with the awesome power to create life. In addition, women must have been revered as the Great Mother's representatives on earth: as mothers, healers and priestesses.

My revised conception of what the earliest human communities were like was also strongly influenced by the findings and assertions of archeologist, Maria Gimbutas. She confounded the male-dominated field of archaeology by suggesting that the many, tiny, ancient female statuettes found in European excavations were not sexual fetishes as male anthropologists had previously thought, but *Goddess* statues— evidence that an *age of matriarchy with its Goddess worship* had indeed <u>preceded</u> the age of patriarchy.

On the basis of her findings of statues, friezes and frescoes, Gimbutas further claimed that the earliest matriarchal civilization in Europe lived in a time of peace, accompanied by the growth of agriculture and the arts. Its people did not produce weapons for killing others nor build forts in hard-to-reach places for protection. Instead, inspired by the gentle influence of the Goddess, they lived in comfortable and accessible houses, in an "age free of strife." Furthermore, similar to Eisler, Gimbutas surmised that in that culture, it was females, not males, who held positions of leadership and high esteem, such as priestesses and judges.

If matriarchy was the first and oldest model of humans living together, why, with the onset of the written word, did the world become patriarchal? Why, thousands of years ago, did *almost* every tribe in the world, at least according to current anthropological research, abandon its valuing of the feminine—its honoring of women as spiritual leaders, and its worshipping of the Goddess as the holy source of life—and turn to the rule of the Father?

No one knows for sure.

Gimbutas theorized that the glorious age of matriarchy ended suddenly and violently with the arrival of Kurgan marauders who brought with them warfare, military technology and patriarchy. For more detail, you can check out her 1974 study entitled, "Gods and Goddesses of Old Europe," as well as her subsequent book, *The Language of the Goddess: Unearthing the Hidden Symbols of Western Civilization.*

Feminist theologian Rosemary Radford Ruether has surmised two possible yet conflicting scenarios of how male citizens may have overthrown the women and ascended to power in those matriarchal cultures. One theory is that hordes of male-ruled clans swept down from the Mongolian desert into the ancient matriarchal, peaceful agrarian Minoan civilization and ruthlessly destroyed it. Since the Goddess and women in matriarchal cultures had been revered for their power to *create* life, the male-dominant hordes had no alternative left but to revere the jealous Father God, the deity who wielded the power to *destroy* life. In place of the earth-related Goddess, the male-dominated tribes established their sky-god who reveled in killing his enemies, especially worshippers of the Goddess or "Great Mother." They esteemed males above females as superior in all facets of public life and leadership.

Ruether's other hypothesis is that, for some unknown reason, men with considerable power *within* the matriarchal society began to take over the leadership.

Perhaps both scenarios occurred simultaneously. We many never know the truth. What scholarship does show is that stories about a jealous Sky-God have been handed down for millennia in the sacred texts of Judaism, Christianity and Islam, the three religions descending from the patriarch Abraham (2000 to 1825 B.C.E.)

So, tell me, my cosmic companions, what is your current creation story?

Whatever it is, and I wish I could eavesdrop on you, I believe it's essential to critique your creation story, no matter its spiritual origin. For example, you might ask the following questions:

- Does the creation story honor of the earth and all her creatures? Or does it privilege some creatures (i.e., humans or males) above all others?
- What role does gender play in the story?
- Does the story end with conflict and domination, or with reconciliation and partnership?
- In other words, does the story foster life in all forms on this planet?

Of course, I realize that God is not a human being. Some of you undoubtedly have an image of God that is non-human. Perhaps you see God as a force that drives Nature, or is Nature herself. Maybe you view the Divine as a Presence or a Spirit. Perhaps your God Light, sparks that animate everything in creation, or energy like electricity. Some theories in quantum physics tend to support this latter view.

I am convinced that there is a spark or essence of the Divine in each thing, person, or natural element. The Lakota call it *Wakan;* the Buddhists refer to it as the Buddha nature. If you are content to pray to a God of pure spirit, my hat's off to you. In fact, I'm a bit jealous. I'm not that evolved yet. I do sometimes pray to this all-pervasive, immanent yet transcendent Divine Spirit.

And yet...

When I'm praying for union with the Holy One, I need to connect with something more tangible than an amorphous energy field. Embracing a field of electricity or receiving a compassionate glance from a vibrational matrix just doesn't work for me. I need a familiar, human-like presence. And because I believe God longs to be *intimate* with us—to be our Beloved—without scaring us to death with divine majesty and power, God takes whatever form will lure each one of us into relationship.

Do you ever long for a relationship with a personal, intimate form of God—in addition to, or beyond, Father God? Where might we go to find such an image?

Worshipping (again)
at the Temple of the Goddess

Growing up, I would never have equated the term "Goddess" with God or even with someone holy. In fact, the only time I heard the term "goddess" was when someone referred to Marilyn Monroe as a "sex goddess." In the 1970s, when I was questing for a new female image of the divine, I eagerly gobbled up the book written by Carol Christ with Judith Plaskow, called *Womanspirit Rising: A Feminist Reader in Religion.*

Christ identifies two major imperatives for people on a spiritual quest, like me or you, dear readers. First, women require a theory of symbol and story about a female god—Goddess—that is congruent *with their own experience.* Second, since most feminist spiritualities use some kind of Goddess symbol, women need to get re-acquainted with ancient goddess symbols, and, when necessary, invent new ones.

The nagging question persists: is the Goddess simply one's own concept of feminine power projected onto a large cosmic screen? One could easily argue that many Christians do the same with the Father/Son God image. Or does the term "Goddess" refer to a divine being "out there" who is not reducible to a human female face but who is indeed transcendent and mystical?

Christ offers three possible responses to these important questions. One is that the "Goddess" is really and truly a divine female, a personification who can be invoked in prayer and ritual. Second, the "Goddess" may be understood as a symbol of the life, death and rebirth cycle in nature and in culture, in personal as well as in communal life. Third, the "Goddess" can be viewed strictly as a symbol pointing to another reality.

No matter which response a woman (or man) chooses, Christ argues that women *need* the Goddess to affirm the authority and goodness of female power, be it divine or human. And brothers, since you have a feminine side, you can benefit, too! Also, you might view your wife, daughters, sister or mom in a totally new way.

Spiritually, worshipping (or honoring) the Goddess can affirm female legitimacy and holiness, as well as the beauty of female generativity and power. Politically, the Goddess symbol supports women's trust in their own power to make smart, life-giving decisions in the arenas of both family and society. Psychologically, when a woman values the Divine Feminine, she helps to defeat patriarchy's view that women are inferior to men and that they are intrinsically sexual temptresses or even evil.

Christ insists that acknowledging and then claiming the power of the Sacred Feminine as legitimate and basically good, is life-giving and life-affirming. The Goddess invites all of us to co-create with Her. When we do, our self-esteem will rise, and we will hold our heads up high, like the gorgeous Greek goddesses of old.

SoulQuesters, you are very lucky to be living at a time when many diverse images of a female Goddess figure are so varied and accessible. Feminine psychologist Jean Shimoda Bolen, offers archetypes of Greek Goddesses in her now-classic work, *Goddesses in Every Woman: A New Psychology of Women*. Each goddess, like Aphrodite or Athena, like each woman today, has to face her own special temperament, talents and temptations, as she seeks to contribute to her family, community and society.

In the Jewish tradition, *Shekinah* is the name of the radiant and beautiful feminine aspect of God, God's visible manifestation to human beings on earth. In Hebrew, *Shekinah* means "the Presence/Dwelling of the Lord," and is often translated as "the Glory of the Lord," or God resting in his house or Tabernacle among his people. The *Shekinah* can also be seen as an expression of *Binah*, the Hebrew Great Mother. Though the term *Shekinah* is not used in either the Old or New Testaments, both scriptures are full of references to God coming in (her) glory.

In the Jewish mystical tradition of *Kabbalah* in the later medieval and modern periods, the *Shekinah* is given great importance. She is often depicted as the Creator's partner who will only be reunited with God when human beings fulfill all the divine commandments, ultimately ushering in the long-awaited Messianic Age.

Feminist Christian theologians have highlighted other names for the Divine Feminine. For instance, in *Sexism and God Talk*, Rosemary Radford Ruether calls her female God, "Divine Wisdom." Divine Wisdom defends the oppressed and critiques the systems of domination in the Jewish and Christian scriptures and traditions. Ruether believes humanity is now at the cusp of a new age of peace and justice, one that will help us

> ...to return Home: to learn the harmony, the peace, the justice of body, bodies in right relation to each other...not from alien

skies but here, in the community of earth. A new thing is revealed: the woman will encompass the warrior. 'Thou shalt not hurt, thou shalt not kill, in all my holy mountain,' says the Lord.

The Shalom of the Holy...Divine Wisdom...She in whom we live and move and have our being—She comes; She is here.

In her book, *In Memory of Her: A Feminist Theological Reconstruction of Christian Origins,* Elizabeth Schussler-Fiorenza names the feminine aspect of God "Spirit-Sophia." *Sophia* is the Greek name for the female Wisdom figure presented in *Proverbs* in the Hebrew Scriptures. A companion and playmate with the Creator God at the beginning of the world, *Spirit-Sophia* continues to call human beings from the marketplace to come and learn of her great wisdom.

Fiorenza asserts that God is revealed not only in the man Jesus, but in the community called forth by Jesus—a community whose mandate it is to feed the hungry, heal the sick, liberate the oppressed, and spread the gospel of God's love. This early community continues to the present day within the many Christian communities around the globe who are dedicated to service and social justice. Commitment, accountability and solidarity are the life-praxis or practice of Christian feminists. The true Christian is the one who walks in the *Spirit-Sophia*, working to bring about God's "new world."

You might remember from your high school or college history class that the Protestant Reformation, begun in 1517, was a vehement response against the abuses in the Roman Catholic Church. While I believe the corrupt practices, such as the sale of indulgences, needed to be stopped, the "protesting" reformers erred greatly when they threw "the baby [Mary] out with the bathwater." Since that time, Protestants have been bereft of an image for the Divine Feminine.

At least the Roman Catholics, from the first century onward, have had Mary to pray to, even worship. Over the centuries, Mary has become the blessed mediator between the almighty judge—Father God, and the poor miserable sinner—man. Millions of Catholics revere Mary, either the Virgin or the Mother, still today, and some Protestants, like me, are joining them.

152

Treat yourself to African-American singer and songwriter Bobby McFerrin as his *a capella* group performs a moving tribute to God as Mother, Daughter and the Holy of Holies in his creative version of *The 23rd Psalm* on his CD, *Medicine Man*.

Around the globe, Mary as the Divine Feminine has many faces and names. For example, in Buddhist countries, she is known as *Kwan Yin,* the Goddess of Mercy. In Poland, she is the *Black Madonna*. In Mexico, she is the beloved *Our Lady of Guadalupe*, with her own feast day on December 12th.

Mother Mary is not the only Christian expression of the Divine Feminine. Since the publication of Dan Brown's thriller, *The DaVinci Code*, many Protestant and Catholic women are excited about the role of another woman in the New Testament—Mary Magdalene. There is much heated conjecture about what role she played in Jesus' life and ministry, and in the life of the early church after Jesus' crucifixion and resurrection. Scholarly researchers alongside devout pilgrims are offering intriguing possibilities. You might read *The Woman with the Alabaster Jar* by Margaret Starbird for a good introduction to "the Tower," the Magdalene.

Native traditions have many female figures in their sacred stories. In the Lakota (Sioux) tradition, White Buffalo Calf Woman bestows important gifts upon her tribe. One oral version goes like this. The Lakota are on the edge of starvation on the Great Plains, so the tribal chief dispatches two scouts to locate the buffalo herd, the main source of sustenance. The scouts travel far and wide with no luck, until they spy a beautiful maiden in a deerskin dress approaching them.

As the maiden draws near to the men, one scout feels lust toward her. She stares at him, causing him to fall dead instantly at her feet. The surviving scout subdues his aroused intentions and humbly requests how he might help her. She asks to be taken to his chief.

Once in the chief's teepee surrounded by tribal elders, she reveals that her name is White Buffalo Calf Woman. She teaches the people many of their traditions, including smoking the peace pipe to resolve their conflicts. When she is finished, she leaves the teepee. A little boy peeks out from under the tent flap, amazed to see that, as she bounds away down the hill, she transforms into a white buffalo calf.

Many Lakota believe that White Buffalo Calf Woman still guides her people, offering comfort, wisdom and strength until her major prophecy comes true—the birth of a white buffalo calf in our land. That mysterious birth will signal the return of the buffalo and the restoration of stolen lands to the Red Race, and will usher in the Fifth Race, the Rainbow tribe, and all humanity will finally live together in peace.

Because I've studied with the Lakota on Pine Ridge and Rose Bud reservations, White Buffalo Calf Woman is especially precious to me. Whenever I'm facing a particularly high mountain to climb or a vast stretch of plains to cross on my life's quest, I pray to White Buffalo Calf Woman for courage and cunning. At other times, she teaches me to walk gently on the earth, paying close attention to the creatures, the trees, open to receive their helpful medicine. She is a gifted trail guide whom you'll want to befriend during some of your wilderness times.

Another manifestation of the Divine Feminine whom I love and honor is that of *Kwan Yin*, the Buddhist Goddess of Mercy. I have several graceful white porcelain statues of her. When I meditate upon her being, I sense a gentle, calming presence, come over me. During challenging times, my dear friend, Pamela, likes to imagine Kwan Yin high in the night sky, pouring compassion like liquid starlight down upon her.

Last but not least, I'm sure you know about the primal Goddess, the Earth Mother, who is widely celebrated in the Wiccan and pagan traditions. Often referred to as *Gaia*, she usually manifests as the Triple Goddess: Maiden, Mother, and Crone, a rough female parallel to the Christian male Trinity.

The Wise Old Crone can be a welcome symbol of female power for those of us who are aging, because she invites us to honor rather than fear our aging process. No wheel chair for the Wise Old Crone! She gives older women permission to be wild and free, dancing and daring. Jenny Joseph paints this picture in her poem, *Warning: When I Am Old, I Shall Wear Purple.*

When I am an old woman, I shall wear purple
with a red hat that doesn't go, and doesn't suit me.
And I shall spend my pension on brandy
and summer gloves and satin candles,
and say we've no money for butter.
I shall sit down on the pavement when I am tired
and gobble up samples in shops and press alarm bells
and run my stick along the public railings
and make up for the sobriety of my youth.

I shall go out in my slippers in the rain
and pick the flowers in other people's gardens
and learn to spit.

*

You can wear terrible shirts and grow more fat
and eat three pounds of sausages at a go
or only bread and pickles for a week
and hoard pens and pencils and beer nuts and things
in boxes.

*

But now we must have clothes that keep us dry
and pay our rent and not swear in the street
and set a good example for the children.
We must have friends to dinner and read the papers.
But maybe I ought to practice a little now?
So people who know me are not too shocked
and surprised
when suddenly I am old, and start to wear purple.

Or perhaps when we are crones, we'll join the *Red Hat Society*, a movement inspired by Jenny's poem. Here's Sue Ellen Cooper, Queen Mother of the *Red Hat Society*, in her own words:

> The Red Hat Society began as a result of a few women deciding to greet middle age with verve, humor and *elan*. We believe silliness is the comedy relief of life, and since we are all in it together, we might as well join red-gloved hands and go for the gusto together. Underneath the frivolity, we share a bond of affection, forged by common life experiences and a genuine enthusiasm for wherever life takes us next.

See what you have to look forward to, young women? Not for ages yet, of course!

So, my time travelers, have fun experimenting with various feminine God images. Read books about various spiritual traditions. Look at art. See what moves you, excites you and uplifts you. The sky's the limit. The earth's the limit. Your imagination is the limit. As you get to know new companions in the unseen world of Spirit, your soul will soar. You will create new myths about the Sacred Feminine, with wisdom and wit, courage and compassion.

155

Here's an ode to Mama God I wrote over fifteen years ago.

The Legend of Golden Sky Mother

First there is the vast blue expanse of space,
      Spreading out to infinity--- silent--- void
      and then a hum begins....low at first,
        and then louder and louder,
          stronger and stronger.

The air begins to vibrate, to shake,
      and a tiny point of light – a spark –
        bursts into rays of light.

From the center emerges Golden Sky Mother,
      her arms, legs and hair
radiating the warmth of the sun
    in all the four directions.
As she floats and grows, so does her belly,
      round and full—
      until she delivers forth
        with great pangs of labor and joy
         the blue/white/green ball of the earth.

The ball goes spinning through space.

Above it, she flings the rainbow,
      and she begins weaving its vibrant colors
      with the deep browns and blacks of the soil
        into all the creatures:
          peacock and parrot,
            leopard and lion.

Then *Golden Sky Mother* scoops up the earth
      in each part of the world
    and lovingly molds the human creatures
      into myriad colors,
    blowing her Sacred Spirit into them
      and into all life

upon the swirling turquoise ball.

She flings tears of joy at her creation
out into the velvet heavens,
where they form into crystals
that quiver even now
with strange and haunting harmonies.

Can you hear them in the stillness of your heart—
that sacred beating drum—
keeping time with the heart
of Golden Sky Mother
as she dances 'round the heavens?

Sharing our Stories around the Campfire

Finally, in addition to inventing new stories about Divine Creators, we need to share our own *human* stories, for "every person deserves to be the star of their own life." Repeat after me: "Every person deserves to be the star of their own life." This means you. You can, and during wilderness times you must, rewrite your life story so that *you are the star*. After all, whether unconsciously or consciously, you are already living out a story you've concocted about your life: its meaning and purpose, its dreams and disasters. So why not write a version that gives you the *kudos*, that honors your strengths and recognizes your amazing gifts?

A few years ago, struggling with self-doubts (broken record, I know), I was scheduled to speak before a group of several hundred people. I consciously decided to pretend to be a stranger in the audience, so that I could listen to my *curriculum vitae* with fresh ears. As the man introducing me read a long and, I must admit, rather impressive list of my accomplishments, I was pleasantly surprised.

"Wow," I marveled to myself. "Pretty cool, woman!"

That night, I experienced what it meant to be the star of my own life.

Any major transition in your life is a good time to create a new script where you are the hero. Some of you know that divorce can be a painful and haunting process. During my separation from my first husband, I found myself feeling like Hester Prynn in *The Scarlet*

Letter. However, instead of a bright red A on my blouse for "Adulteress," emblazoned there was a huge F for "Failure".

After the divorce, the "F" mysteriously morphed into a large "D" for "Divorced." I was shocked to discover that some of my married girlfriends also seemed to read an imaginary neon sign flashing across my chest: "Watch out, ladies. I'm going to steal your husbands." That was the farthest thing from my mind.

The first time that I filled out a medical form in a doctor's office after my divorce, I stared, stumped by those nasty, nosy little "marital status" boxes. Why must I check the box labeled "Divorced," defining my social status by what I've just painfully lost? Then I remembered that I could rewrite my own script. I now have a fantasy that one day soon, I'll add a new box to that darn form, one that offers the option: "Independent, adventurous, wild woman of Spirit." And my checkmark will be huge.

While struggling to find other creative ways to re-frame the traumatic experience of my divorce, I came up with this comparison from the theater world. Let's say a play has had a fantastic run on Broadway, like *The Fantasticks*, one of my favorites. When the show finally ends, certainly the cast members are sad as they strike the set and say their good-byes. But do they automatically presume that the play was a failure? No. It had a successful run, but now it's over. Similarly, I choose to view the end of my first marriage not as a failure but as a pretty good run with many blessings. By doing this, I become my own heroine again.

Here's one last exercise I've adapted from Carol Bridges' *Medicine Woman Inner Guidebook: A Woman's Guide to her Unique Powers*. If you enjoy drama, either watching or creating it, you'll like this one. First, identify a time in your life that makes you mad or sad. Next, make a date to get together with the person involved. If that's not possible, invite a trusted friend to do this exercise with you.

Then, take turns doing the following:

- tell the event as a tragedy;
- tell the event as a comedy;
- tell the event from the perspective of an imagined Higher Being, like the Buddha, an angel, Mary or even God; and finally.

- choose the version you like best, and start living as if *that* version were true—because according to your new script, it *is.*

I admit I've still got a lot to learn about this script-writing exercise, for almost as fast as I rewrite acts from my past, new acts keep arriving. I am just grateful I am more aware of my important role as screen writer, director, set and costume designer, and even casting director.

I am the star of my own life.

You can be, too, my *dah-lings*!

We began this chapter with the importance of sharing stories, and we're coming full circle. You may need to do excavation work, translation work or even a major rewrite of your life story, but what an opportunity to be creative and heal yourself.

Telling part of your past to someone else can help you to grow in your self-worth. When you shine the spotlight upon yourself, you are empowered to take up space on the stage of your life. You can more readily acknowledge the "real" you, with your talents, tricks, foibles and foolishness. Revel in that—be a character!

Second, when you tell your story to someone out loud at least three times, the neurons in your brain start tracing new pathways, you begin to change your brain routing. You no longer cast yourself as the enabler, patsy, controller, worrywart, or _____ (fill in your own word), but as the *heroine* or *hero* of your quest. This is so liberating!

For instance, I have a girlfriend who was pretty beaten down after thirty years in a rough marriage. Today, a few years after her divorce, as she's shared her story with trusted friends, she's begun to blossom—no, to *shine*—in all areas of her life. When she's doing her *rhumbas* or *chachas* with her new partner, you can't get her off the dance floor—and she's just magic to watch.

Sharing your life story with someone can help not only you but another person. I promise that when you share how you overcame an obstacle like alcoholism or hypochondria, or how you forgave a particularly nasty person, or how you experienced a dramatic physical healing, someone's bound to resonate with your situation. Perhaps they'll even become motivated enough to rewrite their own inner script toward the better.

So, storytellers, let's commit to sharing our stories around the campfires of our lives, shall we? It doesn't matter whether we're at the bedside of a sick child, at the kitchen table over tea or at Starbucks over a *latte*; if we're serving at a homeless shelter, running a board meeting, or responding to a friend's panicked voice over the phone in the wee hours of the night. Telling our tales to one another fans the dying embers of our low self-image, and causes our inner spirit-light to glow. Sharing our stories warms us with the sacred fire of companionship, and draws us ever closer to the Holy One in our midst.

Now close your eyes and savor the soft, sticky chocolate of the S'mores, the sweetness of shared laughter and tears. Make no mistake, dear souls. These campfires are on holy ground.

ELEVEN

Dancing in the Meadow to Greet the Dawn:

The Power of Ritual

Picture a tribe of ancient people dancing in a circle on a grassy meadow, singing in ecstasy because they believe that they are *causing* the sun to rise and creating themselves and their world anew. Today, such a notion seems naïve, quaint or superstitious, doesn't it? We're civilized and enlightened, for God's sake. We don't need to dance or sing to help the sun rise. Ritual is obsolete. Dead.

Of course, you probably still sing "Happy Birthday" to your family and friends, maybe even in a restaurant full of strangers. Perhaps some of you are familiar with the Jewish ritual of *bar* or *bat mitzvah* in which, after a period of intense study of Hebrew and the Torah, a 13-year-old Jewish boy or girl is welcomed as a full adult into the faith. Others of you who are Christian have most likely undergone confirmation when you were about thirteen.

Some of you have also experienced the ritual variously called Eucharist, Holy Communion, or the Lord's Supper, Christ's (symbolic) meal of bread and wine, flesh and blood. Christians I've interviewed over the past ten years have admitted that such rites seem rote, boring or even irrelevant to their spiritual lives.

For most of my own life, the purpose of ritual was elusive. Even though every now and then, I enjoyed the high liturgy of an Episcopal Church service with its "smells and bells," or a *bar* and *bat mitzvoth* of my Jewish nieces and nephews, when I entered my doctoral program, I was highly skeptical about the necessity for ritual in our modern-day, streamlined, technologically-based lives.

Perhaps the concept of ritual is foreign to you, too.

In fact, when I tried to recall a good example from my life to give you, I could barely recollect one. Then I remembered my initiation into a sorority back in the late 1960s. It was night. We pledges were blindfolded and then taken by car to an isolated yard somewhere out in the country. During the initiation, our elders placed loops of rope around our necks, with slices of lemons dangling from them. Then they began to interrogate us on different topics. If we answered a question inaccurately, they ordered: "Chow down!" I remember chowing down on those bitter lemon slices more than once.

Next, the "elders" of the sorority taught us the secret meaning of our motto and the esoteric symbolism on our sorority pin. We finished off the evening by singing our favorite sorority songs. The elders hoped that such activities would increase our respect for, and knowledge of, the secret society in which we would soon be full-fledged, responsible members. Mostly, the "hazing" initiation seemed all in good fun, with nothing really earth-shattering or teeth-chattering.

If birthday candles and sorority hazings comprise the bulk of our culture's ritual life, then surely we have outgrown the need for ritual. Our secular lifestyles suit us just fine. Who even thinks about ritual these days?

When I started my doctoral program in Anthropology, I was ritually challenged. As time went on, I was surprised to find that *every* indigenous society I studied, whether the Lakota Indians of the Western Plains, the Kayapo of the Brazilian jungle, or the !Kung of the Kalahari Desert of southwestern Africa, was steeped in ritual. Perhaps, I thought, I should pay some attention to the uncharted ritual waters of my American life.

A decade later, I am thoroughly convinced that we in our technologically oriented culture are missing out on something potentially life-transforming—the ritual process.

But wait.

Let me start by sharing a brief overview of ritual studies.

I am drawing on the fieldwork and writings of the grandfather of ritual studies, British anthropologist Victor Turner (1920-1983). Turner theorized that society in general is comprised in general of basic relationships that are ordered through caste, social class, gender, political parties, division of labor, etc. Each society creates a recognizable system of social control, coupled with prescribed modes of behavior for its members. Over time, members construct specific ceremonies to help preserve their society. Ceremonies name, explain and regulate the society against a potential cultural void or even chaos. This "social structure," as Turner named it, is what keeps a society stable, like pillars of a temple, so that the elders can transmit their values and worldview to future generations.

While every society requires structure to exist and then maintain itself, Turner explained that social structure has some negative effects.

First, members tend to deal with each other as stereotypes rather than as authentic, unique individuals.   Second, citizens are often constrained by laws and conventions; experimental behavior is limited and usually frowned upon.   Third, because social structure maintains order through a hierarchy or class system of some kind, it tends to produce (and re-produce) inequality between members, which can alienate people from each other.   The final and most destructive characteristic of social structure is that it provides a vehicle for leaders (political or religious) to oppress the people they rule, resulting in further alienation, discontent, conflict or even revolution.   We see examples of this globally in the news every day.

What does Turner believe counterbalances and stabilizes this undesirable tendency of social structure to implode?

Ritual.

Early in his career, Turner was highly influenced by Arnold van Gennep's work on "rites of passage"—tribal rites which accompanied every change of place, status, social position or age.   Van Gennep identified three phases in tribal ritual: the separation phase in which initiates are removed from the rest of society; the liminal phase of the ritual; and the initiates' re-entry into society.

Turner decided to focus his anthropological research primarily on the second or "liminal" stage, the transition stage.   He was fascinated by what happened to ritual subjects during what he termed "the ritual process." Think of water turning into steam, a grub into a moth, or an acorn into an oak tree.   Individually, through ritual, a young girl in an African tribe may transform into a woman, or a Lakota warrior may perform the Sun Dance to give thanks to the Great Spirit, *Wakan Tanka,* for his healing.   A whole society might transform itself through a ritual act, for instance, from a state of peace to a state of war.   It is the performance of ritual that enacts and produces the transformation the society desires.

Turner was also strongly influenced by the brain research of his day, especially that of scientist Paul MacLean.   In 1949, MacLean offered a model of the human brain as "three brains in one," each with its own set of intelligences and motor functions.   The "first" brain to evolve was the reptilian brain which includes the brain stem.   This area is concerned with control of movement, such as instinctive behavior, as well as exhibiting emotional displays, territorial defense behaviors, and nest building.   Reptilian consciousness focuses on the body.

The "second" brain is the "old mammalian brain," the mid-brain, comprised of such structures as the limbic system; the hypothalamus which controls and regulates responses to heat, thirst, sex, pain and pleasure; and the pituitary, the master endocrine gland. The second brain deals mainly with emotion.

The "third" and most recently developed section of the brain in MacLean's model is the neo-cortex, the outer layer of brain tissue, rich in nerve-cell bodies and synapses. Iits functions are cognition (thinking) and sophisticated processes of perception and its focus is matters of the mind.

Turner was intrigued by the dual role genetics and brain chemistry play in the ritual process. He wondered, for example: are we human (and not merely animal) *because* we perform rituals, or by performing rituals, do we *become* human? Are we wired in our brains and DNA to create and perform rituals? Or do we construct rituals in order to distinguish ourselves from other mammals?

After decades of fieldwork and brain research, Turner eventually came to believe that both nature and nurture played a strong role in the ritual process. At one point, he wrote:

> We are animals—sometimes rational ones, sometimes divine ones, sometimes social ones—but we are still animals. And our most sacred rituals still concern our 'animal' functions— eating, drinking, moving about, reproducing, dying, mating, fighting.... [Rituals] flow with or without our conscious assent; they are uttered-exclamations of nature and our bodies.

Now, you sisters of spirit might be asking, just how does the ritual process work? At least I hope you're asking that, because I hope you'll become conscious and intentional ritual makers after you read this chapter. Let me break it down for you.

First, there must be ritual elders. Each indigenous culture carefully produces and trains its ritual elders. Second, there must be a carefully designed ritual space. As the ritual begins, the ritual elders lead the participants into the ritual space at a specifically designated ritual time, essentially "betwixt and between" everyday time and space. Turner called this mysterious sacred space "liminality." The ritual space may include a geographic move, a crossing of a threshold either literally or symbolically, or a long and exacting pilgrimage to a shrine, wilderness, or to a holy place like Mecca, Jerusalem or Lourdes.

Ritual space often juxtaposes center and margin. Imagine a tribal village in the Amazon today or on our own Great Plains a hundred years ago. The center of the village symbolizes the socially structured life, while a marginal or wilderness space around the center symbolizes the liminal place where ritual subjects are taken. (Surprisingly, my sorority sisters had a sense of the need for liminality when they took us pledges to a dark place *outside* of the city.)

In other rituals, ritual space juxtaposes surface with depth. That is, the liminal subjects may be taken to a place that is underground, like an "abyss" or a cave. Such liminal spaces may be associated with death (tomb or grave spaces or shapes) or life (womb spaces). Turner even used the catchy phrase "wombs and tombs" to delineate liminality—the ritual space which is "neither this nor that, and yet is both."

Third, there must be the initiates or ritual subjects. Turner listed over twenty-six attributes of liminal subjects, which include being stripped of all signs of status, wealth, or property, being dressed in simple clothing or even stripped naked. Gender distinctions often disappear, rendering subjects nearly androgynous. During the ritual, total silence may be observed or sacred speech may be uttered. In the ritual of baptism, for example, the priest pronounces the sacred formula, "I baptize you in the name of the Father, the Son, and the Holy Ghost."

The totally obedient subjects must be ready to endure pain in order to be transformed into their new state of being. The extreme example for this attribute made me think of the African tribal ritual of Female Genital Mutilation. Finally, the ritual subjects, considered by society to be dangerous and taboo in their liminal state, are kept at a safe distance from the other members.

A true ritual is no mere head trip. Gestures, facial expressions and dance or movement all play a role. The subject's body and senses are fully engaged. One may hear music, chants, prayers; one may look upon visual symbols or read sacred writing. The subject may taste consecrated foods, smell incense, and touch or be touched by, sacred persons or objects. Sacred objects have two purposes: first, to teach the neophytes new ways to think about their religious culture; and second, to give them ultimate standards for their future behavior in their newly gained status. For instance, think of Jewish congregants reaching out during a Shabbat (Sabbath) service to touch the Torah, their Holy Book, with their prayer shawls as the ritual leader parades the esteemed scroll down the aisle of the synagogue, literally reconnecting them with their source of spiritual wisdom.

Finally, during the liminal phase, participants are usually taught some kind of *gnosis* or secret knowledge which has been coveted by their ancestors before them, sacred stories or lore which reveal the origin and nature of the cosmos, the tribe, and the purpose of the ritual. This gnosis does not merely provide the subjects with new information, but is intended to cause a *change in their innermost being*, which leads us to...

The three goals of the ritual process

Turner believed that whether a ritual focuses on an individual or a group or the whole community, the primary goal of ritual is always some kind of *transformation*, whether spiritual, physical, or emotional. A secondary goal of ritual performance is to bring the initiate into closer contact with the Divine. Mostly, though, Turner was captivated by the third goal of ritual performance: the production of *communitas.*

"Communi-what?"

While liminality has to do with physical space of the ritual event, *communitas* has to do with the emotion and change in consciousness that a ritual subject experiences during the ritual. This is why, dear college students, frenzied dancing to wild music at a sorority or fraternity party would not meet the criteria of ritual. There is no change in your consciousness. At least not usually!

What are the characteristics of *communitas*? I know you've experienced something like it, but you didn't realize it had such a fancy name.

First and foremost, *communitas* is "where community happens," where one feels oneself to be uniquely one's self yet experiences a strong sense of unity with others in the group, sometimes described as a "communion of equals." Ideally, said Turner, when even two people experience unity with each other, that feeling expands to include everyone in the world, if only for an instant. Second, subjects in *communitas* experience strong emotions, including a sense of the group's strength. Perhaps the group even thinks that together they can solve their society's and maybe even the world's problems. The example of my 35-year-old niece Rachel springs to mind. Leading groups of young American Jews to Israel, she hopes to build a strong sense of community among them and their counterparts in Israel, as well as motivate them to share their enthusiasm and talents to build a better America.

Third, whereas people in social structures transact business with a mere part of themselves—their minds, status, products or services—in *communitas,* whole persons engage whole persons with body, mind, heart and soul.

Fourth, when *communitas* is present in a ritual, there can be a marvelous sense of playfulness (what my father called "high play" in his book of the same name). Because of this heightened state of awareness and creativity, subjects are able to break out of their everyday social behavior to envision new arrangements of living, working or playing together.

For example, one South American tribe I studied in grad school allowed its men and women to exchange gender roles for one full day every year. The photos of them enjoying themselves in the usually "forbidden" roles were hilarious. Another tribe allowed the lowest members on the tribe's totem pole to play "king for a day." The members proudly bossed their king around and ordered him to perform their common menial tasks. The king was expected to take such treatment gracefully and to comply with their wishes. The purpose of this ritual was to remind the king to be more aware of the condition of his subjects when he resumed his reign, thus keeping the social structure happily intact.

I believe Jesus practiced this kind of social inversion with his disciples when he, the long-awaited Davidic king, knelt before his disciples the night before his arrest, to perform a traditional servant's job—washing their dusty feet.

The sense of *communitas* must have been great in all the above situations.

The concept of *communitas* really appeals to me. As a former hippie and "flower child," I experienced it whenever I was engaged in peace marches or "be-ins," or attended concerts for peace in Vietnam or civil rights. In fact, I could be tempted to seek out a constant state of *communitas.* Fortunately, that's not possible. We can't sustain a *communitas* consciousness for very long. Someone has to carry water and chop wood. Turner was adamant that both social structure and *communitas* are necessary to maintain a flourishing society made up of creative and committed citizens.

One final point about ritual. Turner claimed that rituals helped people in various cultures and tribes to "re-member."

"Get nostalgic, right?" you ask. "Long for the simpler, happier days gone by?"

No. Remembering is not merely about transporting some past lifestyle into the present. It is bringing forth that past *in living relationship* to the present. Thus, ritual helps the community to "re-member", literally to put the body parts back together, and "perform" its unique identity—past, present and future. Turner was prophetic in warning us a half century ago that if our religions and churches begin to die, as many now are, we should examine our (lack of) ritual performance, for

> religion ... lives insofar as it is *performed*, i.e., insofar as its rituals are 'going concerns.' If you wish to spay or geld religion, first remove its rituals, its generative and regenerative processes. For religion is not a cognitive system, a set of dogmas, alone. It is meaningful experience and experienced meaning.

Creating Rituals for Today

Since it is part of my spiritual calling to teach the process and power of ritual performance, soul seekers, I say it's high time to create new rituals to celebrate and deepen the meaning of events in our daily lives in temples, mosques, or churches, or at home, work or play. Turner's theories reveal the necessary elements to create an effective ritual. Though we can only invite but not engineer the appearance of *communitas*, as we devise a ritual, we should at least ask the following questions:

- What is the purpose and quality of the chosen ritual space and time?
- Who are the ritual elders and what is their role?
- Who are the ritual subjects?
- Does the ritual seek to engage the whole person, mind, body, senses and emotions? How? Be specific.
- Is there some time for play, foolishness or laughter?

- Most importantly, what is the goal of the transformation of the ritual's subjects, which will foster the experience of *communitas*—the powerful flow of unity and love between the subjects, elders and the Divine?

In the chapter, "Unwrapping the Gift," in her book, *Women & Ritual*, Sandy Sasso describes the dilemma and the delight available to us when we dare to create new rituals for our time.

> We must navigate a course between a spiritual privatism which asserts that the holy can be completely custom-made, and a religious fundamentalism which claims that custom was made once and for all. We are in need of ritual that both honors the individual and the communal, tradition and change, the repetitive certainty of established acts and words and the refreshing spontaneity of improvisation.

> We are in need of ritual that will give expression to our innermost longings and deepest fears and call us to transcend the personal. Ritual must be more than a sacred affirmation of who we are; it must also be a holy challenge to what and who we may become in solidarity with a community of holy travelers.

In other words, we'd do well to keep all of these elements in creative tension: individual and community; tradition and innovation; and repetition and improvisation.

In her book, *Women-church: Theology and Practice*, Rosemary Radford Reuther insists that we must do more than protest against the old or boring ways of performing traditional rituals. We must create new prayers, symbols, and rituals which reflect our consciousness, values and visions. She advises keeping one foot firmly planted in tradition, one foot in feminist theory, and one foot in women's lived experience. (Uh-oh, is that three feet?) Her book provides re-imagined forms of familiar rituals like baptism and Eucharist as well as presenting new ones: for the onset of menstruation, for divorce, for coming out as a lesbian, or for embarking on a new stage of life.

Here are a few of my own imaginative concoctions to help get your creative juices flowing, my holy travelers.

1. Transforming a young person into an adult

Here is one rather colorful (though admittedly unusual) ritual that I devised years ago to initiate Chelsea and Michael, two thirteen-year-olds in our family, into adulthood. They were the guinea pigs, I mean, the ritual subjects.

The place? Cable Lake, a lovely wilderness lake in northern Wisconsin, our extended family's beloved summer home. The water lapped gently at the shore's edge. The time? One mildly sunny summer afternoon. I had invited the elders of our clan, including several aunts, uncles and cousins, to sit on camp chairs in a semi-circle. The children and teenagers sat on blankets on the ground in the circle facing the center.

Earlier that day, I had struggled with about what to use for sacred objects. Playing around with whatever was at hand, I finally decided on canoe paddles. For generations, our elders have taught the youngsters how to paddle canoes on Cable Lake. Each person, young or old, has sacred canoe lore to share. For example, four of us in my generation remember the time when, as teenagers, we crept out of our cabins against our parents' rules, to canoe over to a local bar. Gliding noiselessly in the moonlight, we kept our eyes on the large branch of the Lollipop Tree approaching us overhead. One by one, we leaned to the left to avoid being hit by the branch. As the last teen leaned over, the whole canoe tipped, spilling everyone out. Our screams of laughter and surprise brought our parents running. Although we didn't reach the bar that night, we'll never forget that canoe trip.

Canoeing is also a great metaphor for sharing Bro clan values: "Be careful. Watch out for one another. Take risks. Have fun!"

We were taught to intentionally tip the canoe over once in a while, as a good metaphor for life—"Get used to the rocking and rolling before being thrown out into the water!" We were taught to use the canoe to pick up our elders to take them shopping in town, or to go on our own adventures, like exploring the Narrows. Last but not least, we all treasured the pleasure of sitting quietly in the canoe at sunset to watch the mother eagle return to her squawking eaglets in their island nest perched stories high above us.

Next, here's the exact ritual process I designed. First, I honored the elders, identifying their role in our Bro tribe over the decades: family historian, physician, advisor or classical pianist. Next, I invited Chelsea and Michael, the ritual subjects, to stand up in front of the paddles laid out on the ground in the middle of the circle, with their backs to the lake. We grownups stood up and encircled Chelsea and Mike. Singing a chant my sisters and I had created earlier that day, we called on the medicine properties of Bear and Eagle—our local power animals at Cable—to bestow their strength, courage, insight, and far-sight upon our two initiates.

The ritual actions? I invited first Chelsea and then Michael to step over the canoe paddle into the liminal space. As each one stepped across, I solemnly placed my doctoral hood upon each, (I rarely had an occasion to wear it, anyway), as I announced their new status—adult members in our Bro clan. As the younger children watched with large eyes, Chelsea and Michael joined the elders on the far side of the circle where they received hugs and whoops of congratulations. We closed the ritual with one final blessing chant. The sense of *communitas* was tangible and full of joy.

2. Moving through divorce to a new single identity

Because divorce is widespread in our society, I want to share an example of a ritual designed by my dear friend, Libbie, to mark the end of her marriage and the beginning of her new life as a single woman. Libby and her husband had shared many years together, raising three children, participating in spiritual communities and taking trips abroad. Now she was going to be on her own again, starting a brand new chapter of her life.

Surrounded by her best friends in her intimate and darkened living room, Libby gave thanks for her marriage, listing the gifts she'd received and the lessons she'd learned. Then she acknowledged her contribution to the break-up of the union and asked for God's forgiveness. Next, we shared a special Holy Communion I had designed just for her.

Then, stripped down to her bathing suit, Libby literally ran out of her home to the nearby Chesapeake Bay, her friends trailing after her with cries of encouragement. She splashed into the waves with a "holler of joy" (Libby was originally from North Carolina) and dove under the water. Symbolically dying to her old married self, she was washed clean, emerging from the Bay newborn and triumphant and ready to face her new single life.

In this ritual, we participants had experienced the liminal space in her tiny, darkened living room. Then we experienced *communitas* as we bonded together, mid-wifing her into her new state of being. What a blessed event of transformation.

3. Honoring the death of a loved one

Ritual can offer great healing and closure to people marking or celebrating the death of a loved one who has moved from womb to tomb to the mysterious womb of the afterlife. For example, on September 13th, 1987, at about 10 p.m., my husband, Chelsea and Kaitlyn, aged 13 and 9, and I learned that my father had died after lying in a coma for ten days. Relieved that his suffering had ended but sad for our loss, I wondered how we might mark his passing with a meaningful ritual. Even though we belonged to a local church community, no one there had known my father. And we were unsure of our friends' willing participation in a spur-of-the moment ritual, anyway. After some thoughtful discussion, we decided to go to a store and buy Dad's favorite food, ice cream, and a bottle of wine, our two sacred objects.

Near midnight, we left our home and walked across the street to a deserted baseball field, our perfect liminal space, where we sat down on a blanket under the stars,. Laughing and crying, each of us shared our favorite memories of Grandpa. We "re-membered" him, put him back together with our sacred stories. Then, emotions spent, we passed around the carton of ice cream and a spoon, and communed with his spirit, giving thanks for how his life had touched ours. Last, we poured the wine into little cups and toasted him on his way: "Godspeed, Grandpa. We love you!" Arm in arm, we strolled back home under the Milky Way, embraced by the spirit of *communitas*. Having tucked Dad's jaunty, larger-than-life spirit into a special corner of our hearts, we were transformed.

Transforming the Ritual of Communion

This example of new ritual practice for a whole spiritual community had its seedpoint one Sunday morning over twenty years ago. I was leading a group of forty or so in worship at Christpoint Community Church. My infant daughter Kaitlyn began to cry and my husband John could not comfort her. After preaching a very distracted sermon punctuated by her howling, I motioned to John to give her to me while some friends prepared the altar for our weekly Holy Communion.

Taking Kaitlyn out to the hall, I nursed her discreetly, marveling as I often did, at this tiny, miraculous being, sucking now on my breast. She quieted down immediately. Handing contented Kait back to John, I walked up to stand behind the altar. As I broke the bread like I had done hundreds of times before, I uttered the familiar words of institution:

"This is my body, given for you. Eat this in memory of me."

"This is my body...." echoed in my head.

Oh, my God.

I was stunned by the epiphany that arose within me. Kaitlyn had grown in my body for nine months, surviving *solely* on nutrients from my body and blood. Now, she was gaining weight and growing strong *solely* on my breast milk, her only source of nourishment. My body had given her life, and was now responsible for keeping her alive!

Like dawn breaking through darkness, a wild and potentially blasphemous notion arose in my head.

What if Jesus had offered us his body and blood, not to remind us of his broken body and violently shed blood, but to feed us, to sustain us, in the same way a pregnant or nursing mother sustains her child's life?

Blown away by this epiphany, I was barely able to finish the service.

When I got home, I sat on the couch, transfixed, while Kaitlyn napped. I needed time to take this revelation in. I also knew I could never perform the ritual of communion with my old consciousness again. I would have to revise my notion of communion within the radical framework of Jesus as my nourishing Mother, for God's sake.

After months of soul-searching, I finally decided to take a sabbatical from pastoring the church to obtain a doctorate in feminism and theology. I also knew I had to pay attention—deep attention—to what this revelation might mean to me in terms of practicing the central ritual of my faith.

Two years later, inspired by that experience, the feminist theologians I was reading and Turner's work on the ritual process, I decided to write my doctoral thesis on the transforming power of Communion as seen through the lens of women's experience.

I interviewed over seventy women asking these questions:

- How do you feel about being female and having a female body?
- Have your feelings changed over time? If so, how?
- What do you think is the purpose of Communion?
- Would you share an experience of Communion that you found memorable, even life-changing?

What inspiring and often puzzling responses the women gave me. After carefully scrutinizing their answers for months, I created three practices of communion, including the one given below. This ritual is not intended to replace the traditional observance of Eucharist but to augment it. Its goal is to help transform a woman's attitude toward her body from one of dislike to one of honor. If you can't get your church to perform it, perhaps a group of your friends could enact it in a private home. If you are not Christian, I hope you will still get a sense of the ritual elements, the liberating process of transforming women's self-image, and maybe even be inspired to create your own rituals.

"The Freedom Meal"

A New Communion Ritual

Before the service begins, the elements would be set upon the altar. The sacred objects would include different types of bread: rye, corn, wheat, *Challah* bread, and wine and/or juice. The service would open with Brian Wren's hymn, *Good is the Flesh* (found in Chapter Six).

The Scripture readings would include *Genesis* 1:27 from the Hebrew scripture, "So God created humankind in his image, in the image of God he created them; male and female, he created them," and from the New Testament, *John* 1:14: "And the Word became flesh and lived among us." The main reading would be taken from *John* 2:1-11.

On the third day, there was a wedding in Cana of Galilee, and the mother of Jesus was there. Jesus and his disciples had also been invited to the wedding.

When the wine gave out, the mother of Jesus said to him, "They have no wine."

And Jesus said to her, "Woman, what concern is that to me? My hour has not yet come."

His mother said to the servants, "Do whatever he tells you." Now standing there were six stone water jars for the Jewish rites of purification, each holding twenty or thirty gallons.

Jesus said to them, "Fill the jars with water."

And they filled them up to the brim.

He said to them, "Now draw some out, and take it to the chief stewards."

When the master of the feast had tasted the water that was made wine, and did not know where it came from (but the servants who had drawn the water knew), the master of the feast called the bridegroom and said to him,

"Everyone serves the good wine first, and then the inferior wine after the guests have become drunk. But you have kept the good wine until now."

Jesus did this, the first of his signs, in Cana of Galilee, and revealed his glory, and his disciples believed in Jesus.

The ritual leader might introduce the communion ritual by exploring how Jesus related to the human body. The numerous Gospel accounts of Jesus performing healings of all sorts shows that he must have cared deeply about people's bodies and minds, especially those that were blind, crippled, twisted or tormented. Also, because Jesus healed people individually rather than in mass groups, he must have valued each body as unique and precious. Jesus held such a strong conviction about the importance of healing a person that several times he disobeyed Jewish law by healing on the Sabbath.

The ritual leader could also examine Jesus' unusual treatment of women. Given his patriarchal culture, it is remarkable that Jesus never belittled a woman because she was a woman—indeed, he never belittled women at all. While the Hebrew faith placed a high value on motherhood, nowhere in the Gospels did Jesus stress the honor of motherhood. On the contrary. In *Mark* 3:31-35, for instance, he expanded the notion of family beyond the ties of blood to include "all people who do the will of God."

Indeed, Jesus' actions with women often directly opposed Jewish customs. For example, Jesus challenged the divorce custom of his time in which a husband could divorce his wife on a whim, merely by writing his wife's name on a piece of paper and tearing it up. Furthermore, while each male Jew prayed every morning, "Thank you, God, that I was not born a slave or a woman," Jesus treated women as equal to men. On several occasions, he spoke with women in public, like the Samaritan woman at the well. He encouraged his dear friend, Mary of Bethany, to sit at his feet alongside his male disciples to learn from him, an act defying the male-centered practice of Torah study.

Jesus healed women as well as men. His first recorded healing was done on his disciple Peter's mother-in-law. Later in his ministry, he raised a little girl from the dead by commanding in Aramaic, "*Talitha, cumi!*" "Little girl, arise!"

Just as radical was Jesus' healing of the woman with the issue of blood, recorded in *Mark* 5:27-34. In that ancient time, Jewish taboos prevented a righteous male from touching a bleeding woman in any way, for she was considered impure and thus able to contaminate him. In the midst of a large throng of people, the desperate, bleeding woman in Mark's Gospel dared to reach out to touch the hem of Jesus' robe, believing that even without Jesus knowing, his power could heal her. However, Jesus felt his power go out from him. He asked his disciples who touched his garment. Knowing the blood taboo and fearful of his wrath, she confessed her deed. In response Jesus not only healed her but commended her for her strong faith in his power to restore her health.

The Gospels record in several places that Jesus lifted up a woman as an example of good discipleship. For instance, the seventh chapter of Luke portrays a moving encounter between Jesus and a brave, unnamed woman. It's one of my favorite Gospel stories.

> And there was a woman in the city who was a sinner; and when she learned that Jesus was reclining at the table in the Pharisee's house, she brought an alabaster vial of perfume, and standing behind him at his feet, weeping, she began to wet his

feet with her tears, and kept wiping them with the hair of her head, and kissing his feet and anointing them with the perfume.

Now when the Pharisee who had invited Jesus saw this, he said to himself, "If this man was a prophet, he would know who and what sort of person this woman is who is touching him, that she is a sinner."

And Jesus answered him, "Simon, I have something to say to you."

And he replied, "Say it, Teacher."

... Turning toward the woman, he said to Simon, "Do you see this woman? I entered your house; you gave me no water for my feet, but she has wet my feet with her tears and wiped them with her hair.

"You gave me no kiss; but she, since the time I came in, has not ceased to kiss my feet. You did not anoint my head with oil, but she anointed my feet with perfume.

"For this reason I say to you, her sins, which are many, have been forgiven, for she has shown great love."

And he said to the woman, "Your faith has saved you; go in peace."

Jesus must also have deeply appreciated the company of the "holy women," like Mary and Martha of Bethany at whose home he often stayed during his travels, and whose weeping at the death of their brother, Lazarus, caused Jesus himself to weep. Jesus also let himself be challenged by the Gentile woman who with her persistent faith in him, begged him to heal her dying daughter, and ultimately persuaded him to expand his mission to include non-Jewish people. Of course, let's not forget Mary Magdalene, whom Jesus must have cherished, because after his resurrection he chose to appear first, not to his male disciples, but to her.

These stories about Jesus—healing bodies, engaging with women in counter-cultural ways—provide a lot of food for thought. After the sermon, the ritual leader continues with the Confession and the Affirmation.

Confession

"Hear the patriarchal curse on women in the words of the church father, Tertullian, passed down to women throughout these past 2000 years.

> O woman, God's sentence hangs still over your sex,
> And His punishment weighs down upon you.
> You are the devil's gateway.
> You are the unsealer of the forbidden tree.
> You are the first deserter of the divine law.
> You destroyed so easily God's image, man.
>> On account of your desert, that is death,
>> even the Son of God had to die.

Participants then respond with the following affirmation taken from Miriam Therese Winter's book *WomanPrayer, Woman Song*, "The Word Made Flesh." Though it is essentialist in its definition of woman, I still find it powerful.

Affirmation

> Flesh of our flesh,
> Bone of our bone,
> God was born of woman alone,
> nursed at her breast,
> clung to her knee.
> shared thirty full years of silence
> with her,
> and broke it
> only for three.

> Women have much in common with God,
> secrets that only women share,
> of the womb,
> of the heart,
> of bringing to birth,
> and sustaining life

and becoming aware.
A giving,
forgiving,
nurturing role,
intent on making whoever is broken
whole.

Is that why men are so afraid?
Afraid to share
prestige or power,
afraid to acknowledge
woman's worth,
because the power
of giving birth
is life,
meaning,
ultimate truth,
and she carries it all
within her?

Word-made-flesh:

God understands
a woman's world
and the work of her hands:
the stress of feeding a multitude
with too many mouths
and too little food.
A wedding feast and no more wine:
"Woman, is that a concern
of mine?"
"Well, yes," she said,
and the vintage flowed;

And sometime later, when a cup would be passed
at a Supper
that would be the last,
a promise was made so there would always be
enough for all.
        'Remember me

    when you eat
    and drink
    in company.'

Thus says God:
"I will be heard!
Make flesh
of my every word!
Give peace, justice, liberty
visible reality;
feed the hungry.
Don't just meet
and plan
what they will one day eat.
Shelter the homeless,
help the poor,
the destitute,
the insecure.
Preach with your hands,
wear out your shoes!
Words alone are not Good News."

Perhaps it is the time again
for women of wisdom
to counsel men;
waging wars,
stating facts
are not the ways
a woman acts.
In giving life,
in meeting needs,
a woman feels,
a woman feeds.
Once in the womb,
once in the crèche,
then again and again,
the Word takes flesh.

180

At this point, the congregants gather around the altar. The leader holds up a loaf of bread, gives God thanks, and breaks it, announcing,

> Today, as we eat of diverse breads, we honor our bodies with their various shapes, sizes, textures and colors. Within the body of Christ, may these bodies be healthy, whole and holy.

Holding up the bread for all to see, she pronounces:

> The bread of freedom—
> the freedom for women to be all that God
> created us to be,
> the freedom to be all that God intends for us to be!

The leader takes the basket filled with various breads and passes it to the person next to her, saying: "The Word takes flesh; the bread of freedom."

After each has received, eaten and passed the bread with the same words, the leader puts her hands in prayer-fashion on her heart, looks into the eyes of the person next to her, and bows in deepest respect. Each person bows to the next around the circle.

Next, the leader pours the wine or juice, and lifts the chalice up to thank God, saying,

> As we drink the cup of wine, may we remember that women bleed monthly, or shed their blood when giving birth, bringing forth new life.

Raising the chalice, she intones,

> This chalice, like Mary's womb, symbolizes woman's body as a holy vessel. Let us remember the realities of blood, feast, wedding, and joy as we drink from this cup at the Freedom Table!

Then each participant passes the cup of blessing around the circle, repeating: "The blood of new life—the cup of sweet joy," and takes a sip.

In closing, the leader and members read the following benediction out loud, a poem by Methodist minister and author, Jan Richardson.

And on the night in which Mary delivered,
Mary placed her hands over her round, full womb
    and whispered,
        "Flesh of my flesh,
        this is my body,
        which I willingly opened to you.
        May you always remember
        to feed on the bread of freedom."

    In the same manner, she whispered,
        "Child,
        you share my blood;
        freely shall I shed it
        in bringing you to birth.
        May you always remember
        to drink deeply from the cup of joy."

O Mary, we remember these your gifts.
O Jesus, we remember these your gifts,
and we join our hearts to yours in rejoicing,
    Glory to the God of generations!
    For heaven and earth have met
        in the womb of a woman.
    Heaven and earth still meet
        within our hearts here.
Peace to all people
    who bring forth the Christ.

The ritual ends with passing the Kiss of Peace as members rejoice in their honored and holy selves.

With my daughter's permission, I will close this chapter with a true story that attests to the healing and transforming power of the communion ritual.

Kaitlyn, age eight, was having a terrible time. Our family had been struggling with her father's bi-polar disorder, the manic phase of which was raging out of control. He had recently returned home from being hospitalized, only to be re-admitted. Kait, who adored him, was devastated by the news.

Kait was also having trouble going to her new school. Not only did she dislike her second grade teacher who ran the class like a drill sergeant, but each morning when we arrived, she'd hug me good-by and then refuse to leave my arms, fearing she might lose me as well as her dad. As her counselor tried to pull her away from me and into the school building, she'd scream and scream as she desperately clung to me. My heart would bleed for her.

This tug-of-war continued for weeks.

One morning as I got ready to drive Kaitlyn to school, she ran out the door of our apartment building, yelling that she refused to go. Since we lived on the third floor surrounded by balconies, whatever way I moved to catch her, she would run the other way. I ordered her to get into the car, but she refused.

Desperate and exhausted, I made a heart-wrenching decision. I lied to her, telling her that if she came to me, she wouldn't have to go to school that day.

Kaitlyn ran into my arms, relieved and smiling. Then with a firm grip on her, I stifled a sob as I told her she still had to go to school. She was furious, understandably so. She felt I had betrayed her. And I had.

On the way to school, I told Kaitlyn that I knew how scary and hard the past months had been for her, for all of us. But I also stated that our family had strong love for each other and we would survive somehow. I suggested that we get some counseling to help us through this hard time. She agreed.

That night after I had fixed dinner, done the dishes and made a small fire in the fireplace, I plopped down, exhausted, on the couch to read the paper. Kaitlyn came over to me, insisting that I stop reading and go sit down on the floor in front of the fire. Puzzled, I obeyed.

I waited, barely breathing, until she emerged from our tiny kitchen, carrying a little candle which she placed on the floor before me. Then she disappeared into the kitchen again, returning with a slice of bread on a plate and a small glass of wine.

Sitting down cross-legged in front of me, Kaitlyn took the bread, broke it, and gave it to me, saying, "This is my body. Eat this."

I watched, stunned, as she took the glass of wine and said, "Here's the cup of blessing, Mommy, for you."

Tears in my eyes, I took a sip, barely able to swallow for the tightness in my throat. Then I held up the cup for Kaitlyn to drink.

Our healing had begun. Thank you, O God, for your holy meal offered to me by your precious child and mine.

A Renaissance of Ritual

SoulQuesters, I hope you are now excited about the possibilities of ritual-making. Please contribute your talents and imagination to the desperately needed renaissance of ritual in our time. I invite you— even dare you—to invent and perform new rituals to mark the crucial times in your lives, whether they be marriage or divorce, a change in health, a new job or a new baby. Design rituals that help your loved ones go through transitions with meaning and purpose, preparing some liminal space here, joining in some *communitas* there.

Don't worry about making the ritual elaborate or even correct. Use what you have on hand that has meaning to your family or your spiritual circle of friends. Choose a few sacred stories to read or act out, or just speak right from your heart. Incorporate two or three objects made special by the love you all share. Play with the symbols and with each other. Invite the Spirit to inspire you and allow the ritual to transform you.

Brothers, sisters, friends—whether in mourning or in celebration, I eagerly await the day when we shall meet somewhere in a grassy meadow, create a ritual to transform us, then dance together to greet the dawn.

TWELVE

_____

Spelunking in Our Soul Caves:

Reaping the Treasures of Darkness

I will give you the treasures of darkness,
riches stored in secret places,
so that you may know that I am the LORD,
the God of Israel,
who summons you by name.   —*Isaiah 45:3*

Darkness

Fearing the dark

Were you afraid of the dark when you were little? I was. Because we moved to a new city every three years of my childhood, I often performed a ritual before going to sleep. I looked under my bed, checked out the closet, shut the door tight, turned on the night-light and propped stuffed animals around me for protection. You can imagine how thrilled I was whenever I got to share a room with one of my younger sisters.

When my own daughters were little, we had a bedtime ritual. You know the prayer. It starts out sounding comforting but ends up pretty scary.

> Now I lay me down to sleep.
> I pray the Lord my soul to keep.
> If I should *die* before I wake,
> I pray the Lord my soul to take.

Why should a little child in her cozy little bed even think about dying in her sleep? So I rewrote the prayer to say with my girls.

> Now I lay me down to sleep.
> I pray the Lord my soul to keep.
> Angels guard me through the night,
> and wake me with the morning light.

Fearing God in the dark

I suspect that many of us, though all grown up, still fear the dark. The Christian scriptures don't help much; sometimes, they even fuel our fear. The *Gospel of John* 1:1-5, for example, pits the God of light against the forces of darkness:

> In the beginning was the Word, and the Word was with God, and the Word was God.... What has come into being in him was life, and the life was the light of all people. The light shines in the darkness, and the darkness has not overcome it.

In addition, the *Letter of First John* 1:5 clearly states, "This is the message we have heard from [Jesus] and proclaim to you, that God is light and in him there is no darkness at all."

Several Hebrew prophets before John, like Amos, predicted that if God does exist in darkness, it will be at the end of the world, the *eschaton.* Pretty scary.

> Woe to you who long for the day of the Lord! Why do you long for the day of the Lord? That day will be darkness, not light.... Will not the day of the Lord be darkness, not light— pitch-dark, without a ray of brightness? (5:18, 20)

Light

People of the light

No wonder we Westerners continually seek more light, more noise, more images. We pride ourselves on being a people of the light, especially since the En-**light**-enment. The Enlightenment has made us citizens of the light. We practically worship it, constantly seeking left-brain, light-oriented satisfaction. So argues Matthew Fox, a former Dominican priest, now Episcopalian, who founded the "Creation Centered Spirituality Movement." And I agree. See his book, *Original Blessing: A Primer in Creation Spirituality,* for further thought-provoking insights on this topic.

Technology and light

The invention of the light bulb and neon lights brought non-stop, 24/7 light into our lives, enabling our eyes to engage the world long after the sun has set. The invention of the radio extending our hearing from shouting across our back yard fences to listening to events around the globe. The invention of television brought exciting foreign images and sounds right into our 1950s living rooms.

Cell phones are omni-present now, too.

Years ago, my family camped out in my great aunt Helen's summer home in northern Wisconsin. I had cautioned my daughter Kaitlyn, then three, that there wouldn't be any color TV to watch. I didn't even know if my aunt's old TV worked at all. Looking up at me with innocent eyes, Kaitlyn asked, "Mommy, will the TV be so old that it will be in black and blue?"

The old world of black and white movies is gone. Our new world offers huge TV screens, lightning fast computers and the World Wide Web, constantly barraging our senses with images, sounds and light, light, light.

God in the Light

Our spirituality too, in the West, has become very light-oriented, especially in so-called New Age communities. Folks are likely to bless each other with, "May the Christ-light protect you" or "May you be filled with love and light." Many people equate light with God. Of course, there's truth to this claim. Teachers from many spiritual traditions have shared their experiences of the Divine as a bright white, even blinding, light. Perhaps some of you have experienced some kind of light in your meditations. Surely God is present in the light.

Experiencing God in the sunshine days

Questers, I'm sure you'd agree with me, if you believe in a God, that God is easily discernible in the good times, in our sunshine days. It's easy to feel God's presence in times of joy.

For example, twenty-five years ago, I was debating whether or not to marry John. We had been dating for almost a year, and I had been wondering where our relationship was headed.

One bright May morning as John and I sat side by side in our local church, Jesus suddenly appeared on the raised platform, his arms outstretched toward us. In my heart, I heard him say that he had work for John and me to do.

Silently, I questioned Jesus, "I hear you. But the real question is: 'Do you want us to do that work as individuals or as a married couple?'"

I waited, listening and watching intently.

Jesus beamed at me and John, and then widened his arms to include us both. Joy started to bubble up within me. Jesus wanted us to work for him *as a couple.* I was thrilled!

On the ride home, I was silent, too shy to say anything to John about my vision.

Later while fixing dinner together, John revealed that during the worship service, he had had a strange sense that Jesus was encouraging us to get married. I gushed out my own revelation. Delighted at this holy coincidence, John swept me into his muscular, sun-tanned arms.

"Should we, Pam? Should we get hitched? Do you want to marry me?"

"Yes, yes!" I cried.

As we waltzed around the room, twirling and hugging each other, our eyes sparkled with tears of joy. For a second, I even sensed Jesus dancing with us, just like he did at that joyous wedding so long ago in Cana in the Galilee.

Several years later, John and I and our new baby girl, Chelsea, were living in the Greystone Mansion on Crystal Lake. One lovely summer day, I sat quietly on our little dock, gazing around the lake. I was startled to see Jesus walking towards me on the water! He was having a ball and seemed a bit chagrined when I spotted his antics. Skimming effortlessly over the water, he stepped onto the dock and sat down next to me. I was so content with my life, my dear husband and precious daughter, that I realized I had absolutely nothing to ask of him. So we sat together, both of us contented and grateful for the sheer goodness of life. After a while, Jesus stood up and headed off, skipping across the lake.

I'll share one more incident with this light-filled Jesus.

Just last year, I was intrigued by the question of what color Jesus' eyes had been. A friend had told me that a Cayce reading had described the Master's eyes as blue or light gray. I, however, reasoned that because Jesus was a Jew, his eyes must have been dark brown.

One day in meditation as I pondered this question, Jesus appeared before me. As though reading my mind, he flashed his "baby blues" at me. "Aha!" I smiled at him, believing he had settled the matter.

Then he switched his eye color to brown.

"Cool," I exclaimed, marveling at his cleverness.

"Of course, I could have one of each!" he teased, as he flashed me one blue and one brown eye

I burst out laughing; Jesus did, too. Then he disappeared.

In my journal, I noted, "I love your fun spirit, Jesus. Show me more. I delight in you!" De-*light*, truly. Light of lights.

Because scripture insists that we Jews and Christians seek the God of light, and because many of us have had such "light" experiences, when the moments of darkness come—and come they will—we flee them. Or we fight them. We grit our teeth, muttering, "I don't want darkness and anguish. I want light and power. I want enlightenment!" We rant and rave and howl at the darkness: "Be gone! Bring me back into the light of God!" We would do anything rather than embrace our despair or loneliness, wouldn't we? We adamantly refuse to enter the light-less cave of our trembling soul.

Finding God in the Darkness

But what price have we paid to be a people who exclusively seek the light and ignore the dark? The November 2008 issue of *National Geographic* featured an article entitled *"The End of Night: Why We Need Darkness."* It argued that, since the beginning of time, human beings and other creatures have needed their world to be dark for at least eight hours a day in order to lead healthy and emotionally balanced lives. Today, however, humanity as a species is becoming increasingly endangered by "light pollution."

Friends, what if we *need* the darkness? What if daylight exists, not to overcome or destroy the darkness, as the Gospel of John claims but to *balance* it? Think of another scriptural passage in the *Genesis* creation story (1:1-5).

> In the beginning when God created the heavens and the earth, the earth was a formless void and darkness covered the face of the deep...then God said, "Let there be light"; and there was light. And God saw that the light was good; and God separated the light from the darkness. God called the light Day, and the darkness he called Night. And there was evening and there was morning, the first day.

True, the Bible doesn't state that God said, "The darkness was good," but God didn't banish the darkness when He created light. God didn't say, "Let there be light 24-7, 365 days a year." No. He left darkness as a large portion of the twenty four hours, for darkness was the place first of chaos and then of creative potential. God ensured that the earth was left with enough darkness for mysterious, magical creation to occur.

Throughout the Hebrew Scriptures, God is sometimes present in the darkness itself. Yahweh led the Hebrews, newly escaped from their bondage to the Pharaoh in Egypt, with a cloud of smoke by day and a pillar fire by night (*Exodus* 40:38). God often spoke from a thick darkness, as in *Deuteronomy* 5:22.

The Sabbath, the holiest day of the week for Jews, is directly connected to the night. *Shabbat* or Sabbath begins at sundown, while the Christian Lord's Day or *Sun*day begins in the morning and symbolically is linked with the sun. Perhaps God's commandment to "Honor the Sabbath and keep it holy" is a weekly reminder to Jews of their origins as a people—*Adonai* leading them from the darkness of slavery to the light of freedom. I love the Torah's requirement that the Sabbath end on Saturday evening at precisely the time when three stars become visible in the deepening violet sky.

The Christian tradition does recognize, though briefly, God's presence in the dark. The New Testament proclaims that darkness covered the earth at the moment of Jesus' death. "From noon on, darkness came over the whole land until three in the afternoon." (*Matthew* 27:45) Preachers often interpret this darkness as the *absence* of God, but I wonder. Might God's presence, at least sometimes, be veiled in darkness so that we are not blinded by its brilliance, or overcome by its power? Perhaps in that agonizing black hole of grief over the crucifixion of Jesus, God was indeed present.

The mystical tradition in Christianity also provides ways to befriend our darkness. For instance, the Spanish mystic, St. John of the Cross, (1542 to 1591 C.E.), coined the phrase "dark night of the soul" to describe a phase in a person's spiritual life which is dominated by feelings of severe loneliness, desolation, and disorientation, even abandonment by God. The use of "night" in the term "dark night" is ironic, since the phase usually lasts much longer than one night, often for weeks, months or even years. The believer's prayer life dries up; her hope shrinks. She may even lose her faith in God altogether. However, if she perseveres through the dark night of the soul and emerges on the other side, she may find her faith even stronger than before. My family has adopted the German philosopher Nietzsche's words to help us get through our hard times, our dark nights: "Whatever doesn't kill you makes you stronger."

Embracing the Darkness

If the Divine can be found in darkness as well as light, then wouldn't it be a good idea to learn to embrace darkness rather than fear it, my sweet companions? After all, we are not really strangers to darkness. *Our lives are already intimately connected with it.*

First, acts of sexual intimacy often occur in the dark. Conception itself takes place in the womb's blackness. Our first nine months are spent, secure and comfortable, with all our needs met, in that small, dark place. Twice in my life I have had the honor and joy of being pregnant. What an incomprehensible and awesome mystery—this little child being formed inside of my womb—all without my conscious effort. Pregnancy is a wonderful reminder of the power of darkness to bring forth new life.

Similarly, the darkness of the earth during the long, cold winter months holds the tiny seeds, allowing them to germinate. While trees and plants may appear to be dead, we know in our bones that in the spring, suddenly out of nowhere, colorful new life will miraculously spring forth. Maybe that's where the season got its name—Spring!

There are miracles of the dark we can gratefully acknowledge. We can contemplate how our internal organs work ceaselessly in total darkness. Our heart pumps like mad, our liver cleanses the blood, and on and on.

Here's another good example. Think about a time when you were lying in the dark next to someone you love. Isn't that kind of intimacy impossible in the bright light of day? I've found that to be true. In the daylight, my husband's body and mine seemed to house two separate, individual entities. But in the dark, snuggled in bed, everything seemed to melt together: the two of us, the bed, the twilight-filled room and the hushed night sky, blended into one sacred body/soul.

Anyone who lives or works in the desert will tell you that after a hard day's work, it's a relief to get out of the glaring sun which can be scorching, even deadly. One would welcome the cool blackness at the end of such a relentlessly light-filled day.

Finally, scientists report that light does not penetrate the whole cosmos; much of outer space is dark. The universe constantly creates new stars out of that very void. Matthew Fox reminds us that all mystery is about the dark and all darkness contains some element of mystery.

Thanks be to the Great Mystery, the Creator of all light *and* dark.

Spelunking in Our Soul Caves

"O.K., I'm following you so far," you respond. "You've convinced me that dark has value, that it's even a big part of my bright and busy life. But what's the big deal for a *Quester*?"

Well, I ask you…have you checked on the size of your soul lately?

Meister Eckhart, a medieval German mystic, suggested that as we humans strive for more and more light, our very souls start to shrivel up. A spirituality that is only light-oriented can very easily become superficial, since it lacks the deep dark roots that "nourish and surprise and ground the large tree" of our spiritual self. Eckhart believed that a human's growth process takes place "in the dark." The very place God works with us is in the "subterranean passages" of our lives. I call them "soul caves."

What gifts may come from our groping in these subterranean passages of our lives, our dark soul caves? Will we find only emptiness and barrenness, isolation and abandonment within them, within us?

Spelunking, the practice of cave-exploring, requires great courage.

I was surprised recently when I stumbled over this passage in the Old Testament. In the seventh century B.C.E., God promised King Cyrus of Persia, a non-Jew at that, through the prophet Isaiah, *"I will give you the treasures of darkness and the riches stored in my secret places."*

Millennia after that promise was given, I believe that promise holds true for us today, Jew and Gentile. But it's up to us to spend some time exploring our dark caves or we won't find those treasures. We'll just bang up our knees, rub up against scary creatures, or bump blindly into blank walls again and again, emerging with nothing but bloodied foreheads. There will be times like that, dear ones.

But we *will* find riches.

Mother Teresa, a Catholic nun called by Jesus to serve the poorest of the poor in Calcutta, India, started the Catholic order, The Sisters of Charity, in 1950. Awarded the Nobel Peace prize in 1979 for her outstanding humanitarian work, by the time of her death in 1997, Orders existed in 130 countries with more than 4000 sisters, who treat over 7000 children and care for four million sick people a year.

Mother Teresa inspired me with her deep relationship to God, inviting me to a similar relationship. I read every book I could get on her life, starting with *Something Beautiful for God*, and used a videotape of her life to inspire my Yale students.

So you can imagine my shock when her "dark" secret was exposed in 2007 in *Mother Teresa: Come Be My Light: The Private Writings of the Saint of Calcutta*. The book, a collection of her letters published after her death *against* her wishes, revealed the shocking truth. We all knew that between September, 1946 and October, 1947, Mother had visions of Jesus instructing her to found the Sisters of Charity. What we didn't know is that Jesus' visits stopped shortly thereafter, causing Mother to sink into deep despair.

"My smile is a great cloak that hides a multitude of pains," she wrote in 1958. "[People] think that my faith, my hope and my love are overflowing, and that my intimacy with God and union with Him fill my heart. If only they knew [the truth]."

Another time, she wrote:

> The damned of hell suffer eternal punishment because they experiment with the loss of God. In my own soul, I feel the terrible pain of this loss. I feel that God does not want me, that God is not God, and that God does not exist.

"God does not exist."

Could this be Mother Teresa speaking, God's beloved servant and disciple?

At one point, she expressed her dilemma to Archbishop Perier of Calcutta this way:

> There is so much contradiction in my soul.—Such deep longing for God—so deep that it is painful—a suffering continual—and yet not wanted by God—repulsed—empty—no faith—no love—no zeal.—Souls hold no attraction—Heaven means nothing—to me it looks like an empty place—the thought of it means nothing to me and yet [I have] this torturing longing for God....

What a terrible struggle Mother Teresa endured through the dark "night"—no, "lifetime"—of her soul. Only her closest advisors were aware of her desperate plight.

Though Mother Teresa died in 1987, she has not abandoned those of us who are hiding in caves or sinking in blackest despair. In one letter to her confidante, she vowed:

> "If I ever become a saint, I will surely be one of darkness. I will continually be absent from Heaven to light the light of those in darkness on earth."

What a beacon you are, Mother Teresa. Bless you, O Saint of Darkness.

Treasures I've found in the darkness

Over the years, I have unearthed "riches from the secret places." It has not been easy. For instance, twenty five years ago, Amy (not her real name), a single mom and dear friend of mine, learned she had breast cancer. For months, she bravely followed a holistic route to healing, but by the time her cancer had metastasized and she turned to traditional methods to save her life, she was beyond cure.

For weeks, I visited Amy and prayed with her. During one visit, she lamented that her greatest sadness was that when she died, her little son would be taken by the courts. I reassured her that somehow God would provide for him. (And God did. After Amy's death, the boy's dad re-appeared and took him back into his life.)

More weeks passed. Amy wasted away. My heart ached for her.

In the midst of my anguish facing her impending death, I found myself sitting in twilight on the dock at Crystal Lake, tears sliding down my cheeks. Underneath my sadness, I was mad as hell at a God who would allow a young single mom to die at all, let alone so painfully.

Suddenly, in the gathering gloom, I felt someone slide his hand into mine. It was Jesus.

"Oh," I gasped. "You're here!"

"Yes," he answered, squeezing my hand.

Then I pouted, "But what about Amy? Why have you abandoned her?"

Soft as the night breeze came his response, "I am holding her hand in my *other* hand."

"O *me* of little faith," I paraphrased to myself, finally letting Amy go into God's awaiting arms.

Yes, God *is* present in our darkness.

My sister, Greta, only in her twenties, had been hospitalized for months as she struggled to overcome her life-threatening colon illness. At one point, she had lost practically half of her blood supply, so the doctors weren't allowed to increase her medication to stop her excruciating pain.

One night, lying alone in her sterile hospital bed, she was surprised to hear herself humming a little tune by the popular children's musician, Raffi. She found herself embracing her illness and pain, even her possible death, as she sang softly to the dark divine presence encompassing her,

"Thanks a lot. Thanks a lot. Thanks for all I've got."

Remember the story of W.B. and me? On a cold and rainy winter's night, I went to a theater alone to see his completed movie. Afterwards, coming home to my dark and empty apartment, I burst into tears and slumped down onto the living room floor. A few short months ago, I had been intimate with a movie star, for God's sake, but now I didn't even have one guy friend to *take* me to the movies.

"What a loser I am," I cried, in my best self-pitying, Oscar-winning, voice.

At that very moment, the phone rang. It was Greta, calling me on one of her intuitive hunches.

Between sobs, I poured out my heart-sick story. Then I apologized for being so self-centered on my miserable love life while she had been fighting for her very life.

"No, Pam," she said, cutting me short. "I've been calling you for months for get your support and now it's my turn to support you."

As I calmed down, it occurred to me that we should light a candle for each other. I'd light a candle for her body to heal completely. I had faith in that prayer for her. I asked her to light a candle for me to find a wonderful mate some day soon. She had faith in that prayer for me. In the inky blackness lit only by a lone street lamp through the window, we lit a candle for each other. Then we prayed together and hung up. That night I received the gift in the old saying, *"It's better to light one little candle than to curse the darkness."* Cursing the darkness, I had grappled with loneliness and despair in my black soul cave and in its place, I ignited a flickering golden flame—hope.

Seekers, whenever we muster the courage to go soul spelunking—
to enter the dark caves of our lives and embrace the darkness;
whenever we struggle to find the riches in its secret places—we will
find presents and holy Presence galore. That's the promise.

Spelunking in our soul caves isn't the only way to find treasures in
the darkness. There is another way.

Surrendering to the Darkness

A man is climbing a really high cliff by himself. Night is
rapidly approaching. Almost to the top, suddenly his foothold
breaks loose. Dangling by his fingernails in the now pitch
black, he calls out in desperation, "Is anybody there?"

A deep, kind voice beckons to him, "I am here, my son. Let go
and I will catch you."

The man looks around, and then whispers timidly, "Is anybody
else there?"

In *Deuteronomy* 33:27, Moses declares that "the eternal God is
your refuge, and underneath are the everlasting arms." Three
millennia later, in the 1970s, the popular version of that was: "Let go
and let God."

Oh, yeah? Let go and fall off a cliff to the jagged rocks below?
Easier said than done.

I can almost chuckle at how much this cliff-hanger and I are alike:
in our hard times, the last thing we want to do is to let go, to fall into
the invisible arms of an unseen God who just might be absent and not
there to catch us.

It's all about trust, isn't it?

Paradoxically, the exact opposite approach to struggling with the
darkness to obtain its riches is to *surrender* to the darkness, to let go—
totally. No struggle. No clenching or grasping. Open your hands.
Open.

Rainer Maria Rilke (1875-1926), one of Germany's finest poets,
was visited by many kinds of darkness: the deaths of young siblings,
the divorce of his parents, ill health and broken relationships.
Ultimately, it seems he was able to move from resisting suffering to
accepting it, as this poem attests.

You nights of anguish.
Why didn't I kneel more deeply to accept you, inconsolable
  sisters,
and, surrendering, lose myself in your loosened hair?
How we squander our hours of pain.
How we gaze beyond them into the bitter duration to see if they
have an end.
Though they are really seasons of us, our winter.

Here are some ways I've used that might help you to surrender with
dignity in our quest for the Dark Divine and its riches.

1. Surrender your mind.

One practice is to surrender your mind, that is, to purposefully turn
off the power to your inner computer screen. We can clearly benefit
from debugging our consciousness, clearing out viruses, then shutting
down and re-booting our psyches. What might happen if we release
our images and allow our minds to be totally blank—dark, silent—so
that God can fill us with something new and helpful and not of our
own making?

Emptying or stilling the mind is pretty hard to do. In fact, I'm a pro
at resisting this process. My mind might actually be a sort of TV
because during meditation, it produces myriad images, storylines and
sound bites, *ad nauseum*. During the early decades of my practice,
even now I admit, as soon as I turn one channel off in my mind,
another program comes on. This can get pretty discouraging.

But I keep trying.

In my early thirties, I was speeding through my life, afraid to slow
down lest I confront my confusion about my current relationships and
career choices. Because speeding seemed to be getting me nowhere
fast (ha), I finally decided to surrender my thought-filled, anxiety-
ridden ego to God. (Ken "Bear Hawk" Cohen says that E.G.O. stands
for "Edging God Out." I love that.)

Sitting in meditation position, I grudgingly admitted: "OK, God, I
know it's your show. I'll stop trying to run it. I'll just sit here and go
blank."

As my inner darkness increased, I anxiously added, "Please fill me
with something that is going to help me."

I still wanted to be filled, not emptied.

After months of an often frustrating practice of surrendering to the darkness in my mind, do you know what eventually arose? The message that God—the majestic, magnificent Creator of heaven and earth—wanted me when I prayed to nickname him "Pokey."

Now at the time I could barely call God "Abba" or "Daddy," let alone use the more formal term, "Father." So addressing God as "Pokey" seemed outrageous, too intimate, too nervy. But, dutiful daughter that I was, slowly and shyly, I began to pray to God as Pokey. Within a few weeks, I came to understand that God had given me that name to counteract the way I was speeding through my life. I could just imagine him saying:

> Trust me, Pam. Trust me to do the moving *in my time*. And if it seems to you that I'm a slowpoke, that's OK. Because no matter how much you speed and try to control life, I am the one who's ultimately in control, not you. The sooner you realize this, the more relaxed and happier you'll be.

For several years, praying to Pokey every day did calm my heart and mind, and slowed down my hectic pace. It was lovely while it lasted. Then, with a new husband and two little daughters, pastoring a church and teaching college, I eventually sped up again, and became Super Woman.

For years now, my best friend Kristy has prayed for me in my dark times, addressing God confidently as "Father." I always felt a bit envious because I still was uncomfortable praying to God as "Father." Like many kids growing up, I confused my father with Father God. While my dad could be loving, teasing, and even brilliant, he could also be punishing, verbally cruel, and emotionally unpredictable. So I never felt safe praying to "Father" God.

Recently, I began to wonder if there was another image of the masculine side of the Divine that I could come to know and love.

So, a few months ago, I tried an experiment. I worked hard on clearing my psychic screen of the familiar male God images: king, judge, father, son, shepherd. I surrendered to the nothingness again, the blank screen. I was nervous. What if nothing happened?

For days, nothing arose.

Then finally, quietly, a name emerged—"Your Grace." I loved it! Most likely because I'm intrigued by the Middle Ages. I imagine "Your Grace" to be a royal king garbed in a purple robe and golden crown. He is infinitely courteous and kind, always respectful to his wife and daughters as well as subjects. He never judges. He only shows compassion and patience when someone makes a mistake. He walks among the people of his kingdom, encouraging peace and harmony. Yet he is also strong and protective. Now, whenever I pray to the masculine side of God, "Your Grace" has become my safe but powerful male image.

I encourage you to experiment with emptying your mind of any pre-conceived images of God, as comforting or scary as they may be. Surrender your mind and let the Holy One surprise you with a new image.

2. Surrender your rage.

Here's a shining jewel I gleaned from one of the darkest times of my life.

While training as chaplain in a New York City hospital, (the same summer I met James Taylor there), I had chosen to work on the unit with terminally ill children. Because I had always loved children, I imagined that I would go into their rooms, cheer them up with my musical theater background, and offer them some joy for their pain-filled days.

After working in the hospital for less than a month, I found myself slipping down into the abyss of the "dark night of the soul." I was losing my grip on the happiness cliff. I was depressed, weepy, sullen. I couldn't bear to witness the children's suffering anymore. I hated listening to their screams while I held them down and the nurses stuck them with needles or pumped them up with medications that burned their tender skin. And God knows I certainly wasn't entertaining them with my so-called cheerful children's songs any more.

However, to my credit (and amazement), I did keep showing up.

And though I tried to cherish every child equally, I admit I had a few favorites on the ward. I befriended a little girl named Tara, a name I had imagined I might give a daughter of mine one day. Tara had already lost one leg to cancer, but she never complained. We loved singing Broadway musicals together, especially *Annie*. We hammed it up gloriously.

One morning as I began my rounds, I eagerly poked my head into Tara's room to see her. Surprised, I saw that her bed was stripped of its sheets. Confused, I found a nurse and asked her where Tara was. Shaking her head, she informed me that Tara had died in the night.

Tara's death pushed me over the edge. Even with my belief that God was all-loving and no soul was ever lost to God, I couldn't bear another one of those sweet young children dying so cruelly.

Back in my dorm room on a sweltering July night, I threw myself on my bed, so furious with God that I yelled right out loud: "It's not fair! It's not fair!"

Sobbing in the pillow over my helplessness to save the children, the words of the Welsh poet, Dylan Thomas, sprang to mind: "Rage, rage against the dying of the light."

And rage I did.

"No more dying! No more! Please, God!"

I don't know how long I screamed and cried.

Finally, sapped of all desire or strength to fight God's inscrutable ways, I gave up. I gave in.

I surrendered.

"OK, God," I thought. "You win. I don't get it. I don't like it. But I give up."

Total silence descended upon me like a soft blanket. Without effort, my heart opened like a lotus to *embrace the darkness*.

Then a kind, gentle voice whispered to me: "My dear Pam, don't you see? You're *all* terminal. It's just that some of you know it and others don't."

Me, terminal?

I was stunned.

After some moments, I realized that the voice spoke the truth. Even though I was healthy and young and felt as if I would live forever, I was going to die someday. I could be hit by a truck tomorrow, but I wasn't mourning the loss of my life today. Yet here I was, mourning these children *before* they were dead.

I found my treasure in the darkness: these dying children were *living* children.

From that day on, I was able to do my ministry with them, singing and laughing with them, teasing them, and hugging and tickling them to death—I mean, life.

3. Surrender your life plans.

"Life is what happens
when you're planning something else."
–John Lennon, one of the *Beatles*

Have you seen the movie where the treasure hunter, Indiana Jones, is being chased through the thick jungle by angry natives who intend to kill him? His only escape is to leap from a high cliff over a deep chasm to an impossibly distant cliff on the other side. The trouble is— there's no bridge. In fact, he's been informed that the only way the bridge will appear is *when* he leaps.

What a great image for us *SoulQuesters*. When your bridge has burned behind you and you're looking into the void ahead, jump! Only then will the magical rope bridge appear.   Sounds impossible, irrational, but it will appear.

Although not always in the shape or form we desire.

As a girl, I discovered the work of the cultural anthropologist, Margaret Mead (1901 to 1978). Mead researched the sexual behaviors of the Samoan tribe who lived on a tiny island in the South Pacific seas, and then shared her enticing fieldwork findings with the American public. I was smitten. I wanted to be just like her when I grew up.

As I matured (I use that word loosely), I was content with my career choice to become a minister and professor rather than anthropologist.. I treasured my life with my husband and two beautiful daughters, the last one being born when I was 41 years old. Still, my daydreams about becoming an anthropologist persisted. Sometimes, I'd find myself fantasizing about living in some exotic land, studying tribes who performed bizarre yet captivating rituals. But I knew that's what it was—a fantasy.

Then, at the ripe old age of 46, I decided I might be able to go for one last dream—to get my doctorate and teach in a university. I was thrilled when I was accepted by a doctoral department in a Chicago school. Its program required me to do one year of theological studies and one year in a cognate discipline. Since I cared passionately about women's well-being in America, I applied to the excellent Women's Studies Department at Northwestern University.

I thought I had everything set up with my primary institution. However, late in August, just weeks before the semester started, my registrar called to inform me that my financial aid package would not apply to Northwestern. I couldn't believe it. Dazed, I asked her which school I was permitted to enroll in. She replied in her most official voice: "The only school we will pay for is our sister school, the University of Chicago."

U. of C.? Of course, I knew *their* reputation—an Ivy League school, one of the best in the country. The problem was that both my father and my aunt had graduated from there in the 1940s. And I had already followed in my father's footsteps by becoming a sixth generation minister in our family. No way was I going to go to his graduate school, too.

But what choice did I have? My financial aid would apply to the University of Chicago and nowhere else. I felt trapped, bushwhacked by God.

I hung up and quickly called the University of Chicago's switchboard to find out what their *Women's Studies Department* offered. I shook my head in disbelief when they answered. There was none. *Rien, nada.*

Anger boiled up in me. I had followed God's guidance every step of the way: moving from Virginia Beach to Chicago, buying our new home, getting our girls in good schools, and reconnecting with our relatives. I had been faithful to the charge Mom had given me in my ordination service in 1982, working to empower women and serve the Christian community. And now no *Women's Studies Department*? What was I to do? Obviously, God was the promise-breaker here. He, and I meant HE, was having a good laugh at my expense.

After a week of ranting and raving at God, (behavior I'm not proud of since I often preached about a God who does keep his promises), I ordered several course catalogs from the University in psychology, sociology and, "What the heck?" I thought—anthropology.

When the catalogs arrived, I took one look at the cover of the anthropology catalog and gasped.

While I had hoped to study women in the United States, God wanted to give me the women in the *whole world.*

I broke down into tears of repentance and thanksgiving. Then I applied to that department and began my journey toward becoming a happy, middle-aged, Margaret Mead.

Through several more synchronicities, I ended up doing my fieldwork with the Lakota (Sioux) Indians on the Pine Ridge and Rosebud Reservations in South Dakota, fulfilling another of my seemingly outlandish childhood daydreams.

With the Universe, my holy travelers, *nothing is impossible.* And usually it's even better than we could ever concoct.

Here's one last story about what can happen when you surrender your life's path to the God of Life.

Several years ago, I noticed a bump on my lower spine. Though it didn't seem to be growing, it wasn't diminishing, either. I was afraid it was a tumor, so I refused to see a doctor. On the day after Christmas, I asked my visiting sister Greta, an energy healer, to see what she made of that bump. She told me to lie down on the floor on my tummy. Then she tuned into my back and, much to my relief, pronounced it merely a knot of tense muscles. After she massaged it, I asked her if she could go into the altered state she assumed when working to obtain spiritual guidance for her clients in Massachusetts. She agreed.

As Greta sat on the floor beside me, she began to moan and wail. Rocking back and forth, she broke out into howls which sounded to me like Indian war cries. At first I felt anxious, but then I realized these were not cries of Indians on a warpath but cries of victory. I joined in their joyous whooping until I found myself convulsed in sobs of relief. I still don't know why.

Still on my tummy, I struggled to sit up and face Greta. Through my blurry tears, I watched in amazement as Greta's facial features morphed into those of a wise and wizened Indian warrior. For a micro-second, I even glimpsed his two long braids. Then Greta's face became hers again. However, in a voice and cadence much lower than my sister's, the figure identified himself as Sitting Bull, one-time powerful chief of the Lakota people.

Sobered now, eyes in awe, I told Sitting Bull that I was honored that his spirit had come to help me. I shyly asked him for vocational guidance. While my pastoral job was very important to me, it was only part-time and didn't provide enough income. Also, I wanted to help more people. Could he please tell me what to pursue?

Sitting Bull replied, "We of the Rainbow Council are proud to be invited to this "medicine meeting." As a spiritual leader, you are part of the Rainbow Way, too. We are pleased that you are offering yourself as a channel for the healing of global diversity, and creating ways of respect and love between different cultures and religions.

"We support you and your spiritual community from the other side. Do what you know to do from your daily alignment [meditation]. More guidance will come. Take up your power. You are a spiritual warrior!"

"But what about my lack of income?" I moaned. I didn't feel like a spiritual warrior at all.

"The bowl in your lap will sometimes be small [like now]," he answered, "but it will fill again. Let the Council do the "providing" and you do the "aligning," casting visions for your people."

"Thank you, Rainbow Council," I replied, though I was still at a loss.

A few weeks later while sitting in meditation, I addressed the Indian teacher, Sun Bear, who apparently had replaced Sitting Bull as my spirit guide. Sun Bear (1929-1992) had founded the Bear Tribe, written many books on earth-based spirituality and achieved popularity with predominantly white audiences from the 1960s through the '80s.

"Thank you, Sun Bear and honored members of the Rainbow Council," I inwardly bowed, "for coming to me today. Can you please give me further vocational guidance?"

"You are the chief of *Living Waters*. So be the Chief. Act the Chief. Don't apologize. Take your power and wear it, as proud and strong as a buffalo calf robe, yet as gentle as the deer-skin dress you love so much. We are with you. Trust the unfolding of Great Mystery."

"Thank you. I will try."

So I tried again to find a second job that matched my skills and passion. I really did. But I found nothing. Weeks later, my spirits plummeted again, along with my energy. I could barely force myself to get out of bed. What now? I finally called my doctor who confirmed that I was suffering from adrenal exhaustion and serotonin depletion. My systems were broken. Wryly, I noted to myself, "No wonder they call it a nervous *breakdown*."

On top of everything, I was lonely. I had no energy to leave the house, and no one had come to visit me for weeks. To be honest, I hadn't let my friends know how low I really was, or I'm sure they would have rallied around me. But I was too proud, or too ashamed, to admit my neediness.

One month later on a cold night in January, I contacted the Rainbow Council again in meditation.

"I miss you, Elders."

The unwept tears stung my eyes.

"I wish you were right here in the flesh, so I could touch you and hug you and see your sparkling black eyes. But you are in Spirit. Still, I am grateful that you're here."

I paused. "Can you give me a clue as to the next step for me on the Rainbow Way?"

"Finish your book. You dedicated it to *Wakan Tanka*, Great Spirit, remember?"

"Yes, of course I do.

"But shouldn't I do something more, like start a weekly women's group?" I asked, knowing full well that I barely had enough energy to feed my cats.

"I don't know what to do. I'm so alone," I complained.

"You *don't* do everything alone," they responded. (Did I sense some irritation with me?) "There is a plan and you contribute to it. Fear not. Do the war cry! Beat the drum! You are a spiritual warrior, a *chief.* Remember that. The path is unfolding. *Trust.*"

For a few days, I pulled on my bootstraps. It seemed like now was the time to step up the program. But as my bank account dwindled, and my energy bottomed out once more, I broke down in tears.

I recorded the following encounter with Sun Bear in my journal.

"My daughter, it isn't easy being a chief, a way-shower. But you aren't alone. And you are not poor. Trust that all is being made ready. You are healing from a big loss, little sister—many losses. You must keep getting stronger so that we can use you for the work of our Rainbow Council."

"What is the work? Where? Give me the details," I pleaded.

"Finish your book, my child. Our young ones are waiting for it. Then you'll get guidance for the next step. Draw on Mother Bear's energy and wisdom. Retreat a little while longer. Then you will start anew."

Mama Bear. I could relate to her. I had been spending my winter days cuddled in furry blankets on my couch. But still I groaned: "I'm sick and scared. I miss all of you!"

"We are with you. Go to your tipi [temple. I love that!] and pray. Smoke pipe. Carry water. Chop wood. Take up your robe again of leadership, vision and courage to teach the young. Gather the elders, too. You don't have to prove anything to anyone anymore!"

Sun Bear finished: "Do the work you love doing, Pamela Anne. Put out the call to the universe for big bucks and it will deliver, so you can help our people."

I thanked him profusely.

Two long years later, as I finish writing this book to you, I *am* stronger: physically, emotionally and spiritually. I continue to grow in trust as avenues of service and abundance open up for me. I proudly walk the Rainbow Path as Chief of my people at Living Waters Sanctuary.

Sisters of spirit, I hope that every so often you will surrender your plans for life to the plans Life has for you.

4. Surrender your heart.

If, on your quest, you find yourself suffering a strong emotion, such as grief, fear, despair, or loneliness, here's a helpful exercise from Tara Brach's life-giving book, *Radical Acceptance: Embracing Your Life with the Heart of a Buddha.* Gently place your hand on your heart. Think of all the people in the world who are experiencing what you are, and repeat several times, "May my suffering increase my compassion." Send out that compassion to those kindred sufferers. Your emotions will eventually calm down, and you will have transformed your suffering into a blessing for others.

Almost six months before the onset of my "nervous breakdown," (I was truly nervous about breaking down), I suffered another condition: painful, irritating diarrhea. I worried I might have *Irritable Bowel Syndrome.* I could have sought medical help, but I somehow sensed that I was in the midst of a spiritual initiation. God wanted me to pay attention to my pain-wracked body *in a new way.*

"OK," I thought.

"If my current life situation were a dream, I'd interpret my diarrhea as a symbol that I have a lot of crap to get rid of. But what crap?"

The answer arose immediately from deep in my gut: "Dig deeper."

I paused, clearing my inner computer screen again. I waited. Responses to my question streamed forth.

"The sh-t of being verbally abused by my dad;
of being hit with a plastic hairbrush until my little legs almost
bled;

of being five years old when, full of rage, he picked me up, lifted me six feet in the air and then dropped me.

I burn with shame, shame, that I must have deserved such treatment."

Along with all this spewing of pent up rage, the truth that my dad loved me came gushing forth. He loved to tease me. Like the time our family was camping when I was little, and I came running out of the outhouse. He yelled to me, "Pam, did you remember to flush it?" I stopped short, ready to turn back when I caught the joke.

My dad also loved teaching me things. He taught me so much about mysticism and about the spiritual traditions of the world. He was an exceptional choral director and he loved me singing with enthusiasm in my strong alto voice. He inspired me with his lectures and sermons. More than anyone else, Dad made Jesus come alive to me.

Whenever I had a nightmare as a child, Dad was the first there to comfort me, and to analyze my dream until I calmed down. When I was a college student, he spent endless hours with his clipboard or chalk board, outlining the pros and cons of my various life choices.

Though as a counselor, Dad was fearless in helping clients deal with their demons, apparently, he had been afraid to deal with his own, and he died in a coma before we truly reconciled.

But I now knew he loved me. And I realized I loved him, too— very much.

But right now, my childhood memories, buried in my bowels, were threatening to destroy my health. All the crap with him needed to be released.

For the first time in my life, I decided to get a colonic. (For those of you unfamiliar with this health treatment, it's a procedure during which a plastic tube is inserted up one's anus, then a gentle flow of water rinses out the lower colon). I was embarrassed to let a physical therapist insert a tube up my butt, especially when I found out that she was a former church member of mine! But she wasn't flustered at all. She loved giving colonics.

During the procedure, she literally cheered me on with comments like: "Look at that brown stuff, wow! How much is in there! How many years! How deep in the colon! It's coming out; it's coming out!"

"Now *that's* a twist on 'riches stored in secret places,'" I smiled to myself.

Afterwards, I wrote in my journal:

"Hurray! I finally understand. The sh-t had to come out so my bowels could be freed from burying and carrying my childhood feelings of shame, rage and abandonment. I needed to go down to the bowels of my childhood despair to clean them out, so I could heal. Thanks be to God for colonics."

During the ensuing weeks, I visualized sending love to my gut, thanking it for all the crap it had held during my sixty-plus years. Still, I wondered, was I truly healed? Had I been cleansed enough? Slowly but surely, I began to trust this shamanic-like healing process. So far, so good.

One night, I decided to give myself a medicine card reading. The first card gave me the same message I had received a few weeks earlier: "Dig deeper. Go down to the roots of your problem."

"Where are my roots?" I questioned, as I closed my eyes and ferreted around in my dark insides. "What is blocking them from helping me grow strong and healthy?"

A picture of my "family tree" roots sprang to mind: Granny and Granddaddy Albin on my father's side, and Nana and Grandpa Larson on my mother's side.

I drew a second medicine card. It advised me to call on my allies and supporters in the unseen world. I breathed slowly and deeply to calm my mind's chatter and my body's shivering.

In the palpable silence, I waited to see what would emerge. Soon, these words formed and spilled out of my heart.

"Nana and Grandpa Larson, please forgive me for overvaluing the Bro side of my grandparents my whole adult life and neglecting to honor you. Now I realize it was you two who offered me the kind, nurturing, cooking, piano-playing side of my ancestral relations. Dear Nana, even though you may not have been a missionary in China like Granny was, you were a pioneer of sorts, too, going to college and teaching piano as a woman back in the early 1900s.

"Grandpa, you're so precious. I always felt safe with you. You were so much fun when we played card games like cribbage and "Shoot the Moon." I ate my first strawberries and snap peas from the little garden you planted in your backyard. I loved it when you gave me a whisker rub!

"I adore both of you. Please forgive me for not honoring your contributions to my life."

That admission made me feel lighter, brighter, as if I had unearthed some sparkling jewel within my dark spirit.

My initiation process wasn't finished, though. The Biblical passage from the sermon I was writing for Sunday sprang vividly to mind:

"Ask and ye shall receive, seek and ye shall find; knock and the door shall be opened."

The door shall be opened.

Just then, with a loud whoosh and a bang—the outside door of my living room flew wide open.

What the....?

I watched in disbelief as the spirits of my four grandparents floated into the room. They gathered sheepishly before the couch where I sat, keeping a safe distance from me. Why? What would happen now?

All of a sudden, the terrified and angry little girl within me burst forth. I screamed at them: "Nana, Grandpa, Granny, Granddaddy, why didn't you save me from Daddy? You did nothing to rescue me. I was only a little girl, for God's sake!"

I put my head down, sobbing bitterly into my hands.

Slowly, my fury abated. My grandparents said nothing. An image arose unbidden within me. One of my dearest friends was struggling with an awful addiction, suffering greatly with her secret. As much as I loved her and wanted to spare her suffering, I realized I couldn't. She would have to get through this herself. Of course, it's true she was a grown up and I had been a helpless child. Still...

Then I had an "aha!" moment.

I realized we can love someone with all our heart and yet still be unable to save them from suffering. We're only human, I realized, as I looked up at my abashed grandparents, and that includes *me*.

"We're sorry, so sorry," they whispered. I could hear them whimpering. They had suffered, too.

My heart flooded with compassion for them. "It's OK. I get it now. I forgive you!"

With that, they vanished, leaving behind traces of glistening tearlight in my watery eyes.

That night, my wounded inner child made a quantum leap into the chasm, into the waiting arms of a healing God.

Unlike the man hanging from the cliff, hesitant to let go, we can choose to drop into the dark arms of God. W*e will be caught.*

You are sure to recognize this story. My girls know how much I love it.

> One night a woman had a dream. She dreamed she was walking along the beach with Jesus. Across the sky flashed scenes from her life. For each scene, she noticed two sets of footprints on the sand, one belonging to her and the other to Jesus.
>
> When the last scene of her life flashed before her, she looked back at the footprints on the sand. She noticed that at many points throughout her life, there was only one set of footprints. She also noticed that it happened at the very saddest and lowest times of her life. This really bothered her, so she questioned Jesus about it.
>
> "Lord, you said that once I decided to follow you, you would walk with me all the way. But I've noticed that during the most troublesome times of my life, there's only one set of footprints! I don't understand why, when I needed you the most, you would leave me."
>
> Jesus replied, "My daughter, my precious child, I love you and I would never leave you. During those times of trial and suffering, when you see only one set of footprints, that's not where I *left* you. That's where I *carried* you."

Rilke offers us one final, golden, poetic gift.

> You, darkness that I come from,
> I love you more than all the fires that dance in the world.
> For the fires make a circle of light for everyone,
> And then no one outside learns of you.
>
> But the darkness pulls in everything—shapes and fire, animals and myself.
> How easily it gathers them—powers and people.
> And it is possible a great energy is moving near me.

I have faith in nights.

We can have faith in nights, my loves. Whether stumbling about, lost and weary, spelunking in the dark caves of our souls, hanging from sheer cliffs in even sheerer despair; or boldly leaping into the void with a faith we didn't know we possessed, we *will* receive priceless treasures. Test God's promise. When all else fails, cry out,

"Teach me, O Darkness! Catch me, O Divine!"

THIRTEEN

Somewhere Over the Rainbow:

The Lure of Far-off Lands

"Somewhere over the rainbow, way up high,
There's a land that I heard of, once in a lullaby."
–Dorothy in *The Wizard of Oz*

CAUTION: You may need your binoculars for this chapter.

In 1968, hitchhiking with my best friend Maggie through Europe, I met and fell in love with Antonio, a handsome student in Milan, Italy. Several years later, in 1971, I decided to go to graduate school in theater at Schiller College in West Berlin, Germany, so that I could be close to him (we would break up a few months later). West Berlin was the site of Hitler's old headquarters and the now-defunct, but then very forbidding Berlin wall, which at that time separated East Berlin from West Berlin and West Berlin from East Germany. East Berlin guards detained me for hours each time I sought to cross East Germany to visit Tony in Milan.

When I first arrived in West Berlin, I heard a bone-chilling police siren which sounded exactly like those I'd heard in old World War II movies. As the weeks turned into months, I began to realize that I had a lot of fear, and even hatred, of the German people for not stopping the slaughter of millions of Jews during the Holocaust, some of whose descendants were relatives on my aunt's husband's side. However, as I began to make some wonderful German friends, including Hans, my smart, fun-loving boyfriend, and as I learned to speak, and eventually even dream, in German, I found my fear unexpectedly diminishing and my love for Germans increasing.

I still experienced some low-grade anxiety daily, however.

No wonder.

Since my dormitory was located only a block from the Berlin wall, every night I struggled to fall asleep to the sound of machine gun fire coming from the East Berlin side.

At 2 a.m. one night, Phil, a drunken student friend of mine, broke through the security of my building, and pounded on my door, yelling, "*Mach auf! Mach auf!*" (the German phrase for "Open the door!")

Startled from a sound sleep, my heart raced with the most terror I'd ever experienced. Jarred awake and soon realizing it was Phil, I opened the door and gave him hell for scaring me so badly.

Throughout the following days, I was plagued by recurrent panic. I asked myself the questions: why had I experienced such ungodly fear? What had triggered it?

I pictured myself standing on a tall German mountain peak, surveying the 25-year valley of my life. With spiritual binoculars, I scanned the wide sweep of the places I'd lived in my childhood, from Wisconsin to New York to Illinois to Virginia, looking for clues to a time I had experienced similar terror.

A distant memory at the far edge of my early childhood came slowly into focus. I remembered that, as a young girl, I had had recurring dreams of myself as a little boy, about five years old, fleeing from darkly uniformed soldiers, desperately seeking a place to hide. When I awoke, my heart was always pounding wildly. Though my parents consoled me after the few bad dreams I had, I didn't dare tell them about this particular nightmare because I was afraid they'd think me crazy for seeing myself as a little boy. Remember, my dad was a psychologist.

The second incident that sprang to mind occurred years later. As an eighth grader in northern Wisconsin, I adored my best friend, Maggie. One day, her father purchased air conditioning for his new car and offered to give us a ride. We were thrilled. As we drove along the narrow country street, he cranked up the AC fan. I began to experience what I now know was a panic attack. I became so anxious that I had to crack the rear window open because I feared I might die from what I bizarrely identified as "fake air."

That same year, the movie *The Diary of Anne Frank* was released. You are familiar with her tragic but inspiring story, aren't you? She was a normal Jewish teenager living in Amsterdam during World War II. When the Nazis started rounding up and exporting Jews to forced labor camps, death camps, really, her family hid for months in their friends' secret attic. Sadly, the Nazis finally discovered the Frank family and hauled them off to various concentration camps. Anne died in a camp, but her diary of her years in the attic miraculously survived. I'll never forget the line she spoke in the movie that touched me to the core: "In spite of all this [war and suffering], I still believe that people are basically good at heart." Talk about a brave soul.

A few days later, Maggie and I were playing make-believe in her attic. We often invented adventures based on the *Nancy Drew* mystery series. That summer day, we decided to act out Anne's story; I chose to be Anne. Things were going fine as we re-played what we'd seen in the movie. Then a bizarre thing happened.

Looking out the attic window, in my mind's eye, I began to see Nazi soldiers dragging Jews out of their homes. Frantically, I called out the names of my "neighbors" in *German* no less, as they were forced one by one onto the trucks. I began to sob hysterically. Maggie stared at me, open-mouthed at my histrionics. As I sank to the floor, she knelt beside me, put her arms around me and comforted me. Finally, my anguish spent, I emerged from what seemed to be an intense, altered state. Maggie muttered, and I nodded in agreement, that I certainly had an over-active imagination.

In the mid-1970s, I visited a good friend in Virginia Beach, who had just installed a sauna on his farm and was excited for me to try it. I was, too. But—you guessed it. After a few minutes in that extreme heat and stifling air, I panicked. Bursting through the cedar door, I lay gasping for air on the cool tiled floor. He'd never expected *that* reaction to his new sauna.

A year later, during a routine physical exam my second year of grad school in West Berlin, my doctor, Herr Doktor Brandenburg, found a non-malignant tumor the size of a grapefruit between one of my ovaries and my uterus. It had to be removed. Since I'd never been hospitalized before, I was afraid to have the surgery he insisted upon. However, because of his confidence and friendly manner, I soon found myself totally trusting him.

As Herr Doktor checked me into the brand-new hospital a week later, he asked me to sign a release form. The form explained that he would do everything in his power to save my uterus, but he might have to remove it along with the tumor.

"Wait a minute," I ordered. Stepping outside of my room onto the balcony of the ultra-modern hospital, I began to negotiate with this capricious God who had cursed young and healthy me with such an evil condition.

"Listen here, God!" I demanded. "You know that ever since I was a little girl, my only wish was to have a little girl of my own. But if I lose my uterus…."

My mind scanned the options.

"OK, it's true I can adopt." I took a deep breath. "All right. I'm ready to face this possibility."

When I went back inside and signed the form, the doctor handed it right back to me.

"Now please sign on *this* line," Herr Doctor requested, "acknowledging that I've informed you that you are a high-risk patient. Chances are higher than normal that you might die during this procedure."

"Just a minute," I gulped, then stormed back out onto the balcony.

"Listen here, God," I fumed, "this is going too far! Dying is *not* an option. I'm young. I have my whole life ahead of me." Engaging in classic "bargaining" with God, I continued, "If I live, I promise I'll serve you for the rest of my life!"

I went back in and signed the release. Waking up groggy after surgery, I learned that Herr Doktor had not only saved my uterus but had thoughtfully made the incision so low that I could still wear a bikini.

Recuperating in my hospital bed, I spent hours continuing to prayerfully contemplate my life's terrain. Eventually, I was able to put the puzzle pieces together, finally determining the source of the terror I felt that fateful night with Phil.

No wonder I had had childhood nightmares of fleeing angry soldiers.

No wonder I needed to breathe fresh air, not "fake."

No wonder I despised studying the German language in high school, even though I had been inexplicably drawn to do so.

No wonder I had resisted going to graduate school in Germany, even though I was irresistibly drawn there as well.

No wonder I had hated those World War II sirens, and Phil had scared me so much.

I had been a young Jewish boy in Nazi Germany in World War II, who had been killed in the gas chambers of a concentration camp.

God was not a capricious God after all. God had almost magnetically drawn me to West Berlin, and then, step by step, guided me through my physical and emotional healing. Love and trust of the Germans replaced my fear and hate of them. I had willingly gone under the knife of a German surgeon, who ended up saving not only my my uterus but my life. Years later, I would give birth to two beautiful daughters.

"Hold on here!" you might gasp. "Are you implying **you were reincarnated?**"

In the '60s, my guy friends rebuilt a Volkswagen into a beach buggy, dubbing it a "rein-car." My friend, Johnny, quipped, "Hey! If everyone owned a rein-car, we'd be a reincar-nation."

OK. I'll be serious now.

Reincarnation is the concept that a person's soul is continuously reborn into a new body over centuries or even eons, until he or she reaches a stage of enlightenment or union with the Divine. Millions of people around the globe—Hindus, Jainists, Celtic pagans, Buddhists and members of several African religions—believe in some form of reincarnation. It's even becoming more acceptable in the United States as I write.

"Still, there's absolutely no scientific proof of reincarnation," you insist.

True. Although there is a growing body of anecdotal evidence, there is no conclusive, verifiable proof that reincarnation occurs—*as yet*. Scientists still don't know what happens to a person after death—or what creates the miracle of new life, for that matter. Neither can scientists provide hard evidence for such qualities as love, joy, or courage, yet you experience those as real, right?

So I ask you—

Have you ever had a *déjà vu* experience where you walk into a place and feel like you'd been there before? Upon meeting a stranger, have you ever found yourself thinking: "Something about this person seems oddly familiar"?

Or if you think that the concept of living in another body during a previous time in history is ridiculous, humor me when I ask you these questions: "Where is your three-year old body now? Your twelve-year-old body?" Sure, you have photos of yourself at those ages, but your actual three-year-old body no longer exists *anywhere on the planet*. Yet, your memory of yourself at those ages survives in the body you currently have.

So maybe it's not such a huge leap to imagine yourself in another body at another time. We actors do that quite eagerly, right, my actress daughter, Kaitlyn? In fact, playing the role of another human being in another time and place sounds a little like *short-term* reincarnation, doesn't it?

Finally, I'm sure at some time in your life you've wondered why evil exists in the world. Theologians use the fancy term "theodicy."

They argue that since evil definitely exists, God must be either all-powerful but not all-loving, or all-loving but not all-powerful. Not much comfort in either choice, huh?

As a child, when I found myself crying because Dad hit me with a plastic hairbrush on the back of my legs to "punish" me, or when I learned about children my age who were starving in far-off Africa, I began to question God's goodness as well as God's power. No sermon I heard in church could rationalize God's unfairness in allowing a young teen's life to be snuffed out by a random bullet, a baby to be born blind, or some folks to be wealthy while others were doomed to starve to death.

What kind of a bizarre Supreme Being created such a world? I know that my daughters struggled with similar objections about God when they were young, too. Each of you insisted to me that you could have designed a happier and more just world than God had. What was God thinking?

Did no one have a reasonable answer to these riddles of human existence?

When my baby brother was born, my parents told us girls that they wanted to give him the middle name "Cayce" after a man they loved who had died fifteen years earlier. We girls agreed. Three years later, at age 16, I came across a book in my father's study, *There is a River: The Story of Edgar Cayce,* by Tom Sugrue. I grabbed it, and read it, fascinated. Here were all the cosmic answers I'd been searching for.

I begged my parents to fill in the blanks about the "mysterious" Mr. Cayce.

In the early 1940s, my dad's mother, Margueritte Harmon Bro, was asked by the Protestant magazine, *The Christian Century*, to review *There is a River*. So intrigued was she by what she read, she wrote an article for *Coronet* magazine on Mr. Cayce, dubbing him the *"Miracle Man of Virginia Beach."* In 1943, my 23-year-old parents were both students, my dad at the University of Chicago in World Religions and my mom a classical piano student at the Chicago Musical College. They moved from Chicago to Virginia Beach to work with the Cayces for nearly a year. My father witnessed Mr. Cayce give nearly five hundred "readings," which included medical and past life information and counsel. Mom and Dad both received readings explaining how their past life achievements or mistakes could affect their present life

218

choices. The encounter with the Cayces changed my parents' lives forever.

Dad shared more of Cayce's biography with me, which he later wrote up in his scholarly and moving life's work, *A Seer Out of Season: The Story of Edgar Cayce.*

Born in 1877 on a farm near Hopkinsville, Kentucky, Cayce at an early age displayed powers of perception that seemed to go beyond the normal range of the five senses. At the age of six or seven, he told his parents that he was able to see and talk to "visions," sometimes of relatives who had recently died. His parents thought he was just a lonely little boy with an over-active imagination. Later, the young Cayce found that by sleeping with his head on his schoolbooks, he could memorize everything in them. (My sisters and I tried sleeping with our textbooks under our pillows but had no such luck.)

At twenty-one, Cayce developed a gradual paralysis of his throat muscles, making it difficult for him to speak. Since several doctors were unable to cure him, he turned to a friend to hypnotize him. In that altered state of consciousness, he not only spoke with a totally clear voice, but he diagnosed the cause of his ailment and recommended medication and therapy which ultimately led to his full recovery.

Soon Cayce learned that, with his strange ability, he could accurately diagnose the source and remedies for other people's illnesses as well as his own. Indeed, the doctors, and eventually Edgar's father, discovered that Cayce needed to be given only the name and address of the patient, in order for him to tune in to that person's physical condition as easily as if they were in the same room together. Cayce would do a thorough mental examination of the patient's bodily systems, scanning for the source of the person's illness or injury. When Cayce found it, he would often recommend osteopathic treatment as well as a regimen of diet, nutrition and exercise, coupled with expressing positive attitudes and emotions toward one's self and others.

These diagnoses were later referred to as "readings." Cayce's wife, Gertrude, conducted the readings and Gladys Davis Turner, Cayce's stenographer, transcribed and numbered each one to protect the name of the client. Cayce gave over 14,000 readings during his lifetime. They are currently available for study, along with his prolific correspondence. See www.edgarcayce.org for more information.

One young doctor in Kentucky who had witnessed Cayce in action submitted a report on Cayce's unorthodox process of diagnosis and prescription to a clinical research society in Boston. In 1920, the *New York Times* carried two pages of headlines and photos of Mr. Cayce.

After that, invalids from all over the country began to seek help from the "miracle man" of Virginia Beach. In addition, many parents, desperate to find the whereabouts of their sons missing in action while World War II was raging, sought Cayce's counsel to locate them. Mom told me that, while she worked as a part-time secretary for Mr. Cayce, she would sit among knee-deep stacks of letters in his home library, opening them and weeping over the pain and despair contained in each one. It seemed that Cayce was their last hope.

Cayce, too, felt overwhelmed by the enormous suffering he found in the letters. By 1943, he was booked for readings two years in advance. He agonized over how many of those folks would be dead by the time he answered their pleas. Against the readings' strong advice, he began to push himself to give, not the usual two to four readings a day, but six to ten. Those who knew and loved him, including my parents, believe he chose to "lay down his life for his friends." He died of pneumonia in January of 1945, at sixty-seven years of age. He left 15,000 documented readings and correspondence out of his soul's desire to help people, especially children.

My friends, while I certainly found Cayce's life story compelling, it was Cayce's story of creation which explained how and why human beings came to be here on earth that gave my life hope, meaning and purpose. How so, you ask?

Companions and co-creators with God

The Cayce story claims that in the beginning, there was only one Source, one Divine Creator, one God, but God was lonely. So God created souls out of God's self. Thus, first and foremost, we human beings are essentially *spiritual*, not physical, beings. Our true nature resides not in our bodies or in our personalities but in our eternal souls, souls that have existed from the beginning of time. Each of us is a unique spark of God, a treasured, holy child.

And our purpose for existing on earth? Mind-blowing. First, we were created to be *companions* with God and with each other. God is always trying to connect with us, to be one with us in some mysterious way. One reading states: "Each soul was, is, and is to be a companion with that creative influence or force called God. Thus each entity is a child of God, or is a part of that whole." Second, because our souls are fashioned in the image of the Creator God, we are destined to be *co-creators* with God—a huge honor.

If all this is true, why don't we remember our marvelous destiny? Cayce claimed that we've gotten so involved with our separate little egos and we've so identified with matter that we've lost sight of the true spiritual nature of our being. Many of us have also forgotten our unique purpose for incarnating into the earth at this specific time in history. More on that later.

Free will

At twelve years of age, I asked my mother why a supposedly loving God would create such a terrible world—full of wars, poverty, suffering, loneliness and pain. She answered, "Ah, Pam, I think God doesn't want us just to be puppets. He wants a *real* loving relationship with us. Therefore he had to give us free will. For only when we are free *not* to love God, are we truly free *to* love him."

The Cayce philosophy and Mom agree. God gave human beings free will—the ability and the power to choose good or evil, life or death. Why? Because it is only by being free to make choices that we can come to know and love our authentic selves, and to know and love God. One lifetime is just too short for most of us to become that wise and caring. Through many lifetimes of trial and error on earth, we make choices: to stagnate or stick it out; to abandon God or to grow in intimacy with the Eternal One. Another reading states: "For the will of each entity, of each soul, is that which individualizes it, that makes it aware of itself; and as to how this is used that makes thee indeed a child of God," a precious, one-of-a-kind child of the Divine.

While the readings suggested that a few "new" souls are entering the earth at this time in history, most of us are "old" souls, having incarnated dozens of times over the past millennia. God is always eager to give us another try. In fact, God offers us *infinite* tries because God's compassion is infinite. God has not willed that any soul should perish. Life is not just a crapshoot after all. There is a purpose in the plan.

The role of karma

The Sanskrit (ancient Indian) meaning for the word "karma" is "memory." Karma is the law of cause and effect. Although I'm far from an authority on Hinduism, the Cayce readings' version of karma differs in three important ways from that of karma in Hinduism. For instance, Hinduism includes a caste system, ranging from the privileged Brahmin or priestly caste down to the lowest caste, the "Untouchables," a concept still accepted by some in India today. Cayce's concept of karma reflects no such caste system.

Second, the Hindu understanding of reincarnation places women below men on the karmic totem pole, based on gender. Cayce's version of reincarnation, in contrast, is not gender-biased. In fact, the readings suggest many souls choose to alternate between male and female incarnations, in order to learn empathy for each gender. God knows we need that!

Third, Hinduism teaches that, in addition to human bodies, souls can re-incarnate into the bodies of animals: cows, monkeys, even insects. Hindus honor animals by refusing to kill them because they might be hurting their relative from a former life. In contrast, the Cayce readings maintain that the soul journeys exclusively through *human* bodies.

In the Cayce picture, whatever we cause others to experience, we will eventually choose to experience in some form, providing us with an opportunity to learn how our actions, thoughts or words have affected someone else, for good or ill. We reap what we sow. Or, as we Hippies were fond of saying, "What goes around comes around." Smile.

I used to be a literalist about karma. I thought that if you killed someone in a past life, you were going to be killed by that person in *this* life. However, I've come to understand that karma isn't as simple as tit for tat. It's much more subtle as Gina Cerminara's intriguing book, *Many Mansions,* taught me.

Cerminara illustrated Cayce's version of karma with two vivid cases from the readings. First, she wrote of a man who had come to Cayce to cure his leukemia, a potentially deadly form of blood cancer. Cayce's reading explained that, two thousand years earlier, this man had been a Roman citizen who had cheered while he watched Christians suffer violent deaths in the Roman Coliseum. Because he had laughed at the spilling of others' blood, this lifetime his soul had chosen his very *own* body as the battlefield, his own cells killing off one another. The reading invited the man to forgive himself and to consider showing compassion for, rather than laughing at another's suffering as he had done in ancient Rome.

The second story I recall Cerminara relating concerned an adult male who came to Cayce because he was tormented and filled with shame by his nightly bed-wetting. Cayce's reading stated that this man had ducked witches in the days of early settlements in the 1600s in the United States. "Witchduck Road" in Virginia Beach testifies to that perverse practice. If a woman accused of witchcraft was tied to a pole and ducked in a pond yet was able to swim to the surface, her persecutors concluded she was a witch and sentenced her to death by hanging. If the woman drowned, however, she was exonerated, her innocence proven. Sadly, she was too dead to enjoy this.

According to Cayce's reading, because of the man's cruel behavior in that past life, the man's soul had chosen before his birth to "duck" himself every night in his own urine—in order to experience humiliation comparable to that which he had caused those women to endure. Through understanding this memory, "karma," and forgiving himself, the man could work towards transforming his behavior from judgment and fear of women to tolerance, perhaps even respect.

When I first encountered Cayce's version of karma, I was elated. I felt free to believe in a good and wise God again. At the same time, I found myself judging others—a lot. For example, if I saw a person in a wheelchair, I decided he was crippled because somehow, in a past life, he had caused another person to become crippled. I thought the same of a person who was blind or suffering from another disability. I didn't like the judge I was becoming, but I didn't see an alternative. The process of karma seemed heartless.

Then I read a Gospel story. Maybe you know it. In *John* 9:2, Jesus and his disciples are out walking when they come upon a blind man. The disciples ask Jesus, "Who sinned, this man or his parents, that he was born blind?" Their ancient worldview believed that a son could indeed be punished for his father's sin. Many peoples of that time accepted a similar notion. I wasn't prepared for Jesus' response.

Jesus answered them, "Neither. He is blind in order to glorify God."

Excuse me? God is glorified by someone being blind?

Jesus' response troubled me for years. I have only recently come to understand that Jesus meant that the blind man's soul was so highly evolved that he chose to incarnate blind in order that others, including

Jesus' disciples, might see through the eyes not of judgment but of compassion.

What a relief. I myself had been blind to this truth. I know now I must *never* judge whether a person is undergoing suffering because of a "karmic" opportunity or because that soul is so highly evolved that she or he has chosen to endure a certain condition to help *others* grow. Any judgment stays between God and that soul.

And when bad things happen to me, I can stop judging myself as well, though that takes years of hard work. Adopting an attitude of humility can help—not being a doormat, but being like "humus" (the origin of the word "humble"), the earth—receptive to whatever falls upon it. And we can even be grateful for it.

Now here is the biggest challenge I've found in working with the Cayce readings, and many spiritual paths teach this truth, as well. To grow spiritually, **you must take responsibility for everything that happens to you.**

"Hold on!" I hear you objecting. "You mean I'm responsible for my mate cheating on me? For my mother abandoning me? For my boss demeaning me? You're crazy."

Now no one knows better than I the temptation to be a victim. It's easy to blame God or someone else for growing up with lousy parents or a mean boss, but by so doing, we only succeed in making ourselves victims, not agents who have the daunting yet wonderful gift of free will. I resisted this teaching for ages; however, I kept bumping into it in various spiritual traditions. I slowly but stubbornly began to entertain the notion. Could it be true?

While I still haven't made peace with situations like child abuse or rape, I do accept, or try to accept *with thankfulness*, whatever suffering or abuse I'm encountering on my path. I believe that prior to my birth, my soul chose it to give me the opportunity to learn and then practice some kind of important spiritual truth. There's no doubt about it, though—accepting responsibility for whatever happens in our life requires maturity and a lot of courage.

How might we gain the courage and strength to face our demons, our karma, so we may heal and grow in our souls?

My father offered two helpful approaches for accepting our "karma." The first was, "If you were creative enough to get yourself into such a *blankety-blank* mess [in a job, relationship, etc.], you're creative enough to get out of it."

I was creative in messing up my life so bad? Cool!

So *bravo to you, SoulQuesters*! You're incredibly creative, too!

Second, when one of us kids was suffering from a failed relationship or a lost job, we'd moan and tease each other with, "Ooooh, bad karma!" Dad would chuckle and remind us, "Girls, *all* karma is *good* karma." Why? Because everything we go through is not for our punishment. It's not random or meaningless. No, it's for our spiritual growth, so we can become the companions and servant leaders God created us to be.

And the good news is that, while the law of karma gives us an opportunity to deal with our addictions, angers, fears and self doubts, we will encounter another spiritual law—the law of grace.

The Waterfall of Grace

Grace. The world is full of it. Ancient scriptures are full of it. The Cayce readings are full of it. Grace—God's love freely given to each of us—is not at all dependent on our earning it. This grace, "Amazing Grace" as the former slave ship owner John Newton put it, is the love the universe has for its creations, the passion of the Beloved for the Lover, which includes you and me. Though we may desperately try to flee from it, ultimately grace is inescapable. It will find us out. It will shower us with new hope and new life.

Cayce is adamant about this. The Law of Karma holds that certain actions and attitudes will set into motion certain results or effects which must eventually be faced. But if we learn the lesson before suffering all the consequences, if we have an "Aha!" moment—for example, if we become sorry for the role we played in causing someone's suffering, if we ask for forgiveness and work towards reconciliation—grace can short-circuit all the pain we might have incurred.

Let's go back to my experience in West Berlin. The fountains of grace continued to shower down on me, "grace upon grace." Because God over-rode my plans to go to graduate school in Milan to be near my Italian boyfriend, so that I would have the opportunity to face and then heal the memory, the "karma," of my frightening, crippling past in Hitler's Germany.. Too, I experienced a full measure of God's grace when Dr. Brandenburg saved not only my life but my uterus (and thus my ability to bear children). This would have been enough grace.

But the waterfall of God's goodness didn't stop there.

Some years after the surgery, I fell in love with and married a man of German heritage, who had grown up speaking German before English. The Jewish side of my family fell in love with him, too, healing some of their hatred of Germans. In addition, I have kept my balcony-promise to God: dedicating my life to serving God to the best of my ability. God has been faithful to me by gifting me with my life-long heart's desire: two exquisite daughters and a wondrous ministry.

Two years before going to West Berlin, I had a powerful dream that puzzled me. (It was a preview of my Berlin experience, but I didn't know that then.) I dreamed that while I was getting into my car in a darkened parking lot, a strange man walked over and stopped me. I recognized instantly that he was some kind of holy person. Later, I came to know that he was Jesus.

The man gently asked me, "Pam, do you know what true loving is?"

I answered with not a little smug self-righteousness, "It means loving everyone, *especially* the Jews."

With infinite kindness but absolute gravity, the man looked right into the core of my soul. "True," he responded. "But, my dear one, real love also means—loving the *Germans*." I woke up, marked forever by Jesus' challenge to love the oppressor as well as the victim, for we are all one in the healing heart of God.

"Lions and Tigers and Bears, O My!"
or
Tracking Down Your Past Lives

My brave soul trekkers, do you remember these words, "Lions and tigers and bears, O my!" chanted by Dorothy and her cohorts as they tiptoed through the ominous dark woods on their way to consult the Wizard? Seeking clues to our past lives can feel that spooky. At the same time, recalling some parts of our past lives might help us discover the roots of a devastating illness, a recurring trauma or disabling fear, and thus present us with an opportunity to grow—physically, emotionally and spiritually.

Furthermore, past life knowledge can help us discern our life's purpose and direction, drawing on gifts and talents we've developed in past lives. What else than the concept of reincarnation could explain a child prodigy like Mozart?

If you're intrigued by Cayce's story of reincarnation, you can go to a library or bookstore and seek out a book. Two classics, written by psychiatrists, no less, are *Return to Tomorrow* by George Ritchie and *Many Lives, Many Masters* by Brian Weiss. Dr. Ian Stevenson researched and wrote *Forty Cases of Reincarnation*, a seminal work on the subject. Trust your intuition to guide you to the right resource. Be open-minded, but as my dear friend, Rev. William Sloane Coffin, always cautioned, "…not so open-minded that your brains fall out!"

When I first started exploring Cayce's view of reincarnation forty-five years ago, I hoped to discover that I had been someone famous, like a queen of England, or some heroic figure like Joan of Arc. After years of exploring possible past lives, I believe most of my lives were just average, although I'm convinced that several ended with violent deaths. I've remembered or viscerally re-experienced being beheaded, tortured on the rack, and disemboweled. Why? Because I ran into conflict with religious authorities like the early patriarchal Roman church or the medieval Spanish Inquisition for holding "heretical," probably mystical, views. No wonder today I have a love/hate relationship with the Christian church!

I've had glimpses of several other incarnations, too, where I've seen myself alternating between nun and prostitute, trying to find a balance between my sexuality and my spirituality. I'm sure I'm not the only person in the world with *that* pattern.

Early in my work through the haunted forests of my past, I hoped to uncover all the *details* of my past lives. I guess I thought it would be exotic and romantic to do so. However, the older I get, and the more I suffer disappointment, loss or illness, the more I am grateful that God keeps most past-life memories blocked from our awareness, at least until we are strong enough to face them and wise enough to integrate them into our present life situation.

Pitfall: When excavating, your past lives, the time or place or personality you once had is not as important as identifying your vocation, your spiritual state of mind, and the relationships you've healed or refused to heal. Remember your high destiny, holy travelers—co-creators and companions with God!

So please tread softly through your psyche's memories. Whenever you take an intentional look into your past for guidance or insight, be sure to surround yourself with protection from higher beings you trust. There are many books and CDs that can help you explore your inner territory safely. If you choose to experiment with hypnosis, always choose a practitioner you trust. Sometimes memories will surface spontaneously, as they did with a friend of mine in the 1970s. He didn't even know about reincarnation, let alone believe in it, when explicit details of his former life as a young soldier in Nazi Germany appeared to him during a time of deep introspection.

Some clues to help recall your past life memories
1. nightmares
2. spontaneous recall (usually while in an altered state)
3. déjà vu (when you're totally awake)
4. movies or books
5. museum exhibits or art objects that attract you
6. historical periods of clothing and décor you adore
7. irrational fears, especially about dying

The time periods of the books you read for fun or the movies you love to see again and again can reveal clues to a possible past life. Or are you attracted to certain exhibits within a museum? For example, when I was six, my first grade class went on a field trip to the Museum of Natural History in Chicago. While my classmates were happily engrossed in the dinosaur exhibits, where was I? Down in the basement, enthralled with the Egyptian mummies in their ancient tombs—not a typical interest for a six-year-old.

Currently, I belong to a Cayce study group on the Temples of Sacrifice and the Temple Beautiful in ancient Egypt. I suspect I was a healer or priestess in one of those temples. Why?

The first gift my first husband gave me was a scarab on a necklace. I had never even seen a scarab before and had to look up its symbolism: the Egyptian symbol for eternal life. I asked him why he had bought that pendant, and he himself was puzzled why he felt compelled to do it. A few years after my divorce, my new boyfriend gave me an Isis necklace and earrings for my birthday—Isis was the famous goddess of ancient Egypt. Unusual gift, since we were living in a campground at the time!

Another clue came two years later. After I led a group meditation with A.R.E. members in a small replica of a pyramid in Virginia Beach, one of the participants confided that she had snuck a peak at me during the meditation and seen me ceremonially garbed in a stunning ancient Egyptian robe and headdress. I was flattered, though

I had experienced no such vision at all. The important thing to remember as we search for past life clues is that we don't get caught up in our egos. Rather, we continue to discern what gifts we bring from past incarnations that will help us in our present lives to make this world a better place.

Objects of art can provide hints to your past lives. Books, fiction or non-fiction, can perform the same revelatory function. I'm a book lover. For instance, as I read the Anita Diamant's description of the ancient Hebrew women's community in her book, *The Red Tent,* I found myself utterly transported back into that time and place, breathing in the fragrances, feeling the textures of clothing beneath my fingers, etc. I'm quite sure I lived in ancient Israel.

These days, I am pleasantly surprised to find myself attending Torah classes and *Shabbat* services at a local Conservative temple, immersing myself in Jewish scripture and ritual. I first felt drawn to Temple to learn more about the life and customs of Jesus as a Jewish rabbi, but I soon fell in love with the people and the rabbi for their own sakes. I continue to be blessed by them on my spiritual journey.

***Excavating Tip*:** Examine not only the cultures and historical periods you love but the ones you *hate,* for they may also provide clues to where and when you've lived before. I've already shared my feelings of revulsion for the Nazis that became a powerful clue for me. In another instance, I've realized that I'm not fond of the Russian Revolution period, either. Yet, at the same time, I'm curiously, even morbidly, attracted to movies about that period, like *Fiddler on the Roof, Dr. Zhivago,* and *Reds.* The cultures about which you feel neutral probably are just that—not relevant to your soul's journey right now. So pay attention to the cultures and times in history that repel you or fascinate you.

Here's one more important insight I've had as I've studied my past lives over the decades. I used to think that certain past life attractions would remain steady throughout one's life. But lately, I've realized that influences from specific past lives change over a lifetime. For example, I used to think that my strong affinity to my past lives in ancient Greece and China would remain constant throughout my life. But then, about fifteen years ago, my passion switched from those ancient cultures to Native American life in the 19th century, culminating in my doing actual fieldwork with the Lakota (Sioux) on the Pine Ridge and Rose Bud reservations in South Dakota. See how the process works? While my love of learning from my Chinese and

Grecian lives enabled me to obtain two masters and a doctorate in my younger life, I'm currently attracted to earth-centered cultures and spirituality, using them in my preaching, teaching, and healing practice.

Finally, a sense of humor helps a lot when encountering your past lives. As a young girl, I dreamed of being *Princess Summer-Fall-Winter-Spring* on the *Howdy Doody* show. Thirty years later, I joined a drumming circle in a Presbyterian church one Saturday morning. As we danced in a circle and the drumming transported me into a semi-altered state, I was surprised to feel something heavy and unfamiliar swinging between my two manly thighs. I gulped as I tuned into my former Indian life as an old man rather than the delicate princess I fantasized about! I still chuckle at that revelation.

I experienced a completely different emotion when I visited a friend on the Pine Ridge Reservation. My friend brought out her mother's beautiful deerskin dress, used only for ceremony, for me to see. I envied her. For a minute, I even imagined myself in such a dress—if there was a deerskin large enough to fit me. Now, ten years later, I believe that I wasn't just yearning that day to wear something more exotic than my customary jeans. I was nostalgic for the days when I actually *did* wear such a dress. My Indian guides have since confirmed this in several past life readings.

I share these stories, Questers, to help you track down your own past lives more easily. The search can be fun and enlightening as well as healing. But you may also be called upon to be fearless and forgiving as well.

Face your fears.

"Fear lives in our reptile brains.
Are you going to take advice from a lizard?"

Columnist Martha Beck made this quip in the June 2007 issue of *O* magazine. Some of us do use our lizard brains to guide us in making decisions. Don't raise your hands. Still, we can choose instead to draw upon our neo-cortex for saner advice.

So take a moment right now to reflect on your greatest fears. For instance,

- What illness do you most fear contracting?

- What's your worst-case scenario of dying?

If you fear dying in a particular way—for example, by knife stabbing, or gunshot wound, or drowning—it's possible that you died in that manner in a past life, and probably recently (as past lives go). The following experience brought this home to me.

I was about ten years old. Mom, Dad, my three sisters and I were watching an episode of *Lassie* in which the blonde little boy, Timmy, gets sucked into a mire of quicksand, and is rapidly sinking to his death. (Good ol' Lassie eventually runs for help and succeeds in bringing back Timmy's dad, who pulls Timmy out of the deadly mud hole with a long branch, just in the nick of time.)

While my sisters watched Timmy sink with only mild interest, I burst into hysterics. Surprised, they mumbled: "What's wrong with *her?*"

I continued to sob. My father pulled me onto his lap and encircled me with his large, strong arms. He whispered calmly into my ear that, while I might have drowned in quicksand in a past life, I wouldn't die that way in *this* life. I didn't look up at him and ask, "What's a past life?" I just took him at his word and let myself be comforted by his reassuring tone. Ten years later, attending the movie, *Lawrence of Arabia*, I watched a young man get sucked to his death in the desert sands. As I watched in horror, I felt my throat constrict and my heart race. Then I remembered Dad's calming words and, repeating them to myself, I was able to keep from rushing out of the theater.

An excellent resource for working with your children's fears is *Children's Past Lives: How Past Life Memories Affect Your Child* by Carol Bowman.

Examine your current relationships.

Much of our life's purpose and mission has to do with the people in our lives—family, friends, or enemies. That's no surprise. The Cayce readings state that souls tend to travel in groups, family groups and larger groups. Even nations have karma. I find it reassuring that my husband, daughters and I are souls traveling together through eons, and we will undoubtedly meet again on earth in the future. Of course, every person can serve as a mirror to us, reflecting what we need to value or to change about ourselves.

The main rule of thumb here is to pay attention to people whom we love and admire, as well as to those whom we just can't stand. For our current relationships can reveal dynamics about our past life relationships. Sometimes our roles will change. In one life, I might be the mother and you the daughter. The next time, you may be *my* mother. Or a man's wife in one life might become his son in another. You can see why we human beings sometimes get our signals crossed, gender and else-wise, for example, desiring to marry the parent of the opposite sex when we're young. Perhaps we have actually been married before!

Identifying a past life relationship with another soul can provide an opportunity to heal the relationship in this life. The Cayce readings are full of such examples, but I want to share one from my own life.

After giving birth to my first daughter Chelsea, I awakened, literally every morning with a song of joy in my heart, eager to see her sweet face again. I cherished every minute I spent with her. As I've told you, when Chelsea turned one and a half, I went on a tour of China for several weeks. While in Guilin, a lovely mystically landscaped village on the Li River, a disturbing past life memory arose.

Many ages ago in rural China, I knew that I had given birth to the soul I now know as Chelsea. Because a girl baby was undesirable in those days, my then husband forced me to take her out on the hillside and leave her there to die. I reluctantly complied, my heart breaking. I know I made a soul vow then and there that if I were permitted to give birth to Chelsea again in a future life, I would never, *ever* abandon her. I would protect and defend her and love her with all my might and heart. I have kept that vow in this life to the best of my ability, and I still adore her, twenty-eight years later.

And you, my magical daughter, Kaitlyn June? I'm not yet sure where or how I've known you before. Our past life together is still a delightful enigma and I trust information will be forth-coming when we need it. I do know that you are very wise and caring, way beyond your twenty-three years. Through my tough times, you have been my faithful nurse and confidante. So maybe you've been my mother in some past life. Too, our passion for music and theater is boundless. There's no one I would rather sing with than you, especially the witches' duet in the musical, *Wicked*. I know that we are best friends, betting on each other's best selves, and cheering each other on. Past life details don't seem to matter when our present relationship is so wonderful.

Indeed, the most important thing, ultimately, is not to spend too much time dwelling on the possibilities of specific past lives. The point is to focus on the blessings of your life *right now*, wherever you live, and whoever you are.

In the *Wizard of Oz*, Dorothy was a *SoulQuester* on that Yellow Brick Road, wasn't she? She traveled with her group souls: the Scare Crow, the Tin Man and the Cowardly Lion. Oh, yes—tag-along Toto, too. She was seeking to get back home to Kansas, Auntie Em, and ultimately her precious, unique self. Eventually, after many tests and challenges, she made it.

Where is your Emerald City, my loves? Who are your treasured companions? After your extraordinary adventures, perhaps in past lives as well, what gifts will you use to bring you and your friends safely back home?

FOURTEEN
_____

Crossing Rivers, Moving Mountains:

Serving the Global Good

"If we just worry about the big picture, we are powerless. So my secret is to start right away doing whatever little work I can do. I try to give joy to one person in the morning, and remove the suffering of one person in the afternoon.... That is the secret. Start right now."
—Chân Không, Vietnamese Buddhist activist

SoulTrekkers, what an important secret Chan Không has shared. Now that we know it, what are we going to do with it? Who might we heal and bless, one precious person at a time? How will we choose to serve the global good—today, now?

We've covered a lot of territory on this quest for your sweet, strong, precious self. I wrote a little poem to sum it up.

You've sharpened your tools for feminist critique.
You decide when you're strong.
You decide when you're meek.
Questing with your body as friend by your side,
a brave heart you carry, your arms open wide.
You're using your brains as you tithe on your trek.
You're telling more stories, though you're also hi-tech.
Ritual helps you to welcome each dawn.
The gifts from your dark times just go on and on.

As we look toward serving the global good, it's time to do one more thing. It's time to abandon the **"either/or"** model of thinking of the past two thousand years: either young or old, self or other, good or bad, merciful or powerful, Self or Others. It's time to replace the dichotomous "either/or" relationships of these opposites with the **"both/and" paradigm** of our new consciousness: both strong and able to surrender; both inclusive and holding firm boundaries; both active and receptive, both full of wisdom and willing to learn. It takes great maturity to be able to dance back and forth between these opposites, or to hold onto them with creative tension. But with practice and perseverance, we can do it.

We live in the tension of another pair of opposites—local and global realities. In women's lib days, our slogan was: "The personal is the political." Today, the political is also the personal. (It was then, too. We just didn't know it.) Whatever benefits the local community advances the wellbeing, the *shalom*, of the global community, and vice versa. My Italian friend, Marco Tavanti, coined the term "glocal" years ago to capture this dynamic, but it hasn't caught on with the public yet.

Friends, our Western worldview teaches that as individuals we are separate and independent from each other and from creation. However, we are so intimately connected to each other and the web of life. The traditional Lakota pay homage to this interconnection every time they perform a ritual like the Sun Dance or the (sweat) purification lodge. Before the ritual begins, each person says, "*Mitakuye oyasin,*" meaning "*All my relatives.*" These relatives include not only human relatives like aunts and nieces but also the Cloud people, the Standing people (trees—I love that), and the Stone people. *All* of creation is kin to us. We are interconnected to everything in the cosmos. How wondrous!

Our planet and her species are struggling to survive the onslaught and disastrous results from over-population, climate change, wars, globalization and technological "progress."

Now is the time for us to become more intentional in our efforts to build a safer and saner world in which everyone and everything can thrive. We don't have a moment to lose. Many people have awakened to this fact and are becoming pro-active, joining together in local and global networks, and combining their visions, talents, resources, and willpower to manifest the changes we can now only imagine.

What image might inspire us in such an endeavor?

In August of 2006, Deepak Chopra, the well-known M.D. turned spiritual author turned peace-activist, lectured to a capacity crowd of five hundred at a hotel in Virginia Beach. At the close of his lecture, he told us that scientists had always longed to understand the process by which a caterpillar turns into a butterfly. The technology had eluded them until recently, but now the technology was in place. Guess what they found?

Five hundred of us leaned towards him as one. You couldn't hear a pin drop.

Each caterpillar has its own unique DNA. For months, it eats and eats and then winds itself up in its cocoon, as every grade schooler knows. But it's the next part that is astonishing. As the scientists monitored the transformation process from caterpillar to butterfly, they witnessed and documented that the brand-new butterfly cells mysteriously had *their own DNA*, different from those of the caterpillar!

The cells eventually form the baby butterfly, which eats its way to adulthood on the dying flesh of the caterpillar. The scientists, usually adept at coining new technical terms, named these butterfly cells "*imaginal*" cells. That is, the cells were somehow able to *imagine* a totally different kind of creature—the butterfly—rather than its former caterpillar self.

Chopra concluded by inviting all of us in the audience to see ourselves as "imaginal cells," capable of transforming humanity from its caterpillar self with the DNA of greed, self-interest, violence, fear and suspicion into its new butterfly self, with the DNA of compassion and cooperation, able to save the earth, to share our resources as we build peaceful ways of living together in one diverse and beautiful human family.

Imagination must be followed by action. There are basically two ways to transform social and environmental ills: acts of charity or justice. What's the difference?

> Some well-meaning church members are standing by the side of a mountain river when they see babies floating downstream in the rapids, in danger of drowning. Frantically, they begin to pull the babies out of the churning water. Finally, after hours of exhausting rescue efforts, one churchwoman cries out that she's leaving.
>
> The others yell at her, "You can't abandon us!"
>
> To which she hollers back, "Hell, I'm not abandoning you. I'm going up the river to stop the bastard who's throwing the babies in!"

The church women are performing an act of charity, that is, rescuing the babies. The lone woman's actions, on the other hand, exhibit social justice: resisting or even stopping the unjust social policy that caused the babies to be in jeopardy in the first place. As a nation, we're better at performing acts of charity than developing just policies, but both are necessary. I love the Hebrew phrase "*Tikkun olam*"—God's command to "repair the world," to serve the common good. Some of you will be rescuers, some reformers. Some of you will do both. God knows there's enough for everyone to do.

Is Hope a Luxury?

Before the invasion of Iraq and the "War on Terror" began, Kelly Anthony wrote an article for the *New Haven Register*. A psychology professor, Anthony had been invited by professors in Iraq to observe firsthand how Iraqis were holding up under conditions of profound and chronic isolation, deprivation and vilification. Her observations are just as applicable and just as heart-wrenching today as they were then.

> I listened as senior academics literally begged me to help protect them and their children from war, spoke with promising young people who had all but given up hope of a future, and observed a rage so close to the surface that it was almost transparent...they do not see any compassion right now in either their own government or ours. Yet even those on the streets seemed stunningly able to draw distinctions between the United States' and United Nations' policies that are slowly strangling them vs. the many people in the United States and the world who oppose this slow, and clearly psychological, torture.

She ends by lamenting:

> I wish my brother [serving in the U.S. military] safety from harm as he gets his orders from our government to potentially do great harm to the friends I made in Iraq. The sadness all this leaves me with becomes so much sometimes I cannot breathe. I hear the words of my new Iraqi friend Bassam, a truly lovely and promising young architecture student about my brother's age...

In a recent email he said we can no longer write [since] we, his new friends in the United States, offer him hope, and *hope is a luxury he can no longer afford.*

We all need hope to survive, don't we? Hope is *not* a luxury. You and I have been blessed with so much in our great country, so we must be the ones to offer hope to others in whatever ways we can. Of course, none of us can save the world alone. But some news clip or Web sound bite will catch your attention one day. The Universe will tug at your heart and lead you to your destiny. Each of you has a mission to accomplish. All you have to do is pay attention, respond and prepare to be transformed in the process.

The most exquisitely made violin makes no soaring music if left in its case. The most cleverly written children's story or the most intricately designed software program accomplishes nothing if left on the shelf. As the wise Naval Officer, Grace Murray Hopper, quipped, "A ship in port is safe, but that's not what ships are built for."

Enough philosophizing. Congratulations if you are already engaged in societal transformation or charity work. If not, it's time to get out there!

Here are some true stories of *SoulQuesters* that I hope will inspire you.

Crossing Rivers

Crossing rivers of prejudice

There are so many creative ways to cross a river or large body of water, most of them fun but all potentially dangerous: wading, fording, swimming, surfing, jet skiing, rafting or pleasure boating. Figuratively or literally, you can bet each new situation will require a new strategy. As you confront challenges, you will change people and they will change you.

Here's a Facebook collection of river-crossing *SoulQuesters*, each one, in their own special way, serving the local or the global good.

Facebook Entry #1

I'll start by telling a tale on myself. For most of my life, I considered myself a goody-goody and was proud of it. I couldn't see myself ever breaking the law. As a follower of Christ, I was eager to help people who had been incarcerated unjustly, but my sympathy stopped cold where the guilty were concerned. They got what they deserved and should learn from their mistakes.

Then, over twenty years ago, I met Jake (not his real name)—a funny, teasing, guitar-playing, poetry-spouting man. For over seven years, we worshipped together in the same church. We exchanged childcare and enjoyed watching our children grow up together.

Then one day Jake made a terrible error in judgment with a young lady friend of his. He was reported to the police who took him to the local jail. He was later sentenced (unfairly) to nine years in various high-security prisons around the state.

When I heard Jake was in jail, I went right over to see him. It was only my second time visiting such a place. I was shocked to see him in an orange jumpsuit standing behind thick glass walls, with armed guards standing around. I asked him how he was. "OK," he said, and then added, embarrassed, that he had been arrested so quickly that he had no time to grab his underwear or socks. Would I please buy him some? A bit taken aback by his request, I agreed. I waved goodbye through the partition and turned to leave.

Now, at that time, my own family was struggling. My husband and I had both lost our jobs because of illness. We had recently applied for welfare while we sought other jobs. Having to feed two young daughters on minimal food stamps, I felt I didn't have a dime to spare on Jake.

"Why was he so stupid to get in trouble in the first place?" I muttered to myself as I walked out the jail doors.

Driving toward K-Mart, I continued to fuss and fume at my dear friend, Jake. Arriving, I parked the car, got out, and slammed the door behind me, still huffing with puffs of righteous indignation.

I almost missed the soft voice that whispered to me these words from *Matthew* 25.

"When did we visit you in prison, Lord?"

"As ye do it unto the least of these, ye do it unto me."

I stopped dead in my tracks.

"Aw, c'mon, Lord," I protested in my defense. "I know that passage. I'm a good pastor. I've been very responsible over the years to people in jail. I support innocent prisoners, like those in *Amnesty International*. That's what you meant by those words, right, Lord? Innocent people. Jake is guilty. You surely couldn't mean I should help *him*?"

Again I heard the words, but this time with a new twist,

*"As ye do in unto the least of these, innocent **or** guilty, ye do it unto me."*

I gulped.

"I get it. I get it."

I repented in sackcloth and ashes, went straight into K-Mart, bought Jake underwear and socks and delivered them to him with a glad heart. I had crossed a mighty river of prejudice of my own making, and found myself transformed.

Facebook Entry #2

My courageous friend, Ursula Corbin, has crossed some pretty rough rivers in her work with death row inmates in the United States. A Swiss citizen by birth, she found herself living in a well-off neighborhood in Argentina in the 1970s. That was a time of great political turmoil. Civilians were frequently kidnapped by various factions, even some governmental agents; many lived in terror for their safety. One day, a male friend of Ursula's disappeared and nobody could find out what had happened to him. He never re-appeared.

That experience planted a seed in Ursula's heart.

When she returned to Switzerland at the age of 36, she watered that seed by joining *Amnesty International (AI)*, an organization that works to free political prisoners and protest the use of the death penalty around the globe.

One day, Ursula's *AI* group in Zurich received a letter from an African-American death row inmate in Texas who asked if someone would write back to him. Ursula was the only one in her group that spoke English, so she volunteered. In a letter to me, Ursula wrote, "This was the start of a very intense and deep pen pal friendship, with many ups and downs, ending with his execution in 1993."

After her friend's execution, Ursula agreed to be interviewed by a Texas radio station. Many death row inmates heard her story and begged her to correspond with them. In response, with the help of two other women, Ursula founded "*Life Spark.*" Still going strong today, it has more than 800 pen pals and inmates in correspondence across the United States. I'm one of them.

When other friends discovered that most prisons provide only one roll of toilet paper and toothpaste per inmate per week, Ursula, along with several men from her *Amnesty International* group, founded "*Reach Out.*" "*Reach Out*" members help to cover the costs of basic needs for death row inmates. Also, because many inmates have lost all contact with family or friends, members exchange letters and build meaningful relationships with the inmates.

Currently, Ursula is still active with *AI,* an honorary member of *"Life Spark,"* and the president of *"Reach Out."* She continues to bring hope and comfort to these all-but-forgotten prisoners. She's told me many times over the years how her life has been transformed by friendships with these inmates who, she reminds me, are children of God, just like us.

Crossing rivers to other cultures
Facebook Entry #3

26-year-old Sveva Gallmann has been crossing rivers in Kenya. Somewhere between an educator, an anthropologist, and an environmentalist, Sveva's philosophy is: "Never let anybody deter you from your position. Make sure you live what you preach and never be complacent." Sounds like the motto of a *Quester*, right?

Sveva grew up on a 100,000-acre wildlife conservancy that her mother developed. Nature was her greatest friend. Her childhood was marred, however, by her father's and baby brother's deaths. Her mother taught her to turn her grief into an appreciation of everything that symbolizes life. Graduating from Oxford with honors in 2002, she has been on the move ever since, from serving a year as a volunteer in a leprosarium in India to rehabilitating dolphins in the Red Sea.

Sveva recently designed the *Four Generations* project in Africa. Increasingly, African children are attending Western schools where they are taught that the old ways of their tribe have no relevance to modern life. The wisdom of the elders, who cannot read or write, is rapidly being lost. Through *Four Generations*, school children learn to record their tribal history, complete with chants and rituals, for the sake of posterity.

When asked in an interview what Americans can learn from Africans, Sveva replied:

> Coming back to the U.S., I am often shocked at the misery that Westerners feel sometimes. I have friends buckling under pressure and taking Prozac, feeling trapped by their jobs . . . depression, insecurity, anorexia. What strikes me about Africa is the resilience that keeps people moving forward even after

the most brutal experiences. Look at Rwanda, and how they've rebuilt. [Africans] are ingenious in how they cope with life's shortcomings.

Facebook Entry #4

Oprah's *"O"* magazine is a great source of inspiring *SoulQuesters*. For example, Lisa Shannnon read and wept when she read the story on the women of the African Congo who had faced rape and brutality from their own country's militia. Then Lisa decided to go the extra mile—literally running a race to earn money to help them.

I love the next part of the story. For, you see, Lisa wasn't much of a runner. In fact, halfway through her first marathon, she quit and called a cab! But her determination to help the Congo women never faltered. Finally, she talked her friends into sponsoring her in a race, this time raising $10,000. Lisa continues to support the Congo women, even down-scaling her photography business to set up similar fund-raising and consciousness-raising events in cities around the globe.

Crossing rivers of racial prejudice
Facebook Entry #5

My dear friend, Beatriz Amberman, has taught me so much about being a *Quester*. Founder of the *Hispanic Community Dialogue of Virginia,* Beatriz advocates for the Hispanic community locally here in Virginia and nationally, most recently focusing on the plight of undocumented workers. She works tirelessly with state lawmakers and advocacy groups to obtain a comprehensive and just immigration policy nationwide. She also serves as past chair and current member of the *Virginia Latino Advisory Board* for the state of Virginia, is an Advisory Council Representative of the *Institute of Mexicans Abroad*, works with the Mexican Consulate in Washington, D.C. and is an Executive Board Member of the *Virginia Center for Inclusive Communities.*

Beatriz, along with her physician husband, George, also a dear friend, is bold in manifesting her vision of equality and respect for all members of our community. She is collaborative in her efforts to build bridges between alienated factions here in Virginia Beach. For example, because Hispanic workers are understandably distrustful of local police officers given the mushrooming occurrences of racial profiling, every year Beatriz sponsors and leads an event where the immigrant community can come without fear of being questioned about their legal status. They listen to local police officials apprise them of their civil rights. Because of her efforts, they and their families feel safer living in Virginia Beach, and police have positive encounters with Hispanic workers.

When Beatriz moderates panels or events, including opposing views on immigration reform, she models the best form of dialogue, encouraging respect for each other's viewpoints as they share their fears in hopes of finding common ground. Though the encounters may get heated, Beatriz always manages to keep her cool. She is inspiring to watch.

Last but not least, Beatriz is a lover of, and advocate for, Mexican culture—dance, food, jewelry and art. In 2004, the Mexican government honored her with the highest recognition given to people of Mexican origin who contribute to opening "The Way," that is, making the road to success more available to future generations of Mexican-Americans. Beatriz is a cultural and civic ambassador, a way-paver *por excelencia*.

Facebook Entry #6

Crossing rivers to connect different or opposed racial groups is such important work, especially because our once white Western world is becoming increasingly multi-cultural. But crossing rivers is not really new and men make great *Questers*, too! I loved to hear my dad tell this story when he lectured.

In 1945, shortly after the end of World War II, my dad was sent to work at an Episcopal church, a Nisei—first-generation born— American Japanese church. The head pastor was Nisei, but the Associate pastor was white. Unfortunately, like many Americans in those days, he feared any Japanese person, even if he or she was American-born.

As a young psychologist, my father was hired by the bishop to observe the associate pastor, for it was rumored that he dealt rudely with his parishioners, treating them with disdain and sometimes undisguised hatred. The church council also ordered my father to do a psychological assessment of the Associate, without raising his suspicions. My dad was to follow the white pastor to meetings and to monitor his interactions with congregation members.

After several months of observation, Dad wrote up his findings and presented them to the church council. His report confirmed their worst suspicions: the associate pastor was indeed hateful, spiteful and bigoted.

The pastor read the report out loud while the council listened in silence. Then he stood up and announced, "That settles it."

Dad paused dramatically. I couldn't wait for that bigoted minister to get canned.

"That settles it," the pastor repeated. "He needs us. He *stays!*"

I'm always amazed at that pastor's Christ-like love.

The story doesn't end here, however.

The church decided to hire my dad as their part-time choir director. Since Dad was going to be working with the associate pastor, he made a decision: whatever little thing the associate pastor did right, no matter how insignificant, he would write him a Thank You note and leave it on his desk.

Dad was true to his promise. Throughout the following months, if the associate pastor did anything right—if he smiled at just one person in the congregation, or if he visited an ill member confined to his home, or if he fixed the kitchen door hanging off its hinges in the social hall—Dad left a little note on his desk, "Good job! Thanks for smiling at that little girl" or "Thanks for fixing that door."

Then, one day Dad found a little note on *his* desk. It was from the associate pastor.

"Good job, Harmon. Whatever you're doing, keep it up! It's working!"

The river of racism had successfully been crossed. The associate pastor's frigid heart had finally melted—from the warmth of the persistent, insistent love of the pastor, the church members and my father.

Moving Mountains

"... I tell you the truth, if you have faith as small as a mustard seed, you can say to this mountain, 'Move from here to there' and it will move. Nothing will be impossible for you."
—Jesus to his disciples, *Matthew* 17:20

It's great to have faith, Christian or otherwise. I pray for more faith daily. Yet faith needs to be coupled with concrete, constructive, and courageous action, especially if we hope to move mountains. Though I'm sure you have some of your own, here are a few suggestions.

- Be a voice for the voiceless on the Internet. You don't even have to leave your computer desk. Using your email, list serves do practically all the legwork, often writing the letter so you just have to sign them. For example, I am on list-serves such as the United Church of Christ Justice and Peace Network, Sojourners, and Americans for Peace Now. Shooting off an email takes minimal effort, but can move mountains of hard hearts or red tape when combined with others' emails.
- Make a phone call to your senator or congress person. Calls are more effective than emails and only take a few minutes longer.
- Donate money to the wonderful groups that are out there working for peace and justice.
- Advocate in person. That is the most effective form of advocacy.

Moving mountains of poverty
Facebook Entry #1

Sometimes listening to a prompting from your inner voice can save a life halfway around the world. This is a true story from a woman mission doctor stationed somewhere in the heart of Africa.

One night I had worked hard to help a mother in the labor ward; but in spite of all we could do, she died, leaving us with a tiny premature baby and a crying two-year-old daughter. We would have difficulty keeping the baby alive, as we had no incubator....

One student midwife went for the box we had for such babies and the cotton wool the baby would be wrapped in. Another went to stoke up the fire and fill a hot water bottle. She came back shortly in distress to tell me that in filling the bottle, it had burst. Rubber perishes easily in tropical climates. "And it is our last hot water bottle!" she exclaimed.

"All right," I said, "put the baby as near the fire as you safely can, and sleep between the baby and the door to keep it free from drafts. Your job is to keep the baby warm."

The following noon, I went to the children to explain our problem about keeping the baby warm enough, mentioning the hot water bottle. I also told them of the two-year-old sister, crying because her mother had died. During the prayer time, one ten-year-old girl, Ruth, prayed with the usual blunt conciseness of our African children.

"Please, God," she prayed, "send us a water bottle. It'll be no good tomorrow, God, as the baby will be dead, so please send it this afternoon."

She added, "And while you are about it, would you please send a dolly for the little girl so she'll know you really love her?"

Could I honestly say, "Amen?" I just did not believe that God could do this. ... The only way God could answer this particular prayer would be by sending me a parcel from the homeland. I had been in Africa for almost four years at that time, and I had never, ever received a parcel from home.

Anyway, if anyone did send me a parcel, who would put in a hot water bottle? I lived on the equator!

Later that day, the doctor received a large box on her verandah. Surrounded by the eager children, she opened the box and pulled out t-shirts and boxes of raisins. The doctor concludes her story:

Then, as I put my hand in again, I felt the.....could it really be? I grasped it and pulled it out—yes, a brand-new, rubber hot water bottle. I cried. I had not asked God to send it; I had not truly believed that he could.

Ruth was in the front row of the children. She rushed forward, crying out, "If God has sent the bottle, he must have sent the dolly, too!"

Rummaging down to the bottom of the box, she pulled out the small, beautifully dressed dolly. Her eyes shining, she asked: "Can I go over with you, Mummy, and give this dolly to that little girl, so she'll know that Jesus really loves her?"

That parcel had been on the way for five whole months. Packed up by my former Sunday school class, whose leader had heard and obeyed God's prompting to send a hot water bottle, even to the equator. And one of the girls had put in a dolly for an African child—five months before—in answer to the believing prayer of a ten-year-old to bring it "that afternoon."

Facebook Entry #2

But we don't have to travel to Africa to move mountains, my friends. And sometimes the quest will take you in the most unsuspected directions.

Mary, a young married woman, mother of two, and member of Christpoint Community Church in Virginia Beach, had decided to go to law school so she could work with the poor as a lawyer. Her constant prayer was: "God, show me the way."

One day in meditation, she received the message, "Don't wait, Mary. Use the money you have saved for law school *now*. Help the poor now."

Puzzled, Mary responded silently in her heart, "No, God, you must be mistaken. I should wait until *after* law school. I'll have more tools, more training then. I need to go to law school. I've saved up thousands of dollars already just for that purpose."

The voice she heard was adamant, and certainly not her own. "Use what you have in hand, Mary. Help them *now*."

Mary had heard of the infamous Brenda, a young single mom who had dedicated herself to helping other single moms and their children. Mary was also aware that working class, as well as poor, families were falling through the cracks of the welfare system. Still, it took her months to get up her courage to contact Brenda. Brenda warned Mary that she needed to be totally honest with herself when she decided she was ready to see the poverty and injustice the families suffered. For once she did, cautioned Brenda, she wouldn't be able to turn her back on them.

A few weeks later, Mary assured Brenda that she was ready. They drove to the home of a single mom who had no rent money and was soon to be evicted. Neither had she anything to feed her children that night. Mary listened to her story, then went home, called up some churches, picked up some bags of food and took them over to the house.

As Mary unloaded the bags from her car, the woman's little five-year-old boy ran out to her, and jumped up and down.

"Oh, is there something in there for me? How did you know it was my birthday?"

Mary was crest-fallen. The bags held only groceries, nothing that would excite a little boy. She drove back home, called up her friends who had little boys, and asked,

"Do you have any toys, preferably new ones, that you could give me for this little boy?"

Several moms pitched in. Then she called up the boy's mother to see if she had a birthday cake for him.

"Are you kidding?" she exclaimed.

Mary called up more friends, imploring, "Someone bake a birthday cake!"

Later, armed with two birthday cakes and several presents, she drove over to the woman's home and celebrated his birthday. The boy was elated.

That night, Mary confided to me with righteous conviction. *"No child in America should have to go without having his birthday celebrated!*

"Pam, you have to allow your heart to be broken and then act. Don't use your pain as an excuse to turn away, but use it to see the face of Jesus in the poor. You'll not only bless others, but you'll be blessed—more than you'll ever know."

After this eye and heart opening encounter, Mary and Brenda started *Mothers Inc.*, an organization devoted to helping single mothers in poverty and their children rebuild their lives. Soon, Mary and Brenda expanded their work to include homeless mothers and families, persuading sixteen congregations to open up their doors on cold winter nights to house them, talk with them, and serve them breakfast. I know. I was a member of one of those churches.

Later that next fall, I joined the board of *Mothers Inc.* On Christmas Eve, a group of church members and I stayed up late wrapping hundreds of Christmas presents to give to children in a local trailer park. The next day, we found a wonderful Santa—from the mall no less—a large, jovial man, who joined us at the trailer park on Christmas Day to sing carols and hand out presents. The children were overjoyed. That night, Christmas spirit overflowed in my heart. I found myself blessed by all of the people involved, especially the children, just like Mary had predicted.

Moving mountains of prejudice against girls
Facebook Entry #3

Joyce Roach provides an inspiring role model for *Questers*. An African-American, Joyce grew up as one of eleven children in a low-income family in New Orleans. She never dreamed she would one day break a race record in the corporate world. But she worked very hard to become the first African-American woman officer for the giant cosmetic company, Avon. For the past six years, she has been the proud head of *Girls Inc.*, a New York-based nonprofit that offers programs to empower young women in the sciences, as well as teaching them how to prevent abuse, others or their own. *Girls Inc.*'s motto is: "Inspiring all girls to be strong, smart and bold."

Facebook Entry #4

Years ago, Oprah Winfrey, the first African-American female to become a billionaire, had an inspiring conversation with Nelson Mandela, the great South African leader. Freed after enduring twenty seven years of imprisonment for his political actions against the unjust system of *apartheid*, Mandela was voted the first black president of his country. He ran on the platform that all of its citizens were worthy of respect and dignity.

That sentiment inspired Oprah to build her dream school for girls in South Africa.

"From the very beginning," Oprah told Mandela in an interview in *O* magazine, "I wanted to create a school for smart girls who will lead this country into glory."

In 2002, Oprah announced her plans to build a leadership academy for the girls there. "When you change a girl's life, it's not just that life," Oprah wisely remarked. "You start to affect a family, a community, a nation. I'm telling you, women are going to change the face of Africa."

Oprah's school for girls was completed in 2007, and continues to make a great contribution to the future of South Africa and the world.

Facebook Entry #5
Of course, you don't have to be famous or rich to move mountains. A few years ago, I attended a talk at a local university. The speaker, Kakenya Ntaiya, was stunning in her tall beauty and quiet confidence. She told us that she grew up in a Masai village in Kenya, Africa, without electricity or running water. Girls were rarely educated at the local mission school because they were expected to become wives and mothers. But Kakenya had other plans—to be educated in the U.S. so that she could return to her village and run a school of her own. She inspired all of us with her courage, vision and determination to better the lives of the girls in her village. Her own village was backing her dream now, too.

Facebook Entry #6
Here's another hero of mine, Greg Mortenson. I met him after his lecture in March of 2011. For an exciting, true-life adventure, read *Three Cups of Tea: One Man's Mission to Promote Peace... One School at a Time*, by Greg and David Oliver Relin. After Mortenson failed to reach the summit of a mountain in Afghanistan in 1993, getting lost and then rescued by a remote tribe in northern Afghanistan, he caught hold of another vision: to build a school for the poor children, especially girls.

Despite years of grueling hard work in the remote, poor villages of Afghanistan and almost being killed at one point, Mortenson finally managed to scale two of the toughest mountains there—illiteracy and poverty.

With his non-profit organization, *Central Asia Institute*, Mortenson continues to work with local villagers to build schools, first in Afghanistan and now in Pakistan. Over the past two decades, Mortenson's organization, *Central Asia Institute* or *CAI*, has helped communities build 131 schools serving 58,000 students, 40,000 of them girls.

Greg's latest book, released in 2009, is called *Stones into Schools: Promoting Peace with Books not Bombs*. He has also started *The Girl Effect* movement (www.girleffect.org), based on his belief that

250

powerful social and economic changes result when girls are allowed to participate in their communities and world.

Facebook Entry #7

Several years ago, lawyer and activist, Mehrangiz Kar, shared her chilling yet inspiring story with several hundred people at a local university women's center. Kar is a human rights attorney who has published widely, especially on the threatened rights of women in her home country, Iran.

In 2000, Ms. Kar took part in a conference in Germany in which female professionals from many fields discussed social and political reform for women in their respective countries. Kar knew it would be dangerous for her to criticize Iran while in Iran, but she felt safe to do so in Germany.

Upon returning to Iran, however, Kar was immediately imprisoned for her comments. When her government reluctantly allowed her to leave Iran to receive medical treatment in the United States, they placed her husband on house arrest.

With a shaky voice, the courageous lawyer admitted to her audience that she didn't know how her husband's health was faring, let alone if she would ever see him again. Still, she pledged to continue her U.S. tour, advocating for human rights for her countrywomen. "I see the women of Iran at the beginning of something far greater than we have accomplished so far." *Insh' Allah*, Mehrangiz. May God be willing.

Moving mountains of war and ethnic hatred
Facebook Entry #8

Next, I want to tell you about Snatam Kaur, a Sufi (the mystical branch of Hinduism). She uses her lovely singing voice in an unconventional way: to contribute to universal peace.

A few years ago, Snatam was a cereal taster for *Peace* cereals. (I didn't even know there was such a job.) Her friends loved hearing her sing the chants of her Sikh faith as well as the modern songs she writes that encourage and celebrate unity among world religions. They begged her to ask the CEO of the cereal company to let her quit her job so that she could sing for peace on a world tour. At first he refused, but then he decided to support her.

I've heard Snatam sing three times now in person. She is one of the most holy women I have ever met and she's just a young woman.

Chanting along with her lovely voice and pure spirit as white as her flowing gown takes me to a place of calm and sometimes even bliss. She has produced many CD's, but her CD *Grace* is my favorite. It's lifted me over many an intimidating mountain of despair into a valley of hope.

Facebook Entry #9

Sometimes we meticulously plan the advocacy action we want to take. At other times, we are thrust into it by outrage and sheer desperation. In the book, *Spiritual Literacy* by Frederic and Mary Ann Brussat, Linda Hogan tells of such a case.

In 1986, I heard Betty Williams, 1977 Nobel Peace Prize laureate from Northern Ireland, lecture in South Dakota. Williams had witnessed the bombing death of Irish children. A little girl died in Williams' arms. The girl's legs had been severed in the explosion and had been thrown across the street from where the woman held the bleeding child.

Williams went home in shock and despair. Later that night, when the shock wore off, the full impact of what she'd seen jolted her.

Betty stepped outside her door, screaming out in the middle of the night. She knocked on doors that might easily have opened with weapons pointed at her face, and she cried out, "What kind of people have we become that we would allow children to be killed on our streets?"

Within four hours the city was awake and there were sixteen thousand names on petitions for peace.

Facebook Entry #10

Remember Chân Không's quote at the beginning of this chapter? I had the honor of studying with her at a week-long Mindfulness Training retreat in August of 2002 on a Massachusetts college campus. Although Thich Nhat Hanh was the main teacher, Chan Khong's calming presence as she sang folk songs in French and Vietnamese belied the rough life she had suffered and triumphed over. Không's book, *Learning True Love,* chronicles that quest. I always assigned it to my students at Yale.

Chân Không was born in 1938 in Vietnam, the eighth of nine children in a well-to-do family. In 1958, she enrolled in the University of Saigon to study biology. She was also involved in political action, becoming the student leader at the University, and spending much of her time helping the poor and sick in the city slums. It was there that she met Thich Nhat Hanh (Thây, "Teacher") in 1959 and instantly considered him her spiritual teacher.

After receiving her B.A. in Paris, Chân Không returned to Vietnam and joined Thây in founding the Van Han University and the School for Youth and Social Service, organizing medical, educational and agricultural facilities in rural areas during the Vietnam War. In1966, she was ordained as one of the first six members of Thây's creation, the *Order of Interbeing*. From 1969 to 1972 she worked with Thây in Paris, organizing and campaigning with the Buddhist Peace Delegation to stop the Vietnam War. In 1982, she worked with Thich Nhat Hanh to establish the still active Plum Village Sangha in France.

Chân Không accompanies and assists Thây whenever he travels. During their three-month return to Vietnam in 2005 after more than three decades in exile, she and Thây spoke to thousands of people throughout the country. Chân Không also conducted mindfulness practices and led the crowds in chanting and song. Soft-spoken and yet strong as steel, she is surely a teacher of true love.

Facebook Entry #11

While my generation is still healing from the Vietnam War, your generation, my daughters and sons, has even more conflicts to deal with, especially in the Middle East. I heard the following true story while attending the regional World Council of Churches annual meeting in Atlanta a few years ago.

Diane, a Christian Palestinian, lived in a small house with her daughter in Israel's West Bank. Israeli soldiers, masked and armed with machine guns, would sometimes break into a Palestinian home and order the family to gather in one room. The soldiers would remain there for days at a time, forbidding the family to leave, even to attend school or buy groceries. Diane and her little girl had experienced such an invasion several times during the past few years.

One day, Diane watched as her daughter looked out the window at Israeli tanks passing by, covered with soldiers dressed in full battle gear. Startled, the little girl cried out, "Mommy! One of the monsters is smoking a cigarette!"

Diane had an "Aha" moment.

The next time an officer came into her home with his soldiers pointing machine guns at them and ordering them to gather in the living room, Diane issued some orders of her own.

"No! I want you to take off your mask, take off your gloves, put down your gun, and shake hands with my daughter. She doesn't even know you're a *human being!*"

The officer was shocked. But because of her moral force, he laid down his gun, removed his mask and gloves, and shook the little girl's hand.

That would have been amazing enough, but there's more. Diane prepared tea and invited the soldiers to sit down and drink it with them. Through this non-violent and very brave act, she learned from the Israeli officer that, when not on soldier duty, he was a psychiatrist who, like Diane, was deeply concerned about the damage the conflict is inflicting not only on Palestinian children but on his own little Israeli ones. Both Diane and the officer both moved mountains that day.

Facebook Entry #12

My youngest hero is Rachel Corrie. On a spring day in March of 2003, one of my Yale students burst into my office in tears. Her friend and fellow student, Rachel, had just been killed in the Gaza strip in Israel.

"What happened?" I asked.

Rachel was a volunteer with the International Solidarity Movement, a group that accompanies at-risk persons in areas of the globe like the Gaza Strip, which was then, and still is, occupied by Israeli forces. On March 16, while Rachel courageously tried to prevent an Israeli bulldozer from demolishing the home of her Palestinian friend, she was run over and killed.

In Rachel's last phone conversation with her mom, she was very upset. She lamented the fact that most Americans don't support and protect the Internationals who are resisting conflict with non-violence. Therefore, they unknowingly undercut the Palestinian non-violent initiatives which are crucial to achieving peace one day with Israel, peace for all—Palestinian and Israeli, Christian, Muslim and Jew.

Since Rachel's tragic death, her mom and dad have continued to petition members of Congress to demand more support for the

International peace workers. They continue to lobby members of Congress to refocus their attention on the Israeli-Palestinian conflict, arguing that U.S. military aid to Israel must be made commensurate with Israel's efforts to adhere to the rules of international law and to end its occupation of the Palestinian Territories.

In an email, Rachel expressed what I'm sure many of you young people are feeling.

> This [war, occupation] has to stop. I think it is a good idea for us all to drop everything and devote our lives to making this stop. I don't think it's an extremist thing to do anymore. I really want to dance around to Pat Benatar and have boyfriends and make comics for my co-workers. But I also want this [war] to stop.

> Disbelief and horror is what I feel. Disappointment. I am disappointed that this is the base reality of our world and that we, in fact, participate in it. This is not at all what I asked for when I came into this world.... This is not the world you and Dad wanted me to come into when you decided to have me.

In one of her final e-mails, Rachel wrote,

> Today as I walked on top of the rubble where homes once stood, Egyptian soldiers called to me from the other side of the border, 'Go! Go!' because a tank was coming. Followed by waving and "What's your name?"

> There is something disturbing about this friendly curiosity. It reminded me of how much, to some degree, we are all kids curious about other kids:

> Egyptian kids shouting at strange women wandering into the path of tanks.

> Palestinian kids shot from [Israeli] tanks when they peek out from behind walls to see what's going on. International kids standing in front of tanks with banners.

Israeli kids in the tanks anonymously, occasionally shouting - and also occasionally waving–many forced to be here, many just aggressive, shooting into the houses as we wander away.

After Rachel's death, her mother mused: "How I wish that the young man in the bulldozer that killed Rachel could have just stopped, hopped out of the bulldozer, and talked to her. He would have met a beautiful soul."

Friends, let's act *now* before we lose any more of our idealistic, courageous young people of any race to such senseless deaths . Choose one culture, become an expert on it, and then advocate for its women, children, and families. Or join a peace-building organization for young people on both sides of a conflict, like *Seeds of Peace* in Maine, *Wi'Am* in Bethlehem, Israel or *Parent's Circle* in Tel Aviv.

Finally, it's a great idea to get trained in non-violent conflict resolution and compassionate listening. Put your *gifts and guts* into action and see what changes you can bring to situations of injustice or violence, perhaps even in your own city. Be creative. Find ways to surprise your opponents into new ways of thinking and acting. Reach out to join hands across mountains of fear and hate to heal the rifts and heartbreak. Though the costs will most certainly be great, the rewards will be priceless.

On the Mountaintop

When we've endured unforeseen hardships and have finally made it to the mountaintop, sometimes—though not always—we are rewarded with a vision. Dr. Martin Luther King, Jr. is one of my heroes. As a college student, I marched with him in 1967 in Cabrini-Green, the slums of Chicago, for better housing for his people. Hundreds of us—black and white, Christian and Jew, old and young—walked peacefully, linked arm in arm, as we chanted peace songs like *We Shall Overcome*. Though our voices were hundreds strong, we barely drowned out the hate-filled names being shouted out at us by mainly young white males lined up on both sides of the street.

I was walking a few rows behind Dr. King when suddenly someone threw a metal can with a jagged edge through the air. It hit Dr. King on the right ear, drawing blood. We stopped short as several policemen rushed up to him.

"Shall we arrest him?" one asked, greatly concerned.

Dr. King was silent for a moment. Then he spoke in that deep, rich voice of his: "We are here on a peaceful march for a just cause. Let's keep on marching."

And we did.

A year later, he was dead, killed by an assassin's bullet. (And we still don't know the whole story behind that tragedy.)

I'm sure you are all familiar with Dr. King's "I Have a Dream" speech in Washington, D.C. But I want to share with you the conclusion of the speech he gave in Memphis on April 3rd, 1968, to the striking garbage workers and their supporters on the eve of his assassination. As I write this, it's the 43rd anniversary of Dr. King's untimely death. Last Sunday, I preached a sermon to honor him and read this powerful testament. I hope it ignites a spirit-spark in you for justice.

> You know, several years ago, I was in New York City autographing the first book that I had written. And while sitting there autographing books, a demented black woman came up. The only question I heard from her was, "Are you Martin Luther King?"

> And I was looking down writing, and I said yes. And the next minute I felt something beating on my chest. Before I knew it I had been stabbed by this demented woman.... And that blade had gone through, and the X-rays revealed that the tip of the blade was on the edge of my aorta, the main artery. And once that's punctured, you drown in your own blood—that's the end of you.

> It came out in the New York Times the next morning, that if I had sneezed, I would have died.

> Well, about four days later, they allowed me, after the operation, after my chest had been opened, and the blade had been taken out, to move around... They allowed me to read some of the mail that came in.... I read a few, but one of them I will never forget....from a little girl...

> It said simply, "Dear Dr. King: I am a ninth-grade student at the Whites Plains High School. While it should not matter, I

would like to mention that I am a white girl. I read in the paper of your misfortune, and of your suffering. And I read that if you had sneezed, you would have died. And I'm simply writing you to say that I'm so happy that you didn't sneeze."

And I want to say tonight, I want to say that I am happy that I didn't sneeze.

Because if I had sneezed, I wouldn't have been around here in 1960, when students all over the South started sitting-in at lunch counters. And I knew that as they were sitting in, they were really standing up for the best in the American dream. And taking the whole nation back to those great wells of democracy which were dug deep by the Founding Fathers in the Declaration of Independence and the Constitution.

If I had sneezed, I wouldn't have been around in 1962, when Negroes in Albany, Georgia, decided to straighten their backs up. And whenever men and women straighten their backs up, they are going somewhere, because a man can't ride your back unless it is bent....

If I had sneezed, I wouldn't have been here in 1963, when the black people of Birmingham, Alabama, aroused the conscience of this nation, and brought into being the Civil Rights Bill.

If I had sneezed, I wouldn't have had a chance later that year, in August, to try to tell America about a dream that I had had. If I had sneezed, I wouldn't have been down in Selma, Alabama, to see the great movement there.

If I had sneezed, I wouldn't have been in Memphis to see a community rally around those brothers and sisters who are suffering. I'm so happy that I didn't sneeze....

And then I got into Memphis. And some began to talk about the threats...about what would happen to me from some of our sick white brothers.

Well, I don't know what will happen now. We've got some difficult days ahead. But it doesn't matter with me now.

Because I've been to the mountaintop.

And I don't mind. Like anybody, I would like to live a long life. Longevity has its place. But I'm not concerned about that now. I just want to do God's will. And He's allowed me to go up to the mountain. And I've looked over. And I've seen the promised land. I may not get there with you. But I want you to know tonight, that we, as a people, will get to the promised land. And I'm happy, tonight. I'm not worried about anything. I'm not fearing any man.

Mine eyes have seen the glory of the coming of the Lord.

Questers, have you had some kind of mountaintop experience on your life's journey so far? Would you even desire one?

Growing up Christian, I did feel close to God, the creator, especially when I was out in nature. But I could never relate to the man, Jesus. In retrospect, I realize that I had such a low image of myself—except for my great brains—that I doubted Jesus would even bother with me. If Jesus did exist—a *big* if—he would not waste his precious time on me. He had bigger fish to fry.

I was twenty-one years old, living in Cambridge, Massachusetts. It was Palm Sunday. Ever since I was a little kid, Palm Sunday had been a favorite holy day of mine. No matter where we lived, from northern Wisconsin to Chicago to Syracuse, New York, I looked forward to Palm Sunday when I could parade with the whole congregation around the church yard, waving palm branches and singing special hymns, especially these lines that I cherished:

All glory, laud and honor to thee, redeemer king,
to whom the lips of children made sweet hosannas ring.

On that particular Sunday, I was sitting alone on the floor of my apartment as sunlight softened into twilight. I had been listening to the music of Ravel's *Bolero*, an orchestral piece that begins slowly with just a few instruments, and then adds instrument upon instrument until the music builds to a glorious climax. The music began to catch me up in its cadence and pull me along with it, in a kind of caravan of joy.

Suddenly, in my mind's eye, people appeared in a ragged procession, following a man astride a donkey. The folks in the crowd danced around the man, and jumped up and down, waving their branches and shouting joyfully.

Like a camera, my mind's eye zoomed right through the throng onto the man's face. For a brief second, he turned and looked at me, locking his eyes right into mine. My heart stopped as I gasped, "Oh, my God, it's Jesus! He really does exist!"

My next thought (such a human one) was, "And I only got to know him the last week of his life."

My heart plummeted.

Just as quickly, I somehow knew in my very bones, that I had met Jesus, if only briefly, and I had been very involved in the work of the early Jesus movement. Tears of joy streamed down my face as I recalled the image frozen in my mind. Jesus had lived. He was real. I had seen him, and he had seen me.

As the decades passed, however, that vision of Jesus faded in my memory.

Years later, I attended a conference at A.R.E. Headquarters in Virginia Beach. I was numb inside. I had been engaged to a wonderful man who had recently broken off our engagement. Adding insult to injury, he and my best girlfriend then hooked up. I felt doubly betrayed, doubly abandoned.

As I sat down in the large auditorium with the other conferees, I found myself shaking my head. I just couldn't make sense out of my earthly journey. If it were true that I had lived before, that I had been married to different men at different times over centuries, how was I ever going to make the right choice of a mate *this* lifetime?

My attention returned to the voice of the workshop leader who happened to be my mother. She was ready to lead us in a reverie, a kind of dream experience while you're awake. Putting on a carefully chosen piece of classical music, she offered the following instructions: "Close your eyes and picture a shoreline, the sea, the sky, and a teacher who has just talked with his disciples. Then let your imagination flow with the music and see what happens."

I took some deep breaths and let the music wash over me. Instantly, I found myself on the shore beside the Sea of Galilee. There was Jesus, just ambling along, with his arms draped comfortably around the shoulders of two male disciples. I was sitting on a very large rock, out of his way, my head drooping.

Catching a glimpse of me, Jesus motioned to his buddies, "I'll be right back."

Looking up shyly, I watched in disbelief as he came over and stretched out his hands to pull me up. As the music took up a lovely ancient melody, we began to dance a beautiful Hebrew dance, our arms stretched above our heads, our palms gently touching. Slowly, we circled round and round, while my heart beat rapidly with trepidation. I dared not look into his eyes.

The music shifted again. Suddenly, Jesus took my hand and up we flew to the mountaintop. Below us in the valley, history stretched out in a wide panorama. I watched, amazed, as I witnessed the rise and fall of empires, war after violent war. People were mating, birthing children, dying. The whole thing was pretty overwhelming, a sharp contrast to Dr. King's gloriously reassuring vision on the mountaintop.

"Jesus," I moaned, "how am I ever going to make a good decision about whom I should marry? How am I even going to make a relationship last longer than a year? It's so hard when I'm down there in the battle!"

I waited, fervently wishing that he would provide me with the exact name of my intended partner and the date we would meet. I needed concrete answers. Foolproof ones.

Instead, Jesus answered, "I know it's hard, Pamela, but you'll just have to learn to trust me. Live your life day by day and you will be given what you need. And..." he paused dramatically, "I'll be with you, *always*."

He started to leave. I became frantic. Unconscious of anyone else in the room but him and me, with tears rolling down my cheeks, I pleaded with him again in desperation,

"*Please* don't leave me. When you're here with me, I believe you, but not when you're gone."

He whispered to me, "Lo, just call me and I'll be there. I *am* with you always."

And he vanished.

That was the most intimate and intense encounter with Jesus I've ever had.

Though it happened more than forty years ago, I remember it vividly. Through those years, in my hard times, when I've asked for

Jesus to come but I don't see him, the memory of this mountaintop vision and his loving assurance to me keeps me going. When I tramp through valleys of doubt or despair, or cross a rough river, or struggle up a steep mountain, I *know* I'm not alone. Seen or unseen, his promise is sure.

On your quest, my children, I pray you reach a mountaintop of your own one day.

FIFTEEN

Blazing a Trail:

Leaving Blossoms and Fruits

Trailblazing is a wondrous adventure! Discovering new territories, building new roads and accessing new terrain, opening up new vistas—going where no woman has dared to go before. Perhaps you're already a seasoned trailblazer. Terrific! Then you'll be pleased to meet a few more of your pioneer partners in this final chapter of our quest together. On the other hand, if you are relatively new to the wilderness, you can look forward to the day you become a trailblazer yourself.

First, if you want to peruse an inspiring book, check out humanitarian and photographer Phil Borges' *Women Empowered*. Every page of it is a tribute to the world's little-known heroines daily breaking gender barriers and triumphing over soul-sapping oppression. Madeleine K. Albright, former Secretary of State under Bill Clinton, introduces the book by stating, "This is a book about hope, based on reality." For example, Howa, age eight, is one of the first women in Awah Fontale, Ethiopia, to be convinced that female circumcision is a 'bad practice.' Thanks to the efforts of her mother, Abay, Howa will be the first girl in her entire family history not to be circumcised. There is hope for the world when an eight-year-old is such a trailblazer!

Marian Wright Edelman is one of my heroes. Born in South Carolina in 1939, she was the first African American admitted to the Mississippi Bar. She began practicing law while working on racial justice issues connected with the civil rights movement. She even represented several activists throughout the Mississippi Freedom Summer of 1964.

In 1968, Mrs. Edelman moved to Washington, D.C. to help Martin Luther King Jr. organize the Poor People's Campaign. In 1973, she founded the Children's Defense Fund to advocate for poor, minority and disabled children. CDF has served as an advocacy and research center for children's issues for almost forty years now. As principal spokesperson for CDF, Mrs. Edelman works tirelessly to persuade

Congress to overhaul foster care, support adoption, improve child care and protect children who are disabled, homeless, abused or neglected.

CDF's base is the old Alex Haley (African-American author of the ground-breaking television mini-series "Roots") farm; where weeklong summer institutes are held. I've attended five of them. Mrs. Edelman's inspiring speeches always motivate me to continue advocating for, and raising awareness about, our at-risk children.

The Freedom School project, now ten years old, trains local churches and other groups to offer a free six-week summer school primarily to disadvantaged African American youth, aged 5-18. This program, based on fostering a love of reading, is designed to empower the youth to make a difference in themselves, their families, their communities, their country and their world. Several years ago, my colleague, Chantal DeJou and I cast the Freedom School vision for the Virginia Beach Parks & Recreation Department and they caught the vision and ran with it. In the summer of 2009, they launched the first Freedom School in Virginia Beach and the second in the state of Virginia. "Good job, good job!"[3]

In addition to her work with CDF and public lecturing around the country, Mrs. Edelman has written many books, including *Lanterns: A Memoir of Mentors* which I used in my Yale women's studies class. She also pioneered *Children's Sabbath*, an annual interfaith community celebration of America's children in places around the country. In 2000, Mrs. Edelman was awarded the *Presidential Medal of Freedom*.

A philosophy of service Mrs. Edelman learned in childhood undergirds all of her efforts. She advises, "If you don't like the way the world is, you have an obligation to change it. Just do it one step at a time." Amen, dear sister.

Another trailblazer to keep your eye on is Eve Ensler, playwright, performer, and activist. She is the author of the play, *The Vagina Monologues.* Based on Ensler's interviews with more than two hundred women of various ages, races and classes, the piece celebrates women's sexuality and strength with pathos, humor and grace. At first controversial, especially because she used the V word, the play has since been translated into more than 45 languages and performed in at least 130 countries.

---

[3] A popular *Freedom School* chant

I was too prudish to attend a production being advertised at Yale. But when one of my students invited me because she was acting in it, I summoned up my courage and went. I experienced both the tragic and the comic in a very compelling, sexually frank and emotionally daring performance. I went from prude to pride in having a vagina in one night!

Several years later, Ensler's experience performing *The Vagina Monologues* inspired her to create *V-Day*, a global movement to stop violence against women and girls. It is a catalyst that promotes creative events to increase awareness, raise money and revitalize the spirit of existing anti-violence organizations. In 2008, *V-Day* celebrated its 10-year anniversary as *V to the Tenth* in New Orleans. Featuring two days of speakers, art, performances, makeovers, massage, medical testing, yoga and healing circles, the event was attended by over 30,000 women and men and reached millions of people all over the word—raising over $700,000 for local efforts to end violence against women and girls.

Eve's latest work, *I Am an Emotional Creature: The Secret Life of Girls Around the World,* was released in early 2010. In conjunction with *V-Day*, *V-Girls* goal is to engage young women in an "empowerment philanthropy" model, igniting their activism and providing them with a platform to lift up their voices.

You can almost smell the smoke rising from the trail Ensler blazes.

Another powerful *SoulQuester* and trailblazer is Dr. Wangari Muta Maathai, born in 1940 in the Ihithe village of Kenya She died of complications of ovarian cancer in 2011, but she has left a strong legacy.

Wangari was an environmental and political activist. After receiving both a bachelor's and master's degree in the United States, Wangari returned to Kenya. Against great opposition from male teachers and students, she was able to earn a Ph.D. She then worked her way up through the academic ranks at the University College of Nairobi to become the head of the veterinary medicine faculty, a first for a woman in any department at that prestigious school.

In 1977, Wangari founded the Green Belt movement in Kenya, comprised mostly of village women who have planted more than 10 million trees to prevent soil erosion and to provide firewood for their cooking fires.

Wangari's work with the Green Belt Movement, as well as with environmental and women's causes, cost her greatly. For example, in

1997, she ran for the presidency of Kenya, but the party withdrew her candidacy a few days before the election without even letting her know. In 1991, she was arrested and imprisoned for her work. Thank goodness, an Amnesty International letter-writing campaign helped free her. In 1999, protesting against continuing deforestation in a public forest in Nairobi, she was attacked and suffered head injuries.

In January of 2002, Wangari accepted a position as Visiting Fellow at Yale University's Global Institute for Sustainable Forestry. Though I was a pastor at Yale during that time, I regrettably wasn't aware of her presence. In January, 2003, back in Kenya, Wangari was elected to their Parliament as Deputy Minister in the Ministry of Environment, Natural Resources and Wildlife.

In 2004, Wangari became the first African woman to receive the Nobel Peace Prize for her contribution "to sustainable development, democracy and peace." From 2009 until her death, she served as Co-Chair of the Congo Basin Forest Fund and is the United Nations Messenger of Peace. She was indeed a Messenger of Peace on a self-blazed trail of vision, passion and commitment to a green world of hope.

Some of you have surely attended a *Bat Mitzvah*, the Jewish rite of passage from girlhood to womanhood to become a "daughter of the Torah." But how many of you know that it wasn't until 1960, fifty short years ago, that the first girl, Sandy Eisenstein, was allowed to become such a "daughter"? This was nothing short of revolutionary.

Active in her Reform Philadelphia congregation as a little girl, Sandy dreamed of becoming a rabbi, unaware that throughout several thousand years of Judaism, no woman had ever been rabbi. In fact, only since the last century have Jewish women even been allowed to study Torah. In the Middle Ages, for example, one rabbi instructed his male pupils, "If a woman has touched the Torah, it is better for you to burn it than to touch it."

Sandy was to be a trailblazer of firsts.

Fortunately for Sandy, the new Jewish Reconstruction movement had just opened a rabbinical school. In 1969, she was accepted into its second class, and in 1972, she was the *first* woman ordained by a rabbinical seminary. Sandy soon became a prominent voice in feminist Judaism. She also married her classmate, Dennis Sasso.

In 1977, along with her husband, Sandy took a position as co-rabbi of Beth-El Zedeck, a temple in Indianapolis, and became the first woman to serve a Conservative congregation and the *first* woman to serve as co-rabbi with her husband! When her son David was born, (I love this), she became the *first* rabbi to become a *mother*. Sasso and her husband continue to serve the Indianapolis congregation where she also writes and teaches. She's a true trailblazer in thought, word and deed.

After working on this book for more than five years and closely reviewing my life in the process, I realize that I, too, in a modest way, have been a kind of trailblazer.

As a little girl, I never daydreamed about becoming one, however. I was much too interested in being a people pleaser and a mommy. In my thirties, I realized I was a round, mystical, feminist peg trying to fit into a square male chauvinist career hole. Though the road I've travelled has often been rocky and sometimes lonely, it's been an exciting journey, nonetheless, filled with amazing surprises, twists and turns, and guides and angels hovering 'round me. Allow me to share one last trailblazing adventure.

From 1993 to 2005, I reaped rich benefits in being part of the academic and religious communities like the University of Chicago or Yale University. I enjoyed the high caliber of students and colleagues, with their progressive values and viewpoints, as well as their excellence in music and the arts. I learned a great deal from my Yale students and congregational members. At the same time, however, I found myself in a sort of spiritual exile from people I considered "kindred spirits." Almost all of my friends and colleagues seemed disinterested in the mystical life or in *any* life outside the traditional Christian box.

I longed to find some folks who loved exploring the far-out dimensions of human existence: angels, near-death experiences, psychic phenomena, reincarnation. Even our daughters, whom we had tried to raise with open minds, were skeptical of such topics. At times, they threw the same "That's too weird!" glance at me that I used to throw at *my* parents. Thank God, I could discuss such things with my open-minded husband.

In the years following my resignation from my pastoral post at Yale, our family spent our summer vacations in Virginia Beach, and I decided to interview for any available ministerial position. Time after time, sitting in search committees of several denominations, I was met by resistance to my passionate, progressive, and I believe Jesus-based, values and vision for the larger church.

Late one night, in desperation, I pleaded to a heretofore unresponsive divinity, "God, can't you please just give me just one clue, one tiny clue, as to which congregation you want me to serve?"

Crickets chirped. The fan whirred. In the dark and hushed room, these words arose in me, clear as a bell, "*Living Waters.*"

"Hmmm," I mused. "What a lovely name!"

Then puzzled, I added,

"However, I don't recall seeing a church with that name on the UCC website."

It took days for me to realize that God was calling me to start a second spiritual community, like I had so many years ago with Christpoint.

I recalled the story of Jonah, the ancient prophet in the Hebrew Scriptures, commanded by God to warn the sinful city of Nineveh to repent of its actions or God would destroy it. Jonah considered his calling and decided he preferred to be swallowed by a whale.

Just like Jonah, I stubbornly resisted God's call, hiding in the whale's belly for two long years.

"Please, dear God, don't choose me. I'm too old, too tired, too poor..." (You name it, I listed it.)

Frustrated by not being able to find a congregation which embraced both the mystical path and the path of social justice and peace-making, I finally gave in.

"OK, God! I'll do it!" I announced.

Besides, I had roped my 16-year-old Kaitlyn into agreeing to be the youth choir leader, recruiting some teens from her drama department to sing in the choir. (She did and we all had several gloriously fun, Broadway-tune filled years before they headed off to college.)

"Now what, God?" I wondered, having no clue as to how to proceed.

I decided to write out the vision statement God had planted in my heart. Then I let the whole thing go.

At that time, I was singing with an excellent choir in a local Episcopal church. One day, unbeknownst to me, my choir director friend shared my vision statement with the rector. Shortly after this, the rector called me into his office, told me that my vision was in line with his church's vision, and offered me their small chapel for services right then and there.

I blinked in disbelief.

I had no *people*. No hymnals.

But I did have a lovely space and a gracious host. With the Spirit's help, everything came together, and on March 3rd, 2006, *Living Waters Sanctuary* was born.

At *Living Waters*, most of us are Christian—that is, our service is Christ-centered and biblically based. But we are far from being traditional. For example, we have no creeds and no membership requirement except to love God, your neighbor and yourself. Everyone is welcome. To interpret scripture, we use the lens of feminist theology ("women and men are equal in God's eyes") and liberation theology ("God has a special preference for the poor").

Also, we challenge or re-interpret some of Christianity's traditional truth claims, such as Jesus is the *only* way to God, or Jesus needed to die so that God could be reconciled to the rest of humanity (the theory of atonement). Many of us in *Living Waters* believe that yes, Jesus was the Way-Shower who attained Christ consciousness and revealed Christ-like actions to the world. At the same time, many of us believe that each and every soul is destined to become an enlightened, Christ-like being like Jesus with the purpose of serving others and healing the world. We are called to become Carol Christ, George Christ, or Heather Christ.

This notion is similar to the Buddhist ideal of the *Bodhisattva*, the person who refuses to enter *nirvana* (enlightenment) until every blade of grass is also freed from suffering and becomes enlightened.

In addition to the term Christian, we at *Living Waters* identify ourselves as *interfaith*. We recognize and honor that each spiritual tradition, i.e., Buddhist, Muslim or Native American, has a precious part of God's truth. So the more we share our truths and practices with each other, the more quickly we can bring peace to the world and safety to all children and creatures.

Too, those of us who accept reincarnation know we have walked various spiritual paths in former lifetimes, so we are not really strangers to them. Each of us is as multi-faceted and lovely as a sparkling diamond—how we shine! Dad used to love telling audiences, "Turn around and look at the person sitting next to you. That's not just a person; that's a whole string of civilizations!"

Take me as one small sample. To name a few, I have retrieved soul memories of my being an ancient Egyptian priestess, an ancient rural Chinese woman, and a Lakota Indian (male or female in different lifetimes). I also have memories of being a black woman in the rural

South during the time of slavery. As my husband and I walked down a dirt path, reveling in the beauty of the moonlit night, several white men jumped out from the bushes and slit his throat. He fell dead at my feet. And as I revealed earlier, I believe I was a little Jewish boy killed in a gas chamber in the Holocaust.

Because the term "church" carries harmful historical and emotional baggage for many people, *Living Waters* identifies itself not as a church but as a "sanctuary," a safe space where members and guests can try on various spiritual approaches without fear of being judged by others. Our lesbian sisters and gay brothers are warmly welcomed for their gifts and beautiful spirits, as well.

I love the freedom I possess in being pastor of an independent faith community. I treasure being able to preach on peace-making and social justice issues, as well as on the mystical paths of different religions like Sufism (the mystical branch of Islam), Buddhism, Judaism or Native American traditions.

I also relish being able to share stories from the Cayce readings about Biblical characters. For example, there is Sarapha, the innkeeper's daughter, who attended Mary in labor that first Christmas Eve but only after her evening chores were finished, and then cradled the new-born Jesus in her arms to the anthems of angelic choirs. Or the story of Judith, the strong, unexpected female leader of the Essenes, a desert Jewish sect of Jesus' time Cayce referenced in quite a few readings, later to be validated in 1947 after his death with the discovery of the Dead Sea scrolls.

In the *Living Waters* community, we are committed to loving and protecting the earth and the miracles of creation. I am touched by Cayce's musing in one reading, "Who can teach a rose how to bloom? Who can teach a baby how to smile?" We can't teach those things, but we can appreciate and hallow them.

Finally, during worship, we engage the mind-heart-body-spirit connection, with circle dancing, body prayers, and with Broadway tunes or Gospel songs often replacing sacred anthems. My mother, now a young ninety-two and an ordained minister, contributes often as pianist. We have warm and spirited members who are eager to welcome you. So when you're in town, come worship with us!

Final Words of Encouragement:

"Stay True to the Journey"

In my "olden days," as my young daughters referred to the days of my youth, I believed that it was possible to veer off one's spiritual path and get lost. Today, I believe that *the whole world is our path,* our school, our training ground—so we can never get off of it. That's a relief!

Several years ago, a little boy looked up at his mother after church, pointed to me and said, "She's the most alive person I've ever met." That was quite a compliment, even coming from one so young, and one that keeps me striving not to disappoint him. After all, an early church father once proclaimed, "The glory of God is a human being fully alive."

How do we walk ourselves into such newness of life?

Ask Jumping Mouse.

I heard the story of *Jumping Mouse* from a wonderful Methodist minister, Rev. Ray Buckley. Though it took his grandmother's Lakota people three days to perform, he presented the shortened version.[4]

May you encounter this tiny, spunky *SoulQuester* somewhere on your journey, dear friends.

> There was a mouse who lived on the prairie and she was a very good mouse. She gathered seeds and she stored them in her cheeks and each day she would count them, but one day she heard a roaring sound, so she said to the other mice, "Brother and sister mice! Don't you hear that sound?"
>
> They would say, "Foolish mouse! There is no sound. Go back and count your seeds."
>
> But day to day, she would still hear that roaring sound in her ears. So one night, in the middle of the night, she stuffed her cheeks full of seeds and followed the sound.
>
> On her journey, Mouse touched plants she has never seen before; strange plants and trees and rocks brushed against her.

[4] I've changed the mouse from male to female for inspiration.

Her perspective of the world which had previously been so small became enlarged, and as it became enlarged, the roaring sound became louder, and she found herself on the banks of a great river. She heard a voice from the water that asked,

"Who are you, little sister?"

"I'm a mouse and I've heard a roaring sound and I've followed it to this place, but I don't know what it is."

The voice, which was the voice of Frog, said, "You have come to the banks of a great river which flows from the top of the shining mountain. But I want to tell you of something even more wonderful.

"If you crouch as low as you can and leap as high as you can, you can see the reflection of the shining mountains in the river."

So the mouse crouched as low as she could and leaped as high as she could, but she couldn't see anything. So she crouched lower and leaped higher and she still couldn't see anything. On the seventh time, she crouched as low as she could and she leapt as high as she could into the air, and there, reflected in the Great River, were the Shining Mountains.

The mouse rushed back to the mouse village and she said, "Brothers and sisters! I must tell you what I have seen. I have touched things that I have never touched before. I have heard a roaring sound! I have followed the sound to the banks of a Great River.

"But what is more important—when you get to the Great River, if you crouch as low as you can and leap as high as you can, you will see the reflection in the river of the Shining Mountains!"

They said to her, "Foolish mouse! There are no plants we have not seen. There is no Great River. There are no Shining Mountains. Now go back to counting your seeds."

And to make fun of her, they changed her name to "Jumping Mouse" or "The Mouse that Jumps."

Each night when Jumping Mouse went to sleep, she could not forget the vision of the shining mountains. And one night in the middle of the night, she got up, put seeds in her cheeks, and began the journey to find them.

On the way, she met an older mouse with a nice mouse house, who was a very wise Grandmother. And Grandmother said to her:

"Foolish mouse. There is no Great River. There are no Shining Mountains. There are no new things that touch you in the world. Stay and count seeds with me and do what we have always done and we will gather the seeds together."

Because Jumping Mouse was a polite mouse, in the middle of the night when she got up to leave, she took the seeds from her mouth and left them for the grandmother. And once more, she began the journey.

On the way, Jumping Mouse bumped into something big and brown and furry. And a deep voice said to her, "Who are you, little sister?"

And she said, "They call me Jumping Mouse. Who are you?"

And he said, "I am *Tatanka*, the bull buffalo, but I am dying and they say that only the eye of a mouse can heal me. But I have never seen a mouse before."

Jumping Mouse stepped back and she thought, "My eye could heal this buffalo. But if I lose my eye, I will lose my way of seeing. I will not be able to count seeds and I will not be a good mouse."

But then she thought, "On my journey, the Creator has placed this buffalo in front of me. And since I have two eyes, I will give him one."

And no sooner had she thought this than her eye went to the buffalo and the buffalo was made whole.

The buffalo walked as slowly as he could and Jumping Mouse walked under him as fast as she could so that the eagles and the hawks could not get her.

At the base of the Shining Mountains, she continued the journey alone.

Halfway up the mountain, Jumping Mouse met a coyote who was chasing his tail, or, as Native people would say, he had lost his identity. Spiritually, he did not know where he was in the world.

Jumping Mouse said to him, "Who are you?"

And the coyote said, "… are you? *(echo)* … are you? … are you?"

And Jumping Mouse said, "Coyote!"

And the coyote said, "Coyote! … *(echo)* Coyote!.... *(softer still)* Coyote!"

Now Jumping Mouse knew that coyotes ate mice, and she thought,

"If my eye healed the buffalo, perhaps my other eye can heal the coyote.

"But if I give my other eye, I will be blind. I will not be able to count seeds, and I will not be a good mouse. I will not be able to complete the journey."

But then she said, "The Creator in all this world has brought me to this place. I will give my eye."

And no sooner had she thought it than the eye left her head and it went to the coyote, and the coyote was made whole.

And in the mouth of the coyote, Jumping Mouse was carried to the top of the Shining Mountains which she could not see and left there, blind and alone in the snow.

It was cold and it was dark and she could feel the shadows of the eagles and hawks flying overhead, and she knew the end was imminent. And then, suddenly, the world went black.

And then she began to see—but it was not the snow of the Shining Mountains. She was looking down on the peaks. She could see the great grasslands where the mouse village was. She could see the Great River and the old mouse house. She could watch the river flow as it flowed past Frog's dwelling.

And when she looked out to see her paw, there was no paw, but feathers and bone as far as she could see. And she looked to find her other paw, but there was only feather and bone as far as she could see.

And the voice of *Wakan Tanka*, the Voice of Creator, said, "You have been faithful, little one, to the journey. I give you a new name. You are eagle."

Chelsea and Kaitlyn, apples of my eye, and all of you sisters and brothers of spirit, we've come to the end of our journey together. I feel honored that you have welcomed me as guide and companion at this stage of your life. I pray that you, like Jumping Mouse, will stay faithful to the journey, to your own unique soul's quest.

In the first chapter of this trail guide, I shared Hazel's prediction for me as an infant: "There's something wonderful about this child." In closing, I want to add that there's something wonderful about *every* child.

And while the results are still out about my life's contribution to the world, I promise you to keep doing my best to stay true to my path:

advocating for women's worth and children's well-being locally and globally, building bridges between faiths and cultures, and collaborating with others for human rights and peace for all peoples. I ask the Holy One to bless the desires of my heart and the work of my hands.

My closing prayer for each one of you, precious companions, echoes the poem that began *SoulQuest*:

> ...I choose to risk my significance:
>> to live
>> so that which comes to me as seed
>>> goes to the next as blossom,
>> and that which comes to me as blossom
>>> goes on as fruit.

May you continue to risk your significance, discovering and using your vision, your gifts and your spiritual power in creative ways to heal yourselves, others and Mother Earth.

> *To a weeping, lost and lonely world, may you add your fragrance and beauty to the blossoms of my love for you.*

> *To a hungry world, may you deliciously increase the fruit of my labors.*

> *And with your wisdom, grace and love, may you lead the elders and children in the sacred dance of life.*

May *SoulQuest* continue to flourish!

276

Acknowledgements

There are so many people I want to thank for helping me bring *SoulQuest* to birth. First, I want to thank my sweet Mom, who gave the first rough draft an enthusiastic yet critical read-through and encouraged me up through the book's completion. Thanks to Lynn Rogers, Crystal and Elizabeth Waitekus and Pearl Batista for constructive feedback on the early chapters.

How can I ever thank you, Mary Boyd, dear P.B., with your sharp eye and wise suggestions in the final stages of editing? You taught me so much about the fine art of writing, even if I did have to delete most of my exclamation marks!

Deep thanks to Marcus Walther for helping heal my body and spirit so I could persevere and finish *SoulQuest*. For family, Erika, Greta, Alison and John, and friends too numerous to mention, including Jim Conway and the BBA Foundation for their hearty support, Kristy DiGeronimo, Carol Hodies, Anne Racher, Libbie McDowell, Pamela Fitzgerald, Charlie Zamzow and Jim Dial (now cheering me on from the other side). You believed I had something of value to say and you cheered me on to the finish line—thank you all from the bottom of my heart.

Many thanks to Phil Neff for his exquisite cover photo, more lovely than I could have envisioned, and to Kaitlyn, my Wild Woman, goddess-like daughter on the cover.

I remain forever grateful to John Benetz for his faith-filled companionship through 25 years of marriage and raising our precious two daughters, and for his endless *post-it* notes and cups of coffee while I was writing and rewriting this labor of love, revealing his faith in me and my message. I remain forever blessed.

To my precious daughters—Chelsea, the first light of my life, for the joy she gave me every day when she was little, and for her words of counsel to me in her young adulthood beyond; for the pride I feel when I watch her as a clever businesswoman and now compassionate and upbeat social worker, for our special bond as mother-daughter and her loving support of *SoulQuest*. And Kaitlyn, for the beauty of her inner spirit, for her prodding me again and again to take risks, for her priceless friendship, and for her courage in heading to L.A. after college to go for her dream to become a movie star. They both bless me beyond words.

Finally, I offer this book for the well-being of women, children and men around the globe in humble gratitude to the One God with many names: Mama God, the Holy Spirit, *Wakan Tanka*—Beloved Companion on the Holy Quest.

Mitakuye Oyasin.

278

Reader's Guide
Questions for Discussion

<u>Chapter 1</u>
1. What is your gut reaction to the word "feminist." How do you define feminism?
2. How do you understand "power"? What is your current personal relationship to power?
3. Do you see your life as a "quest" or in some other way? Explain.
4. Do you divide your life into sacred and secular? Why or why not?
5. Where are you now in your spiritual journey? What spiritual or philosophical traditions or teachers have influenced you? Are you part of a spiritual community at this time? What are you gaining from it? What might you like to change?

<u>Chapter 2</u>
1. Do the imagination exercise on your self-image. What confirmations did you receive about yourself? What surprises?
2. What, if anything, are you doing to boost your self-esteem?
3. Do you make an effort to boost others' self-esteem? When and how?
4. This chapter offers several ways to boost your self-esteem. Try one for a week and report to the group.

<u>Chapter 3</u>
1. What is your response to the three views of human nature: universalist, evolutionary or social construction? In which camp do you place yourself and why?
2. What is your realistic assessment of gender relations today? What do you hope for in the future and what are you actively doing to make that hope a reality?
3. Do you detect patriarchy in your religion or spiritual tradition? Might you challenge or enlarge your tradition regarding the Divine Feminine and women's roles and worth? How?
4. Has anyone ever tried to put a period after your name? How did you respond? What would you do differently now?

<u>Chapter 4</u>
1. Why is knowing the history of racial relations between black and white women important in the discussion of sisterhood? If you are

male, do some research on the history of the relationship of black and white men in the U.S. and report to the group.

2. What role, if any, do you think race plays in people working and playing together in our culture today?

3. Have you learned something eye-opening from a woman of race different than yours? If so, share.

4. Who are your "sisters" or "brothers" in your work, spiritual or social life today? How might you intentionally strengthen that bond?

Chapter 5

1. What practices do you use for self-examination and guidance in your daily life? Do you find the use of altars, journaling, dream interpretation or medicine cards helpful? Why or why not? Choose one, experiment and report on it.

2. Share your vision or some of your goals with the group. No critiquing or questioning. (You can do that over coffee later.) Just listen and be supportive.

3. This chapter list six attitudes to take on your quest. Which are your favorites? Which ones are you already good at? Try "Isn't that fascinating?!" for a week and share the results.

4. Are there attitudes you would add? What are they and why are they important to you?

Chapter 6

1. How do you feel toward your body in general? If you are female, how do you feel about being in a *female* body? Has your view changed over your lifetime? If so, how?

2. Has your faith life or spiritual worldview affected your treatment of your body? Explain.

3. How do (did) you experience your period, or *moontime*? If you have a daughter, or plant to, what might you like to teacher her when she begins menstruation about becoming a woman?

4. What value do you place on your sexuality? With whom do you choose to be sexually intimate and why? Is trust a factor?

5. What do you think of Estes' *Wild Woman*?

Chapter 7

1. What role, if any, does forgiveness play in your spiritual life?

280

2. Share a time when you successfully forgave someone or they forgave you. How did that experience change you?

3. If you want to forgive someone right now but can't do it, pick a heart-opener from the chapter and try it. Share with the group.

Chapter 8

1. Share a joke on yourself when you thought you were being so clever and it backfired.

2. Brag about your brains. Be specific.

Chapter 9

1. What is your current attitude toward money? Has it evolved over time?

2. What is your response to the practice of tithing? Is Edwene crazy or on to something?

3. Have you tried tithing? What happened?

Chapter 10

1. What is your current creation story, how the universe was made? Has it evolved over your lifetime? Explain.

2. How do you picture the creator God, if at all?

3. Do you see any point in reviving or creating an image of God that is female? Explain.

3. Rewrite an episode of your life story modeled on Carol Bridges' exercise. Share with the group any new insights or feelings about yourself or the situation.

Chapter 11

1. After reading this chapter, do you have a greater appreciation for the transformative power of ritual? Why or why not?

2. If your group is Christian, celebrate the Freedom Meal Communion Ritual. Share your responses.

3. Following the guidelines in the chapter, design a ritual, read it to the group and then enact or perform it together. Discuss afterwards. Did you sense *communitas*? What transformation, if any, did you experience, either personally or as a group?

Chapter 12

1. Have you encountered God in the Light in your meditation or in your good times? Share an experience if you wish.

2. Have you ever experienced a "dark night of the soul"? How did you make it through?

3. On your quest, what place, if any, does the practice of surrender hold for you?

4. Do you find it more of a challenge to surrender your mind, your anger or your life plans? Elaborate.

5. Did one of the surrender stories in the chapter especially touch you? Why?

Chapter 13

1. How do you envision your life purpose, your reason for being alive? Perhaps you have several.

2. What do you think about the concepts of Free Will? Karma? Grace? Explain.

3. What do you think about the concept of reincarnation? If you accept it, share a memory if you wish. If you've never entertained the notion, are there any clues from this chapter that you might now wish to explore?

Chapter 14

1. Why is it important to have role models in general and female role models in particular?

2. Which of the *questers* in this chapter particularly inspires or touches you?

3. Have you ever had a mountaintop experience? If you are comfortable, share it with the group.

Chapter 15

1. What wisdom or folly do you find in the *Tale of Jumping Mouse*? What is your favorite childhood fairy tale? Grown-up tale? (Think of movies, books or grandparents or parents' stories, either real or fictional.) How does it guide or influence your life?

2. Identify and share one gift or talent you have, and how you plan to offer it to the world in the near future. Be specific.

3. If you are a trailblazer or know someone who is, share the story and celebrate!

Extra Credit

1. Seriously learn a language or spiritual tradition other than your own. Share some of what you've learned with someone.

2. Challenge yourself to worship at a place you've been judgmental about. Open your heart and mind to find one positive practice or person you meet there.

3. Foster a young person in their spiritual journey, either formally or informally. (i.e., Big Brother or Big Sister) Be sure to commit yourself for a specific time (say, bimonthly) and specific duration (one year). Commitment and follow-through are essential in this extra credit task.

Happy SoulQuesting!

* * *

If you are interested in engaging Dr. Bro
for spiritual life coaching (on the phone or in person),
booking her for a lecture, retreat or workshop,
or just want to comment, please contact her at

pamelabro22@hotmail.com

or visit

WWW.SOULQUESTNOW.COM

Made in the USA
Charleston, SC
14 March 2015